Nazek Khalid Matty
Sennacherib's Campaign Against Judah and Jerusalem in 701 B.C.

Beihefte zur Zeitschrift für die alttestamentliche Wissenschaft

Edited by
John Barton, Reinhard G. Kratz, and Markus Witte

Volume 487

Nazek Khalid Matty

Sennacherib's Campaign Against Judah and Jerusalem in 701 B.C.

A Historical Reconstruction

DE GRUYTER

ISBN 978-3-11-044788-0
e-ISBN (PDF) 978-3-11-045104-7
e-ISBN (EPUB) 978-3-11-044937-2
ISSN 0934-2575

Library of Congress Cataloging-in-Publication Data
A CIP catalog record for this book has been applied for at the Library of Congress.

Bibliographic information published by the Deutsche Nationalbibliothek
The Deutsche Nationalbibliothek lists this publication in the Deutsche Nationalbibliografie;
detailed bibliographic data are available in the Internet at http://dnb.dnb.de.

© 2016 Walter de Gruyter GmbH, Berlin/Boston
Printing and binding: CPI books GmbH, Leck
♾ Printed on acid-free paper
Printed in Germany

www.degruyter.com

MIX
Papier aus verantwor-
tungsvollen Quellen
FSC
www.fsc.org
FSC® C083411

Acknowledgments

This book represents a slightly revised version of my doctoral thesis, which was written at Oxford University and submitted in 2013. My deepest gratitude goes to Professor John Day, my thesis supervisor, for his patient guidance, enthusiastic encouragement and invaluable nuanced critique of this research project. My gratitude also extends to Dr Frances Reynolds for her priceless advice and assistance in matters concerning Assyriology. A debt of very great appreciation is owed to Dr Richard Conrad, Blackfriars graduate tutor, for his valued constructive suggestions during the development of this research work. I am also deeply thankful to Professor Kevin Cathcart and Dr Stephanie Dalley; their willingness to give their time so generously and to share their immense expertise has been very much appreciated.

I owe huge thanks for my Congregation for granting me the time and financial support necessary for the execution of this research. The love and encouragement of my Dominican Sisters and the members of my family have strengthened my motivation to complete the research every step of the way.

In addition, I wish to thank Blackfriars Hall for providing a supportive and intellectually stimulating environment. The librarian Dr Michael Black and the fantastic library that he directs deserve special note.

The following friends have been especially helpful and encouraging throughout the years of my research: Sister Maria Hanna, Sister Marie Therese, Fr James Swetnam S.J. and Sister Rose Ann Schlit, who were there for me in the times of dryness. I would also like to express my gratitude to the friends and companions who have made these years special.

I am grateful for the editorial assistance of Professor John Day, Dr Richard Conrad, Mr James Disley and Mr Ralph Weir.

The completion of this work would not have been possible without the financial support of the Missionswissenschaftliches Institute Missio, The Dominican Sisters of Saint Chatherine of Siena Newcastle Natal "Bushey Sisters", The Dominican Sisters of the English Congregation of Saint Catherine of Siena, The Catholic Women's League, Samfundet Dominikansystrarna, Sisters of the Love of God, Charitable Trust, Pfarrer Markus Wagemann and Dr. Robert Hauger Ms Cornelia Starks, Mr Kamal Jacob, and the benefactors who assisted me anonymously. I am very grateful for their help.

Contents

Appendix

Abbreviations

ÄAT	Ägypten und Altes Testament
AB	The Anchor Bible
ABD	*The Anchor Bible Dictionary*
ABRL	Anchor Bible Reference Library
ABS	Archaeology and Biblical Studies
AfO	*Archiv für Orientforschung*
ALSPM	Abhandlungen zur Literatur Alt-Syrien-Palästinas und Mesopotamiens
AO	Analecta Orientalia
AOAT	Alter Orient und Altes Testament
AS	Archaeological Studies
ATD	Das Alte Testament Deutsch
AUM	Andrews University Monographs
BASOR	*Bulletin of the American Schools of Oriental Research*
BCSBS	*Bulletin of the Canadian Society of Biblical Studies*
BCTP	Bible Commentary for Teaching and Preaching
Bib	*Biblica*
BKAT	Biblischer Kommentar: Altes Testament
BM	*Baghdader Mitteilungen*
BWANT	Beiträge zur Wissenschaft vom Alten und Neuen Testament
BZAW	Beihefte zur Zeitschrift für die Alttestamentliche Wissenschaft
CAD	*Chicago Assyrian Dictionary*
CDA	*Concise Dictionary of Akkadian*
CHANE	Culture and History of the Ancient Near East
COHP	Contributions to Oriental History and Philology
Ébib	Études bibliques
ÉgT	*Église et théologie*
EHAT	Exegetisches Handbuch zum Alten Testament
FHTB	Facultas Hierosolymitana Theologiae Biblicae
FOTL	Forms of The Old Testament Literature
HALOT	*Hebrew and Aramaic Lexicon of the Old Testament*
HBM	Hebrew Bible Monographs
HKAT	Handkommentar zum Alten Testament
IASH	The Israel Academy of Sciences and Humanities
ICC	International Critical Commentary
IES	Israel Exploration Society
ITC	International Theological Commentary
JAC	*Journal of Ancient Civilizations*
JBL	*Journal of Biblical Literature*
JCS	*Journal of Cuneiform Studies*
JDds	Jian Dao Dissertation Series
JNES	*Journal of Near East Studies*
JSOTSup	Journal for the Study of the Old Testament: Supplement Series
MC	Mesopotamian Civilizations
MAJTh	*Mid-America Journal of Theology*

Ms	Monograph series
Ms	Moreshet series
MThA	Münsteraner Theologische Abhandlungen, Altenberge
NAC	The New American Commentary
NICOT	New International Commentary on the Old Testament
OA	*Oriens Antiquus*
OIP	Oriental Institute Publications, Univ. of Chicago Press
OTL	Old Testament Library
OLZ	*Orientalistische Literaturzeitung*
PBM	Paternoster Biblical Monographs
PEQ	*Palestine Exploration Quarterly*
OS	*Oudtestamentische Studiën*
PIA	Publications of the Institute of Archaeology
RINAP	Royal Inscriptions of the Neo-Assyrian Period
SA	Studia Asiana
SAAB	*State Archives of Assyria Bulletin*
SAAS	State Archive of Assyria Studies
SAOC	Studies in Ancient Oriental Civilizations
SB	Sainte Bible traduite en français sous la direction de l'École Biblique de Jérusalem
SBL	Society of Biblical Literature
SBT	Studies in Biblical Theology
Ser	*Serapis: The American Journal of Egyptology*
SHCANE	Studies in the History and Culture of the Ancient Near East
SO	*Studia Orientalia*
StPol	Studia Pohl, Series Maior
SubBib	Subsidia Biblica
VT	*Vetus Testamentum*
VTSup	Vetus Testamentum, Supplement
TB	*Tyndale Bulletin*
TBSAW	Topoi. Berlin studies of the ancient world
TCS	Texts from Cuneiform Sources
ThDOT	*Theological Dictionary of the Old Testament*
VB	Vorderasiatische Bibliothek
WBC	Word Biblical Commentary
ZA	*Zeitschrift für Assyriologie und vorderasiatische Archäologie*
ZAW	*Zeitschrift für die Altestamentliche Wissenschaft*
ZDPV	*Zeitschrift des Deutschen Palästina-Vereins*
ZThK	*Zeitschrift für Theologie und Kirche*

Chapter One: Introduction

1. Preliminary remarks

Sennacherib's campaign against Judah in 701 BC[1] is a topic that has interested biblical specialists, Assyriologists and archaeologists for many years. This can be ascribed to the fact that the event has been recorded and well documented in a remarkable variety of sources. The campaign is recorded in Sennacherib's annals more than once, and also in the Bible in three different accounts (2 Kgs 18–19; Isa 36–37; and 2 Chr 32). Also, there is archaeological evidence that tells us more about the event. Yet there is no consensus about what happened in 701, simply because the sources we have present the event in different, even contradictory, ways. This causes diversity in the way scholars read and interpret these sources. These factors have prolonged the debate about what really happened in 701, with people continuing to ask which account is historically realistic. Therefore, the more the topic has been investigated, the greater the number of divergent issues that have emerged.

In the midst of all these opinions, there is one thread running through all the studies: a fascination with what happened in 701. What is historical and what is theological? Which text is more reliable? In order to answer these questions, there have been a variety of approaches to this issue. Some scholars have focused their efforts on the historical aspect of the text, and others on the theological aspect. Some have approached it archaeologically, and some linguistically. Some have been concerned only with the Assyrian sources, while others have found the solution in the biblical accounts. Some scholars have explored additional sources, which are related to the event, such as "Sennacherib's letter to God"[2] and the narrative of Herodotus (*History* 2. 141), while others have dismissed these sources, considering them of no value in this regard. All in all, it is obvious that the approach used to deal with Sennacherib's campaign against Judah is decided by what the researcher seeks to understand from the texts that relate the event. Therefore, it is important, I believe, to make clear what this research aims to discuss while investigating the texts related to the events of 701.

This study seeks to reconstruct Sennacherib's third campaign against Judah and Jerusalem. I am aware that knowing exactly what happened in 701 is far from realistically possible. After all, in investigating the event under discussion,

---

1 All dates are assumed to be BC unless noted otherwise.
2 Na'aman, N., "Sennacherib's 'Letter to God' on his Campaign to Judah", *BASOR* 214 (1974), 25–39.

we deal with texts drenched with theological and propagandistic content, whose aim is not to relate history but to express ideology. In this regard, A. Kuhrt considers the attempt to know what has exactly happened as "a fruitless exercise", since the Assyrian and biblical accounts are dealing with a version of events which were depicted to serve the interests of the scribes of both sides, despite the fact that the presence of factual data is undeniable.[3] Kuhrt's statement might be useful in reminding us that caution is in order when we seek historical information from the texts; nevertheless, it is worth persevering since what is required is not to know exactly what happened but rather to understand how much the data we have can help us in reconstructing the events of 701.

Therefore, this study will discuss historical questions about the campaign. The chief concern is whether Sennacherib had really accomplished his mission. Was there any reason for receiving Hezekiah's tribute in Nineveh? Did Sennacherib return to Nineveh unexpectedly? If so, what was the reason for his return? Some scholars have assumed that Sennacherib was successful in his campaign. He quelled the rebels, punished the enemy kings and received their tribute, reestablishing peace in the region. Other scholars, however, assume that Sennacherib suffered a setback and returned to Nineveh unexpectedly. Still other scholars assume that both sides had a kind of victory: Sennacherib received tribute and Hezekiah remained on the throne with Jerusalem remaining intact. Each of these arguments is based on some reason that someone sees as supporting it. But none of the studies seems to me fully comprehensive. Previous works on Assyrian inscriptions have tended to focus only on Sennacherib's third campaign. They do so at the cost of anything that can be learnt from the broader context in which this campaign took place, and the habitual way in which such campaigns were carried out under Sennacherib. We find a similar situation concerning the biblical account which narrates the return of Sennacherib. Previous theories have tended to limit themselves to one or two items of evidence to the exclusion of the rest. In doing so, scholars have consistently offered explanations of Sennacherib's return which are in tension with the remaining evidence. For example, many scholars appeal to a rumour about a Nubian military advance as the reason for Sennacherib's return, based on the combined evidence of 2 Kgs 19:7//Isa 36:7, and 2 Kgs 19:9//Isa 36:9. However, this is difficult to square with Hezekiah's payment of a large tribute, mentioned in 2 Kgs 18:13–16. In my opinion, the best historical hypothesis concerning the reason for Sennacherib's return

---

3 Kuhrt, A., "Sennacherib's Siege of Jerusalem", in A.K. Bowman *et al.* (eds.), *Representations of Empire: Rome and the Mediterranean World, Proceedings of the British Academy 114* (London, 2004), 13–33.

should attempt to give equal weight to each piece of evidence in each relevant area, whether it be literary or archaeological in origin.

Therefore, my justification for returning to this much-discussed area is that previous scholarship has failed to meet the criteria required for providing the best historical hypothesis. Over the course of my investigation I shall examine the relevant Assyrian inscriptions, not merely those relating to the third campaign, and the purported instances of biblical evidence, as well as engaging with archaeological and literary considerations. I will show that the most important theories offered up to this point contradict or contend with an important piece of other evidence. Having shown this, I will then suggest a view of my own which does, as far as possible, take all the available evidence into due account.

2. Past research

2.1. Scholarly opinions

Several monographs and many articles have been dedicated to following the course of the campaign historically and answering the question of what happened in 701. One has to admit that the insights and conclusions of these studies must be taken seriously. However, in my survey, I shall present the theories of those who have pursued independent lines of research on the historicity of 701. The aim of this survey is to gain an understanding of the way scholars have dealt with the historical aspect of the events and to ask whether the perspectives have changed through years of studying this matter.

In 1967, B.S. Childs made a survey of the major historical reconstructions that had been suggested from the nineteenth century up to his time. His survey demonstrated that the theories are divided into three groups. The first group is those scholars who accepted the order of events as narrated in the Bible. Sennacherib attacked Hezekiah, and Hezekiah paid him tribute but it was not enough. Sennacherib, therefore, sent his official to threaten Jerusalem but something mysterious happened that then made Sennacherib withdraw. The second group are those scholars who argued that there were two campaigns. The tribute payment and the prophetic narrative are two stories narrating different events separated by a period of time. The third group are the scholars who assert the authenticity of the tribute episode and Sennacherib's annals. Hezekiah lost the war and capitulated in the end. Childs was not satisfied with those arguments.[4] Even after proposing the form-critical method as suitable for the text, at the end of his study he states: "The results of our study in reference to the historical problem have been mainly negative."[5]

In 1980, R.E. Clements discussed the events of 701 and, in opposition to Childs, he asserts that "we know much of what happened in 701," basing his confidence mainly on the tribute episode in 2 Kgs 18:13–16 and Sennacherib's annals. In his view, the historical side of the problem is less important.[6] He therefore directs attention to the literary origins in the prophetic narrative and to its theological ideas. He agrees with L.L. Honor's suggestion that the prophetic narrative is "a late legendary version"[7] and thus studies it as narrative theology.[8]

Despite these two contradictory views—i. e. the strongly negative conclusion of Childs about the efforts dedicated to the historical reconstruction of the event and Clements' affirmation that the matter is very obvious—there have nevertheless been some attempts to discuss the historical aspects of the campaign. Some of these attempts, one must say, came in the context of other challenges and issues that scholars dealt with when they studied the deliverance of Jerusalem.

In his lengthy study, F. Gonçalves presented a significant literary critical study of 2 Kgs 18–19 and parallel passages in Isaiah and Chronicles. He accepted the traditional division of A (2 Kgs 18:13–16), B1 (2 Kgs 18:17–19:9a, 36–37) and B2 (2 Kgs 19:9b–35) as three versions of the same event. Regarding the historical value of each part, Gonçalves seems somewhat tentative. In his view, the purpose of A is to show how and on what condition the war ended.[9] B1 preserves historical memories, although it does not allow us to answer the question of what happened.[10] B2 is a later addition and is to be regarded as secondary.

---

4 Childs, B.S., *Isaiah and the Assyrian Crisis* (SBTh 3; London, 1967), 11–18.

5 Childs, *Crisis*, 118.

6 Clements, R.E., *Isaiah and the Deliverance of Jerusalem. A Study of the Interpretation of Prophecy in the Old Testament* (JSOTSup 13; Sheffield, 1980), 18. Recently, Clements published another significant book where he discussed the deliverance of Jerusalem in 701. Five chapters are dedicated to a discussion of the literary and theological aspects of the accounts of Sennacherib's attack. See Clements, R.E., *Jerusalem and the Nations. Studies in the Book of Isaiah* (HBM 16; Sheffield, 2011).

7 Clements, *Deliverance*, 14. See Honor, L.L., *Sennacherib's Invasion of Palestine. A Critical Source Study* (COHP 12; New York, 1926).

8 Clements, *Deliverance*, 20.

9 Gonçalves, F., *L'expédition de Sennachérib en Palestine dans la littérature hébraïque ancienne* (Ébib 7; Paris, 1986), 371.

10 Gonçalves, *L'expedetion*, 443.

W.R. Gallagher's conclusions about the historical aspect of the narrative are stronger, although his study is in a way similar to that of Gonçalves. He started by solving the problem of the contradictory portrayal of the prophet Isaiah in the prophetic narrative and in proto-Isaiah by establishing the historical background of some of the texts in Isaiah. Then, he moved on to discuss the historicity of A and B; in his view, both are reliable and they do not contradict the account of the campaign in the annals of Sennacherib. Hezekiah surrendered when Sennacherib was at Lachish, but Sennacherib did not accept that surrender immediately because it "did not conform to Sennacherib's military goals".[11] However, he later accepted it as a result of two factors: first, he heard a rumour about an Egyptian army coming to fight him and, secondly, a setback occurred perhaps because of an epidemic.[12]

A refreshing new attempt has been made by P.S. Evans to solve the puzzle of 701. He dedicated his study to undertaking a rhetorical-critical analysis, which in his opinion is the only way to tackle the text.[13] Aware that rhetorical criticism has tended to be ahistorical in its focus, he advanced his study with an eye on historical questions. Furthermore, he believes that the biblical account in 2 Kgs 18 – 19 provides significant evidence for the historian if it is read as a whole. In order to achieve that, he studied the structure of the whole story and posited that 2 Kgs 18:13 – 19:37 has syntactical integrity, containing as it does discernible units within the narrative linked to temporal progression. He did not believe the text is describing the same event three times (A, B1 and B2), but rather reflects a sequential progression. In the light of his structural analyses, Evans reread the story and resolved the tension between A and B. Having accomplished that, Evans turned to a discussion of the historicity of 2 Kgs 18 – 19. His treatment in this part is strongly dependent on his conclusions of the first part. The flow of the events is the same as they are narrated in the biblical account. However, he confirmed their historicity by comparing the biblical material with Sennacherib's annals and reliefs.[14] In his view, the role of the Egyptian aid was significant in the war.[15]

Another author who focused on the historical events of 701 without examining the biblical or the Assyrian texts comprehensively is H.T. Aubin. Aubin ascri-

11 Gallagher, W.R., *Sennacherib's Campaign to Judah. New Studies* (SHCANE 18; Leiden, 1999), 257

12 Gallagher, *Sennacherib's Campaign*, 261.

13 Evans, P.S., *The Invasion of Sennacherib in the Book of Kings. A Source-Critical and Rhetorical Study of 2 Kings 18 – 19* (VTSup 125; Leiden, 2009).

14 Evans, *Invasion*, 167 – 177.

15 Evans, *Invasion*, 177 – 179.

bed a significant role to the Kushite army led by Tirhakah against the Assyrians. His work is based on the story related in the biblical account in 2 Kgs 19:9, which describes Sennacherib hearing that Tirhakah King of Kush has come out to fight him. The author suggests, "it seems likely that this would have been a second expeditionary force that the pharaoh had mustered after sending off the one that fought at Eltekeh."[16] His point of departure is data given about the Egyptian role in 701 by Egyptologists.[17] Aubin's monograph is quite thorough and detailed, but his main argument is encapsulated within chapters 10 and 14 where he offers six reasons that lead him to the conclusion that troops dispatched as part of an Egyptian-Kushite army caused the Assyrian withdrawal.

An interesting solution to the problem is offered by S. Dalley, who looks at the events of 701 from a different angle. She emphasizes the favourable Assyrian foreign policy towards Judah, which reached its apex with Sennacherib's unexpected treatment of Hezekiah's rebellion after the former invaded Judah in 701. Her proposal differs from those of other scholars in that she suggests that Sennacherib's positive conduct towards Hezekiah arose from the assumption that there was a family relationship by marriage between the Assyrian royal family and Jerusalem. Dalley's proposal is first presented in her article "Yabâ, Atalyā and the Foreign Policy of Late Assyrian Kings", where she asserts that the two Assyrian royal ladies, whose names Yabâ and Atalyā were found in grave 2 at Nimrud and who were the consorts of Tiglath-pileser III and Sargon II respectively, were originally Jerusalemites from the royal family.[18] Her claim is primarily based on the argument that the names of the two ladies are not Assyrian names: Atalyā, Dalley argues, is a Hebrew name because it contains the Yahwistic theophoric yā, and Yabâ is a West Semitic name and it is possible to understand it as a Hebrew name.[19] Beside the etymology of the names, the author discusses other evidence which reinforces the Jerusalemite identity of the two consorts. This evidence leads her to some conclusions about Sennacherib's

---

16 Aubin, H.T., *The Rescue of Jerusalem. The Alliance between Hebrews and Africans in 701 BC.* (New York, 2002), 12.

17 Mainly Yurco, F.J., "Sennacherib's Third Campaign and the Coregency of Shabaka and Shebitku", *Ser* 6 (1980), 221–240; and Kitchen, K.A., *The Third Intermediate Period in Egypt (1100–650)* (Warminster, 1986), 385. Kitchen asserts that when Sennacherib divided his army between Libnah and Jerusalem, Tirhakah regrouped his own forces to re-attack Sennacherib's dispersed army. But Sennacherib regathered his army smartly which made Tirhakah retire again to Egypt. Of course, Aubin does not agree entirely with this scenario, but at least he is convinced that there was a second Egyptian force led by Tirhakah.

18 Dalley, S., "Yabâ, Atalyā and the Foerign Policy of Late Assyrian Kings" *SAAB* 12 (1998), 83–98.

19 Dalley, "Yabâ", 94.

mild treatment of Hezekiah. These are as follows: diplomatic marriages are documented in Neo-Assyrian inscriptions. In addition, the names of foreign women who had a role in the royal court are known: Semiramis and Naqiiya. There are also signs of a peaceful relationship between Assyria and Judah in that Tiglath-pileser III's attack against southern Palestine bypasses Jerusalem. Furthermore, there is the non-involvement of Ahaz in the anti-Assyrian coalition of 733, the silence of the Judean kings towards the Assyrian military action in the southern area in 732, 720 and 713, and Isaiah's advice to Jerusalem (7:18–20) not to turn against Assyria. The message of Ahaz in 2Kgs 16:7 further indicates the peaceful relationship of Judah with Assyria.[20] Thus, the period of the Judean kings from Uzziah through to the reign of Manasseh was marked by a peaceful and favourable relationship between the two states, which was one of the reasons for the mild treatment of Hezekiah by Sennacherib.

The conclusions of this proposal are discussed again in a later article in which Dalley offers further explanations concerning the background to the unexpected alliance between Assyria and Judah. Assyria used foreign agents to manage trade operations as part of its strategy to maintain peaceful relations with its neighbours in the late eighth century. As for Hezekiah, Dalley puts her hypothesis in this way: "Judah... was in a position to benefit from this trade, so it was in its best interest to allow safe passage through its territory." Hezekiah was obliged to pass on some of the profits to Assyria under Sargon II, whether as a tax or as a friendship payment.[21] After the death of Sargon, however, when the balance of power shifted against Assyria, Hezekiah found an opportunity to stop paying the tribute, which Sennacherib interpreted as an anti-Assyrian activity that demanded punishment.

N. Na'aman too looks at the text from a different point of view.[22] He draws attention to the changes Hezekiah made to his predecessor's policy of submission and loyalty to Assyria, leading a coalition that tried to break the Assyrian yoke. He asserts that Hezekiah not only broke the yoke and refused to pay the tribute but also that he showed a hostile attitude towards the Assyrians and formed an anti-Assyrian alliance. In spite of these actions, however, Sennacherib left him safe in his city. To explain Sennacherib's behaviour, Na'aman first asserts that the assumption that Sennacherib intended to annex Judah and did

---

20 Dalley, "Yabâ", 87–89.

21 Dalley, S., "Recent Evidence from Assyrian Sources for Judean History from Uzziah to Manasseh", *JSOT* 28 (2004a), 389.

22 Na'aman, N., "Forced Participation in Alliances in the Course of the Assyrian Campaigns to the West", in M. Cogan *et al.* (eds.), *Ah, Assyria: Studies in Assyrian History and Ancient Near Eastern Historiography Presented to Hayim Tadmor* (SH 33; Jerusalem 1991).

not succeed in his goal is not supported by the evidence. According to Na'aman, the policy was designed to gain a balance of power, not to expand the Assyrian territory. The plan was only to weaken Judah, the strongest kingdom near to the Egyptian border. Sennacherib's success enabled his heirs to dominate the western territories without being threatened by local rulers. This explains why there was no anti-Assyrian alliance after that. The other reason for the campaign was to rescue the attacked vassal Padî, King of Ekron, who had already made an oath of allegiance to Assyria. In his argument, Na'aman discussed the military policy that was used during the time of Tiglath-pileser III and Sargon II. This policy—of not annexing states—was not new in the Neo-Assyrian period. In his campaign against Damascus and Israel, Tiglath-pileser III did not annex Israel in its entirety. The same policy was applied to the kingdom of Hamath in 738: despite the fact that most of its areas were annexed, the reduced kingdom of Hamath remained a vassal state under the new king, Eni-ilu. The reason, Na'aman thinks, was a long-standing loyalty to Assyria that began in the days of Shalmaneser III. For this reason, they were given another chance to behave properly. Forgiving the rebel, then, was possible if it served the Assyrian policy, and such a policy would make sense in relation to Hezekiah. Sennacherib did not intend to annex Judah, as that would not do him any good in his relations with Egypt.[23]

Having noted that discussions about the matter have revolved around the biblical accounts, A.R. Millard and A. Laato turn to the Assyrian inscriptions to answer historical questions about the campaign. In his 1984 article, Millard[24] makes some interesting observations about Sennacherib's treatment of Hezekiah. He notes that in the context of Assyrian royal inscriptions, Hezekiah's treatment seems to be unusually light. At the same time, Millard states that there is no sign given in Sennacherib's annals that Hezekiah was forgiven. If Sennacherib had forgiven Hezekiah, it would be logical to expect that he would mention it in his inscriptions, just as his grandson Ashurbanipal did with the Tyrian king Ba'alu.[25] The absence of such a statement leads Millard to doubt Sennacherib's success.[26] When he turns to the biblical text, Millard argues that the story of the Angel of the Lord is historically reliable, even if it is theological.[27]

---

23 Na'aman, "Forced", 93–98.
24 Millard, A.R., "Sennacherib's Attack on Hezekiah", *TB* 36 (1985), 61–77.
25 Millard gives an example of how the Assyrian kings could be merciful sometimes and forgive the rebels if they repent and admit their sin. King Ashurbanipal forgave the Tyrian king Ba'ali, but then he mentions that in his record. Cf. Piepkorn, A.C., *Historical Prism Inscriptions of Ashurbanipal* (AS 5; Chicago, 1933), 40–45.
26 Millard, "Hezekiah", 68–70.
27 Millard, "Hezekiah", 76.

Similarly, A. Laato questions the historical accuracy of Sennacherib's account.[28] Through a comparison between Sennacherib's inscriptions and the Babylonian Chronicles he shows that the historical accounts differ. For Laato, the fact that Sennacherib's own inscriptions were written a year after the event does not change the propagandistic nature of the annals. Laato goes on to present the particular literary and stylistic devices used in the inscriptions when military setbacks are being concealed. These involve hiding the reason for the sudden withdrawal to Nineveh, mentioning Hezekiah's paying of tribute so as to give the impression that his campaign to Judah had been successful even though the main rebel was not dethroned, not destroying Jerusalem, and exaggerating the number of deportees in order to bolster his campaign. These coded statements prompt Laato to conclude that Sennacherib did not achieve his goal, but had to abandon the siege.

2.2 Discussion

This survey illustrates the main directions that research on the historical issues of the campaign has taken. One can recognise three ways of conducting the research, which have not changed radically since the time of Childs. I will now present these three lines of enquiry and then discuss their validity and invalidity.

The approaches of Gonçalves, Gallagher and Evans are representative of the most prominent scholarly approach to the narrative. In this kind of study, the interest lies in the biblical accounts for two primary reasons: first, because of the various sources and layers of composition that characterise the narrative and, secondly, because part of the narrative is connected with the book of Isaiah as a result of the prophecies they share. Therefore, scholars who have sought to do exegetical justice to the diverse biblical texts have simultaneously kept an eye on questions of historical fact. While Gonçalves and Gallagher utilize the source-critical method, Evans focuses on the rhetorical. In both cases, the main focus of the research is to examine the overall literary unity of the text and the source(s) behind the text. Being somewhat tentative in his approach, Gonçalves does not help us to form a clear idea about the course of the events. Gallagher and Evans, however, rely on the historicity of the text, but their reasoning in regard to the events that happened during the campaign is not convincing. The efforts have not been really to reconstruct the historical course of

---

28 Laato, A., "Assyrian Propaganda and the Falsification of History in the Royal Inscriptions of Sennacherib", *VT* 45 (1995), 198–226.

the events but rather to study the character of the narrative and the relation between its different units. In other words, the historical reconstruction came in the context of reconciling the sources within the narrative and with other extra-biblical texts in the form of Sennacherib's annals.

Aubin's study presents a different methodology. The focus there is not on the analysis of the text but rather on the events. Clearly, his study is concerned more about history than the other studies and he has some illuminating insights that can help us to direct our research, particularly in his focus on the possible reasons for Sennacherib's withdrawal. Unfortunately, however, Aubin's study does not give all the possible reasons equal weight. From the beginning of his discussion, he directs the reader to think about the Egyptian-Kushite aid as a reason for Sennacherib's return. Neglecting other possible reasons means questions must be asked about the validity of his argument. Moreover, arguing that there was Egyptian-Kushite aid without dealing with the implications of what that might entail in the wider context of the narrative leaves the argument rather lacking in solid premises.

Although they use different methodologies in their studies, Na'aman and Dalley come to similar conclusions about the behaviour of Sennacherib in relation to Hezekiah. They both argue that Sennacherib forgave Hezekiah and withdrew after reducing the kingdom, quelling the rebels, and receiving a large tribute. One has to say that this explanation for the events has been the most acceptable to scholars. Given the fact that "in the Assyrian history this was not a moment of imperial expansion but of consolidation, re-asserting dominance over the Levant and paving the way for the following kings to move into Egypt,"[29] one might think that it was no surprise to see Sennacherib return without destroying Jerusalem. However, I see this theory as not convincing. Even if we assume that Hezekiah was forgiven, and find it unsurprising that Jerusalem was not destroyed, the question remains why Sennacherib did not enter Jerusalem and receive the tribute in the palace there, or alternatively why Hezekiah did not come out of his city to show submissive behaviour as other kings in the region did. The oddity in Sennacherib's behaviour is that he neither entered Jerusalem nor received the tribute in the region of Judah. If Hezekiah was forgiven, why did he not come out of Jerusalem to show submissive behaviour? The "forgiving theory" thus needs more discussion, in my opinion.[30]

---

29 Millard, "Hezekiah", 68.
30 It is worth mentioning that Dalley's argument is discussed and her evidence evaluated by K.L. Younger "Yahweh at Ashkelon and Calah? Yahwistic Names in Neo-Assyrian", *VT* 52 (2002), 207–218; and A. Achenbach, "Jabâ und Atalja – zwei jüdische Königstöchter am assyrischen Königshof. Zu einer These von Stephanie Dalley", *BN* 113 (2002), 29–38. The two schol-

The last proposed solution to discuss is that of Millard and Laato. Both scholars seek to understand Sennacherib's behaviour in the context of Assyrian inscriptions and the Babylonian Chronicle. In other words, they study the events from the Assyrian point of view. Although their conclusions have been very significant, their studies are brief and do not give the subject the weight it deserves. Laato consulted the Babylonian Chronicle, which looks at Sennacherib's campaign from a different angle. This methodology could be of great help in studying Sennacherib's campaign. However, the Babylonian Chronicle clearly only deals with Assyrian events in connection with Babylonia. Thus, consulting other Assyrian texts should support what we learn about the third campaign from this Chronicle—but such a comparison is missing from Laato's work. Moreover, placing the third campaign in the wider context of other campaigns just to look at one aspect (as Millard does) could be seen as giving only a narrow picture of the event. A more comprehensive study, therefore, is needed to look at the possibilities that the texts present in order to help us to understand the third campaign.

3. Methodology

The discussion above leads us to outline the methodology this research employs to deal with Sennacherib's third campaign. Needless to say, the scholarly arguments and theories presented above will be thoroughly discussed and elaborated upon. However, the methodology of Millard and Laato in particular contributes significantly in shaping this research. Before going further in that direction, however, I would like to discuss other issues in need of clarification. First of all, the

---

ars are not convinced that the two Assyrian queens mentioned in Dalley were of Judean origin. Younger bases his argument on a detailed study of a Neo-Assyrian transcription of a Yahwistic theophoric element. After presenting a number of non-royal Hebrew names containing the Yahwistic theophoric element and investigating the way these names are transcribed in the Neo-Assyrian cuneiform documents, he states that there is a certain way of denoting the theophoric element in the Neo-Assyrian transcription and that such an indicator does not exist in Atalyâ's name. Thus, he concludes, "it is very far from certain that the name of Sargon II's queen, Atalya, contains the Yahwistic theophoric element".

Beyond the etymological issues surrounding the two names, Achenbach's study addresses additional matters. For him, the Bible does not give a reliable account of a marriage between a Judean king's daughter either with Tiglath-pileser III or with Sargon II. Moreover, the mention of Ahaz and Hezekiah as tributaries among other kings in the Assyrian annals, and the insignificant role that Jerusalem played that made the Neo-Assyrian kings spare it, are all possible evidence to suggest that Judah did not enjoy the special treatment that Dalley suggests.

main concern of this research is the historicity of the events. The text and its theological aspects, therefore, will not receive the same level of attention that the historical issues do. The present study keeps in view the comprehensive literary examinations that have been undertaken on the text over a long period and which have reached an apex in recent years. In his 2010 thesis, P. Song-Mi applies source redaction and form criticism to the biblical accounts of Sennacherib's campaign within a wider context of what he calls the Hezekiah complex. His study comprises and embraces a large corpus of opinions and arguments concerning the text and its layers. His main interest is in discovering what theological and ideological concerns drove the progression of the complex.[31] Another attempt has been made by D. Bostock to direct attention not to the layers of the text but rather to the final form in which the text has been received. The author employs narrative criticism with special reference to the theme of faith.[32] One has to say that these two studies present the dominant method in dealing with Sennacherib's attack against Judah. Therefore, finding another methodology is desirable, especially if our interest is no longer the unity or theme of the text but rather the historical questions it raises. Nevertheless, it is important to reaffirm that this study will not apply traditional critical methods unless they are significant for the discussion.

The other issue that needs to be discussed before proceeding is the historicity of ancient texts, and how much we can rely on these texts to gain knowledge about what happened centuries ago. In this regard, the most obvious step to start with is the fact that the variety of sources available mentioning Sennacherib's campaign makes it impossible to regard the event as a rhetorical fiction or artificial construction to serve certain aims, even if the way it is recorded might incline the reader to think so. Needless to say, it is almost certainly impossible to know what really happened because we know about the event only through those who conveyed what they understood of the event and, more importantly, who only told us what they wanted us to know. However, if more than one source records an event this gives one the means to trace the flow of different lines and see where they come together. In this context, C.K. Telfer's words are helpful in framing our discussion:

> "To reject literature (biblical or extra-biblical) simply because it is saturated in religious ideology is to condemn oneself to ignorance of much of ancient near eastern history. A

---

31 Song-Mi, P., *The Development of the Hezekiah Complex: Literature, History and Theology* (Ph.D Dissertation, Harvard University, 2010).
32 Bostock, D., *A Portrayal of Trust: The Theme of Faith in the Hezekiah Narratives* (PBM; Milton Keynes, 2006).

more responsible and fruitful approach is to engage in a thorough literary study of the texts at hand to determine as exactly as possible what they may affirm… a comparative approach should be employed throughout.[33]

There are two points worth dwelling on here in Telfer's statement. First, it is implausible to dismiss the ancient texts because of their ideological and propagandistic nature; they are actually important evidence for historical events. Secondly, it is vitally important to use a suitable methodology to deal with the texts. It is obvious that in our case we are dealing with a variety of texts with annalistic and narrative characteristics and, thus, more than one way of studying a text is needed in our investigation. Before going further in our discussion about methodology, further clarification about the historical value of our texts is due. As for the Assyrian annals, it is true that they are meant to present a royal ideology; they certainly do not simply present a historical report of events that happened at a certain time. Thus, one might question the value of any historical knowledge we might get out of them. However, H. Tadmor's definition of the annals supports our use of them as a source in our study, in that he conceives of them as "official royal texts that describe the events of each year, written in the first person."[34] This means that these annals, though certainly permeated with ideology, do nevertheless narrate historical events. The main risk we might have in dealing with the annals is to regard the whole text as historical when we find a piece of historical information, or alternatively to consider the whole text as historically worthless when we find propagandistic and religious biases.[35] On the other hand, concerning the biblical accounts, the matter is more problematic as the text has gone through an elaborate history of writing, editing and refining. Yet extracting some sort of historical information is not impossible in the texts we are dealing with. Fortunately, the availability of the archaeological and extra-biblical sources helps us to evaluate the text. Moreover, the oddities in the text and the presence of more than one way of recording the event suggest some authenticity within the text.[36]

---

[33] Telfer, C.K., "Toward a Historical Reconstruction of Sennacherib's Invasion of Judah in 701 B.C. with Special Attention to the Hezekiah-Narrative of Isaiah 36–39", *MAJTh* 22 (2011), 9.

[34] Tadmor, H., "Observations on Assyrian Historiography", in M. Cogan (ed.), *"With My Many Chariots I Have Gone Up the Heights of Mountains". Historical and Literary Studies on Ancient Mesopotamia and Israel* (IES; Jerusalem, 2011), 47.

[35] See Kofoed, J.B., *Text and History. Historiography and the Biblical Text* (Winona Lake, 2005), 164–170.

[36] Grabbe, L.L., *Can a 'History of Israel' Be Written?* (JSOTSup 245; Shefield, 1996), 30.

In the light of this, I am going to present some information about the methodology I will employ in this research, while simultaneously clarifying the reasons why I will seek to examine critically the historicity of the texts we have.

The first point that is important in terms of my methodology is that equal attention will be given to the Assyrian and the biblical accounts; as a result, the work will be divided into two main parts. The first part deals with Sennacherib's campaign from the Assyrian point of view and the second with the same event from the biblical point of view. Nevertheless, reconciling both accounts is not the most urgent target in this research, although it will be discussed at certain points within the study. Instead, the Assyrian accounts will be treated separately from the biblical accounts so that we can learn what each account tells us about the campaign.

The second key point is that the study will not use the same methods to deal with the Assyrian accounts as it does with the biblical ones. Fundamentally, this is because the two accounts are different in genre and in their ideological aims. While the Assyrian royal inscriptions focus on the king and his deeds (thus emphasising the victory of the king), the biblical accounts—although there is a certain focus on the theological aspect of the events—place more emphasis on Sennacherib's return and also provide more than one reason for that return. Therefore, the two main questions that this study investigates are: Did Sennacherib really end his third campaign victorious? And, what was the reason for Sennacherib's return to Nineveh?

In relation to the first question, it should be noted that studying only the text of the third campaign is not really enough to decide whether Sennacherib was defeated or not. In this respect, L.D. Levine's statement is very significant: "a sample of one campaign is not sufficient to draw wide-ranging conclusions. It is the repetition of patterns that must be observed as well as the deviation from these patterns. One campaign may be anomalous, and thus, it is dangerous to use it as a basis for generalizations".[37] This study, therefore, will read the third campaign in the context of all the royal campaigns of Sennacherib. Comparing the patterns the Assyrian scribes used to present each campaign will help us recognise the deviations that can indicate irregular situations.[38] In other words, comparison will have a substantial role within this study. The subject of this

---

37 Levine, L.D., "Preliminary Remarks on the Historical Inscriptions of Sennacherib", in H. Tadmor and M. Weinfeld (eds.), *History, Historiography and Interpretation. Studies in Biblical and Cuneiform Literatures* (Jerusalem, 1983), 69.

38 Tadmor, H., "History and Ideology in the Assyrian Royal Inscriptions", in M. Cogan *"With My Many Chariots I Have Gone Up the Heights of Mountains". Historical and Literary Studies on Ancient Mesopotamia and Israel* (IES; Jerusalem, 2011), 25.

comparison is the literary conventions and formulaic patterns used to describe the political, military and economic aspects of each campaign.

Part One:
Sennacherib's Third Campaign within the Context of the Assyrian Inscriptions and Reliefs

Preliminary remarks

The Assyrian records from the ninth to seventh century demonstrate the Assyrian policy that was carried out at that time to achieve certain goals. The inscriptions of the most prominent kings like Ashurnasirpal II (883–859), Shalmaneser III (858–824), Adad-Nirari III (810–783), Tiglath-pileser III (744–727), Shalmaneser V (726–722), Sargon II (721–705) and Sennacherib (705–681) display the kind of strategy used by those kings in relation to the neighbours of the Assyrian Empire. The Assyrian Empire included tribute paying, vassal states and also exerted some influence over states independent from it.[39] Enlarging the empire and extending its boundaries, monitoring the influence of the neighbouring enemy states like Elam and Urartu, and establishing the Assyrian hegemony over other states, when possible, were the major aims of the Assyrian kings.

One of the most effective ways to achieve their aim was the regular launching of military campaigns, using the army that was famous for its highly advanced state. Therefore, the special attention that the Assyrian royal inscriptions paid to those campaigns is not surprising. That policy of conducting campaigns, however, was not arbitrary or careless; on the contrary, the Assyrians kings were clearly veteran politicians who knew how to plan for their military enterprises in advance. Accordingly, their treatment of the states around them differed according to their interests—the states that were a direct military threat to the empire were treated more carefully and harshly than states valued for their economic vitality. There was even a difference in Assyrian treatment of the states that were controlled by them and the rival civilisations that were independent. In fact, military actions were conditioned by certain factors; they had to meet certain political and economic values. M. Liverani draws our attention to the various themes of Assyria's imperialistic and colonial ideology.[40] He realised that these ideological themes were applied differently according to different areas because "what can be said of the Mannean mountain-dwellers cannot be said of

---

39 Cogan, M., *Imperialism and Religion: Assyria, Judah and Israel in the Eighth and Seventh Centuries B.C.E.* (SBL 19; Missoula, 1974), 42.

40 Liverani, M., "The Ideology of the Assyrian Empire", in M.T. Larsen (ed.), *Power and Propaganda. A Symposium on Ancient Empires* (Mesopotamia 7; Copenhagen, 1979), 297–317.

the Arab nomads, what can be said of the Syrian town-dwellers cannot be said of Babylon."[41] J. Reade similarly asserts that according to the Assyrian perspective "foreign states were grouped in categories and treated accordingly".[42] Thus, the varied conduct of the Assyrian kings and the different outcomes of their campaigns should not puzzle the reader. On the contrary, this variety could lead to better understanding of the Assyrian kings' special treatment of certain kings.

However, it is important to note that when the military campaigns were represented in Assyrian literature, these were not meant to narrate the events of each campaign only, but rather they presented them in a way that served the royal ideology. Hence, like other royal texts they took "the form of eloquently composed war reports,"[43] with a certain compositional structure and lexical-ideological conventions employed to narrate both the historical event and express the Assyrian ideology. Therefore, close attention is required when reading the Assyrian reports of the campaigns. This will be helpful in understanding the historical events described through the formulae and conventions.[44] Moreover, it is important to note that the Assyrians did not represent their campaigns via literature and texts only, but also used mural art to express visually what the inscriptions could not convey. Studying the reliefs, then, enriches our knowledge about the representation of their military activity.

When it comes to the representation of the campaigns, Sennacherib is no exception. Like his ancestors, he authorised writing and depictions of the military campaigns conducted during his reign. The texts and the reliefs, accordingly, came to demonstrate his victor's prerogative, when they narrate the episodes of the campaigns. This does not exclude the fact that there were certain ideological-literary conventions and particular techniques used in the texts and in the reliefs.

Hence, going through the representations of the campaigns will give us the opportunity to have a look at all the campaigns, and then to see the commonalities and irregularities in presenting the military activities. This, however, is not the main aim of the literary reading of Sennacherib's campaigns. The aim of going through the inscriptions of Sennacherib is to look at the third campaign

---

41 Liverani, "Ideology", 304.
42 Reade, J., "Ideology and Propaganda in Assyrian Art", in M.T. Larsen (ed.), *Power and Propaganda.. A Symposium on Ancient Empires* (Mesopotamia 7; Copenhagen, 1979), 333–334.
43 Tadmor, H., "Propaganda, Literature, Historiography: Cracking the Code of the Assyrian Royal Inscriptions", in M. Cogan (ed.), *"With My Many Chariots I have Gone up the Heights of the Mountains": Historical and Literary Studies on Ancient Mesopotamia and Israel* (IES; Jerusalem, 2011), 3.
44 Tadmor, "Propaganda", 326.

in the wider context of Sennacherib's campaigns and other similar military activities so as to understand better Sennacherib's behaviour towards Hezekiah and Jerusalem. To be more precise, it is obvious that the Assyrian scribes and sculptors did not present exactly what happened during each campaign, but rather how they were meant to perceive each campaign. The scribes used particular language to express the official perception of the campaigns, and the sculptors used particular ways of visual narration to convey these official perceptions of the campaigns. So, going through the literary texts and reading carefully how each campaign was written about can help us interpret the sources. Thus, our literary investigation will help us weigh the evidence and lead us to a conclusion about historical issues concerning the third campaign. Investigating the reliefs, especially the Lachish reliefs, will strengthen the study and provide an opportunity to compare the representation of the campaign in the written texts with that in the mural art. In the course of this investigation, archaeological evidence will be consulted to help us evaluate what the written texts and the reliefs tell us about the campaigns.

This part of the study is divided into three chapters. In the first chapter, I investigate the literary conventions used to represent the campaigns that Sennacherib conducted during his reign. In the second chapter, the reliefs of Lachish will be studied thoroughly. And in the third chapter, Jerusalem's blockade is compared with other cases of blockaded cities. The aim of this is to look at the third campaign in a much wider context in a way that has never been undertaken before and compare the data so that we may have a clearer idea about what made the third campaign special. This enables us to try to discern, from the language and the way it is depicted, what happened in that campaign.

Chapter Two: Literary Reading of Sennacherib's Campaigns

1. Introduction

Many military campaigns were conducted during Sennacherib's reign. They are recorded in inscriptions; these inscriptions, however, represent the campaigns using literary modes to explain different issues within each campaign, like the introductory formula, the motive of the campaign, the fate of the enemy king, the strategy used by Sennacherib to defeat his enemy, and the economic outcome of the campaign. In the following study, therefore, I present the texts of these campaigns so that we may have an idea of the way Sennacherib desired his campaigns to be expressed. The different themes presented in the campaigns will be discussed in order to understand the main features that the written texts focused on.

For methodological reasons, the episodes of all the royal and non-royal campaigns are presented. Doing so will provide the study with the necessary data about each campaign. From this the work proceeds to discuss the common motifs and conventions presented when narrating the events of the campaigns. Unsurprisingly, the military activity and the economic exploitation will make up a large portion of the discussion, as they were prominent motives for the campaigns. Afterwards, a conclusion will be drawn about the campaigns in general and about the third campaign in particular.

2. Preliminary considerations

2.1. General notes about the campaigns

The Assyrian inscriptions give witness to the fact that Sennacherib started his military activity before he was crowned as the king of the Assyrian Empire. It is not surprising then that his first campaign occurred fairly soon after his coronation. The main purpose of the campaigns was to confirm that the Assyrian Empire was in control of all the neighbouring states. Like his ancestors, Sennacherib put much effort into quelling the danger of the powerful and threatening states like Babylonia, the land of the Hittites and Egypt, and to ensuring that the vassal states showed submissive behaviour and demonstrated their loyalty to Assyria. Conducting military campaigns was one of the well-known and often successful ways to achieve such aims. Therefore, the military campaigns comprised a large portion of the inscriptions of Sennacherib.

However, tracing all the details needed about all the military campaigns is not a straightforward task for several reasons. These include the fragmentary nature of the tablets or items that contain the accounts of the campaigns; the dearth of sources; and the fact that Sennacherib did not record all the campaigns he conducted, as we find out about those other campaigns from other sources that were inscribed from a non-royal perspective. More importantly, Assyriologists put effort into categorising and dating the campaigns. A.K. Grayson asserts that "the problem of dating arises out of the fact that Sennacherib's campaigns are generally not dated by eponym or regnal year, but are merely numbered sequentially as first, second, third, etc. The official numbering, which goes up to eight in the exact corpus, included only expeditions personally led by the king. Campaigns led by Sennacherib's officials were usually excluded from royally sponsored compositions."[45] Additionally, excavations have yielded no (textual) information about Sennacherib's campaigns after 689. So, it is unknown whether Sennacherib stopped campaigning after 689 or whether we simply do not have the relevant information.

Nevertheless, some serious attempts have been made to synchronise data about the military campaigns of Sennacherib. In his 1924 book, D.D. Luckenbill presented the campaigns recorded in the annals of Sennacherib.[46] More recently, R. Borger has presented a reliable edition of some of Sennacherib's campaigns in his *Lesestücke*.[47] At the end of the same century, E. Frahm made a very comprehensive study of the inscriptions of Sennacherib with much more extensive explanation about some texts of the campaigns and the military activity of Sennacherib.[48] In *The Prosopography of the Assyrian Empire*,[49] Frahm gives a brief account of Sennacherib's biography, including his military actions. And most recently, Grayson and J. Novotny published the first volume of *The Royal Inscriptions of Sennacherib*.[50] Although Grayson and Novotny's book provides basic editions of texts that can serve our study, we still need the previous literature because the first volume does not contain the texts of all the campaigns.

---

45 Grayson, A.K. and Novotny, J., *The Royal Inscriptions of Sennacherib, King of Assyria (704–681)* (RINAP 3/1; Winona Lake, 2012), 9.
46 Luckenbill, D.D., *The Annals of Sennacherib* (OIP 2; Chicago, 1924).
47 Borger, R., *Babylonisch-Assyrische Lesestücke* (AO 54; Rome, 1979).
48 Frahm, E., *Einleitung in die Sanherib-Inschriften* (AfO 26; Vienna, 1997).
49 Frahm, E., "Sîn-aḫḫê-erība", in H. Baker, *The Prosopography of the Assyrian Empire*. Vol. 3, Part I: P-Ṣ (Helsinki, 2002), 1113–1127.
50 See n. 44

2.2. Counting the campaigns

Despite the fact that the last numbered campaign in Sennacherib's inscriptions is the eighth, apparently there were more than eight campaigns. The Assyrian scribe numbers the royal campaign against the Babylonians that took place in 704/703 as the first campaign. But from other sources we know that the first campaign took place right after the coronation in 704 against the Kulummeans in the north and was led not by Sennacherib himself but by his magnates.[51] There is no mention of that campaign in Sennacherib's inscriptions so far. The other two campaigns, undertaken not by the king but by his military officers, took place in the years 696 and 695. These campaigns are narrated in the inscriptions but they are not numbered as the other eight campaigns are; they are titled *ina limmu PN*, "in the eponym of PN".[52] Moreover, the inscriptions report two other campaigns, one against the Arabs in 690 and the other one against the Babylonians in 689, when Babylon was sacked. So far, there is no full account of the campaign against the Arabs; and the destruction of Babylon is not related to the other campaigns in the annals, but in other inscriptions called Bavian inscriptions. So, whether or not these last two campaigns were numbered like the others is uncertain. Regardless, I am going to present all the campaigns, making use of the data made available to us by the sources mentioned above. It might be bold to claim that a pattern can be concluded from presenting the different elements of each campaign because, as mentioned above, we do not have the full accounts of all the campaigns. However, certain features can be discerned about the strategy of Sennacherib in his military activities if we look carefully at the data provided by the sources available. On these grounds, I am going to present the campaigns.

2.3. Texts used in the investigation

In presenting the military campaigns of Sennacherib, this study will depend on the earliest versions available. Later versions will be used when needed in our investigation. This is because the earlier versions contain fuller accounts of the campaigns. A later version of a campaign tends to be shorter and reduced to give space to narrate the campaign following it. Utilising the earliest versions

---

51 Millard, A.R., *The Eponyms of the Assyrian Empire 910–612* (SAAS 2; Helsinki, 1994), 48.
52 Frahm, *Einleitung*, 251.

available will enable us to have clearer ideas about each campaign and, accordingly, to trace the military strategy that Sennacherib used in his campaigns.

It is worthwhile mentioning that this study is aware of the difficulty in choosing a certain text to present the episodes of any campaign. The task of the scribe was not to list the events, but rather to present them in an historiographical framework. In this regard, Levine directs our attention to an essential point in studying the campaigns. In dealing with Sennacherib's campaigns to the south he demonstrates that:

> the term *girru*, often translated by "campaign," does not correspond to the usual meaning of that term in military history. It is not clear in the historical records of Sennacherib what mechanisms operated to divide events in *girru*'s. Whatever these mechanisms, different lines were drawn in different sources as to where a connected series of events should be cut off and a new series begun.[53]

One can understand from Levine's statement that using other sources presenting the campaign is important. But the point I would like to make is that in this part of the study, I am not trying to reconstruct the campaigns of Sennacherib; rather, I seek to understand the literary presentation of these campaigns. Thus, I take the annals as "literary documents that have formal structures."[54] Examining these structures, therefore, will help us understand the purpose of the representation of each campaign. It will be necessary to consult other sources in order to know what was desirable to keep and what was omitted.

3. Presenting Sennacherib's campaigns

In the following part the main military actions of the campaigns and their outcome, viz. economic exploitation, are presented. Doing so will give us an idea of the main focus of Sennacherib, or, to be more objective, it will help us know the way Sennacherib perceived these campaigns and wanted them to be represented. Outlines of each campaign will be sketched and a very brief explanation about which version is used to describe each campaign will be given.

---

53 Levine, L.D., "Sennacherib's Southern Front: 704–689 ", *JCS* 34 (1982), 53.
54 Levine, "Sennacherib's Southern Front", 52.

3.1. The campaign against the Kulummeans

There is no account of this campaign. The eponyms of the Assyrian Empire record its date in 704.[55]

3.2. The first campaign against Babylonia in 704

Sources
The longest and earliest account of the operation of the first campaign is preserved in the earliest inscription of Sennacherib, called *First Campaign*, which was inscribed on barrel-cylinders, probably in 702.[56] Also, the campaign was recorded later in other inscriptions that described the events of the operation in less detail, e. g., Tarbiṣu Cylinders: 5–61[57]; Bellino Cylinder: 5–19[58]; Rassam Cylinder: 5–17[59]; Bull 2/3: 7–10, 13–15[60]; Bull 4: 3–9[61]; Chicago Prism: I 20–64[62]; and Nebi-Yunus: 6–8, 12.[63] In addition, the campaign is mentioned in the Eponym Chronicle[64] and in Babylonian Chronicle ii 9–25.[65] The account used in this study is that in the First Campaign Cylinder translated by Grayson.[66]

Episodes of the campaign
A. Introduction (at the beginning of my reign)... line 5[67]
B. Mentioning the motive of the campaign

---

55 Millard, *Eponyms*, 48
56 Frahm, E., "New Sources for Sennacherib's 'First Campaign'", *ISIMU* VI (2003), 131. In his article, Frahm re-edits the earliest royal inscriptions that describe the events of the first campaign.
57 Suleiman, A., *Al-kitāba al-mismārīya wal-ḥarf al-'arabī* (Cuneiform Writing and Arabic alphabet) (Ph.D. Dissertation, Mosul n.d), 138–66.
58 Grayson, *Sennacherib*, 51–52.
59 Grayson, *Sennacherib*, 61–62.
60 Luckenbill, *Annals*, 76 f.
61 Luckenbill, *Annals*, 66 f.
62 Grayson, *Sennacherib*, 172–173.
63 Luckenbill, *Annals*, 85 f.
64 Millard, *Eponyms*, 49.
65 Grayson, A.K., *Assyrian and Babylonian Chronicles* (TCS 5; Locust Valley, 1975), 76 f.
66 Grayson, *Sennacherib*, 32–37.
67 The first four lines of the account contain the epithets given to Sennacherib. This part of the inscription is not going to be included in the episodes of the campaigns presented in the study.

     a. Merodach-Baladan appeals to the Elamite King Šutruk-Naḫḫunte II ... lines 6–7

     b. The Elamite king responds...lines 8–9

     c. Merodach-Baladan organises to fight and gathers together the Aramaean tribes that were living along the rivers...lines 10–15

C. Sennacherib's military reaction

     a. Sennacherib marches into Babylon...line 16

     b. Merodach-Baladan creates the powerful units for war and brings them to Cutha...lines 17–18

D. Date and the itinerary formula (on the 20ᵗʰ of Šabāṭu (XI), I set out of the city of Aššur)...line 19

E. First set of military actions

     a. Sennacherib sends men to find out about Merodach-Baladan in Kish... line 20

     b. Reaction of Merodach-Baladan: combat in Kish...line 21

     c. Sennacherib's magnates send messengers to Sennacherib asking for aid...line 22

     d. In Cutha

        i.   Assaulting Cutha

        ii. Slaughtering (*ṭabāḫu*) the warriors...line 23

        iii. Taking the city (*ṣabātu*)...line 23

        iv. Taking booty (*šallatiš manû*)...line 24

     e. In Kish

        i.   Sennacherib moves to Kish...line 25

        ii. Merodach-Baladan flees to Guzummanu...line 26

F. Second set of military actions

     a. Sennacherib defeats (*dabdû*) the Elamite, Chaldean, and Aramaean army...line 27

     b. Sennacherib takes booty...people and animals...lines 28–29

     c. In Babylon, the capital city

     d. Sennacherib enters (*erēbu*) the palace and takes booty...people and goods...lines 30–33

     e. He sends after Merodach-Baladan, but cannot capture him...line 34

     f. Sennacherib gathers the rest of the booty...line 35

     g. In the course of his campaign

        i.   Sennacherib besieges, conquers and takes the spoils (*lamû, kašādu, šalālu*) of 88 strong cities and 820 small cites...36–50

        ii. He has his soldiers take the goods of the cities, which he destroys, devastates, burns and turns into forgotten mounds (*napālu, naqāru, qamû*)...line 51

iii. He brings forth the irregular bands from four cities and takes them as spoils...line 52

h. He has his troops devour the harvest of these four cities...line 53

G. Placing a puppet on the throne: Bēl-ibni...line 54

H. On the way back, Sennacherib captures the tribes which were not submissive and takes booty (*kašādu, šalālu*) ...lines 55–56

I. Third set of military actions

    a. He receives tribute from the official of Ḫararatu...line 57

    b. He cuts down the subjects of the city of Ḫirimmu...line 58

    c. imposed annual tribute ...line 59

    d. Carrying off booty to Assyria and smiting subjects who had not immediately submitted...lines 60–62

3.3. The campaign against Zagros in 702

Sources

The earliest accounts of the second campaign are reported in two texts, both inscribed in 702: the Bellino Cylinder and another text combining elements of the First Campaign Cylinder and the Bellino Cylinder.[68] Also, the accounts are recorded in other inscriptions with fewer details, e.g. Rassam Cylinder: 18–31;[69] Bull 2/3: 15 f;[70] Bull 4: 9–17;[71] Chicago Prism: I 65–ii 36;[72] Nebi-Yunus: 12f;[73] K 1280: 1–10;[74] and Jerwan no. 34 (+).[75] Since the text in the Bellino Cylinder is the earliest version of the campaign, this study will use it to examine the events of Sennacherib's campaign against the region of Zagros.

Episodes of the campaign

A. Introduction (on my second campaign)...line 20[76]

B. Itinerary formula (against the Kassites and the land of Yasubigallians); and the motive of the campaign: not being submissive...line 20

---

68 Grayson, *Sennacherib*, 41–55.

69 Grayson, *Sennacherib*, 62–63.

70 Luckenbill, *Annals*, 77.

71 Luckenbill, *Annals*, 67–68.

72 Grayson, *Sennacherib*, 173–175.

73 Luckenbill, *Annals*, 86.

74 Luckenbill, *Annals*, 156.

75 Frahm, *Einleitung*, 157.

76 The lines before the description of this campaign narrate the account of the previous campaign after presenting the names of Sennacherib.

C. Description of proceeding through a mountainous region...line 21
D. In Bīt-kilamzaḫ
    a. Besieging and conquering Bīt-kilamzaḫ, the stronghold...line 22
    b. Taking booty (people and animals)...line 22
    c. Destroying, devastating and ruining the small cities...line 23
    d. Setting the tents on fire...line 23
E. Making Bīt-kilamzaḫ a fortress again, strengthening it, and settling people in it...line 24
F. Kassites and Yasubigallians
    a. Settling the people of Kassites and Yasubigallians in ḫardišpu and Bīt-Kubatti...line 25
    b. Joining them to Arrapḫa...line 26
    c. Placing a stele there...line 26
G. In the land of Ellipi
    a. The king Ispabāra flees...line 27
    b. The two royal cities with 34 strong cities and the small cities are destroyed, devastated and burned...lines 28–29
    c. The orchards are cut down...line 29
    d. Bringing the people of Ellipi to naught... line 29
    e. Taking booty (people and animals)...line 30
    f. Two strong cities with small cities and the district of Bīt-Barrû added to Assyria...line 31
    g. Elenzaš is made a royal city and stronghold of the district. And its name is changed... line 32
H. On the return, a tribute is received from Medes and they submitted to Assyria for the first time...line 33

3.4. The campaign against the west in 701

Sources

The earliest known account of Sennacherib's campaign against the Levant is the Rassam Cylinder. The account was written in 700.[77] In addition, the accounts were recorded later in other inscription, e.g. Bull 2/3: 17–22;[78] Bull 4: 18–32;[79]

---

77 Grayson, *Sennacherib*, 63–66.
78 Luckenbill, *Annals*, 77.
79 Luckenbill, *Annals*, 68–70.

Chicago Prism: ii 37–iii 49;[80] and Nebi-Yunus: 13–15.[81] This study, therefore, is using the accounts in the Rassam Cylinder translated by Grayson.

Episodes of the campaign

A. Introduction (on my third campaign)...line 32
B. Itinerary formula (against the land of ḫatti)...line 32
C. In Phoenicia
    a. The attitude of Lulî, king of Sidon: being overwhelmed by fear, he fled... line 32
    b. Eight fortified cities were overwhelmed by the weapons of Aššur, and submitted at the feet of Sennacherib...lines 33–34
    c. Tu-ba'lu is seated on the throne...line 35
    d. The king imposes annual tribute and taxes...line 35
    e. Eight kings of the Westland bring fourfold gifts to Sennacherib and kiss his feet (the names of the places are listed)...lines 36–38
D. In Philistia
    a. Dealing with Ṣidqâ , who had not submitted to the Assyrian yoke (moved the gods from his father's house, himself, members of the royal family... all to Assyria...line 39
    b. Placing of another person on the throne (Šarru-lū-dāri)...line 40
    c. Payment of tribute is imposed...line 40
    d. In the course of the campaign, four cites (names are mentioned) are conquered and spoils are taken from them...line 41
    e. The officials of Ekron feared...their sin is that they handed their king Padî, the Assyrian vassal, to Hezekiah; they banded together with the kings of Egypt and the king of Meluḫḫa ...lines 42–43
    f. The battle in the vicinity of Eltekeh...(the enemy was defeated)...line 44
    g. Collecting booty from the enemy after the battle...line 45
    h. Two cities (Eltekeh and Tamnâ) are conquered and spoils are taken from them...line 46
    i. Drawing near to Ekron (officials are tortured and killed; those who sinned were taken as spoils; the innocent ones are released)...lines 46–47
    j. Padî is brought out of Jerusalem, placed on the throne and tribute to him is imposed...line 48
E. In Judah

---

80 Grayson, *Sennacherib*, 175–177.
81 Luckenbill, *Annals*, 86.

    a. Dealing with Hezekiah, who did not submit to the Assyrian yoke: 46 cities are besieged and conquered...lines 49 – 50

    b. Booty is brought out of the cities ...line 51

    c. Hezekiah is enclosed in his city...line 52

    d. Fortresses are erected around Jerusalem to prevent anybody getting out...line 52

    e. Cities which Hezekiah conquered are taken from him and given to the kings of Philistia...line 53

    f. Again tribute on the kings of Philistia is imposed...line 54

    g. The attitude of Hezekiah: he was overwhelmed by the radiance of the lordship of Sennacherib, and sent to Nineveh a large tribute to Sennacherib...lines 55 – 58

F. Forming a large military contingent from the prisoners...lines 59 – 60

3.5. The second campaign against Babylonia in 700

Sources

As for using the earliest edition of this campaign, the matter is more complicated than in the previous campaigns. Frahm suggests that the earliest version of the account of the fourth campaign is K 2627+ r. 23 and DT 320: 1'–7', of which almost nothing remains.[82] So we do not have an account recorded shortly after the campaign. The text where the account about this campaign can be read is in the Octagonal Clay Prisms, which were inscribed in 697–691, several years after the campaign. In these Prisms, the accounts of the campaign in question are almost identical. Therefore, I will use the text in Cylinder C, which was inscribed in 697, to recount the campaign. Also, the accounts of the campaign were recorded in Bull 2/3: 11–13;[83] Bull 4: 33–37;[84] Chicago Prism: iii 50–74;[85] and Nebi-Yunus: 8–12[86]. In the non-royal inscriptions, the campaign is recorded in the Babylonian Chronicles,[87] as well as some king lists.[88]

---

82 Frahm, *Einleitung*, 61 – 62 and 200.

83 Luckenbill, *Annals*, 76 f.

84 Luckenbill, *Annals*, 71.

85 Grayson, *Sennacherib*, 177 – 178.

86 Luckenbill, *Annals*, 85 f.

87 Grayson, *Chronicles*, 77.

88 Grayson, A.K., "Königslisten und Chroniken B. Akkadisch", *RlA* 6/1 (1980), 93:16; 101; 120:12; 122:1.

Episodes of the campaign
A. Introduction (on my fourth campaign)...column iv, line 15'
B. Itinerary formula (against Bīt-Yakīn)...lines 17'–18'
C. In the city of Bittūtu
    a. The enemy king Mušēzib-Marduk, the Chaldean who dwelt in Bittūtu, flees because he feared Sennacherib's weapon...lines 19'–23'
D. In Bīt-Yakīn
    a. Merodach-Baladan flees to Nagīte-raqqi because he feared Sennacherib's mighty arms...lines 24'–34'
    b. Booty is taken...only people and members of the royal family...line 35'-column v, line 2a
    c. His cities are destroyed and set on fire...lines 2b–4
    d. Placing Aššur-nādin-šumi on the throne, and making the land submit to Assyria...lines 5–9
C. Conscripting the prisoners into the army...lines 10–15

3.6. The campaign against Urartu in 697

Sources
The case with the campaign against the northern region is similar to that of the previous campaign. The earliest text available is in Cylinder D, which was written between 696 and 695. The account of the campaign is also related in the Judi-Dagh inscriptions: 12–51;[89] Bull 2/3: 22–3;[90] Bull 4: 37–47;[91] Chicago Prism: iii 75–iv 31;[92] and Nebi-Yunus: 16 f.[93]

Episodes of the campaign
A. Introduction (on my fifth campaign)...column iv, line 70
B. Mentioning the motive of the campaign: the populations of seven cities on Mt Nipur have not been submissive...lines 71–77
C. Mentioning the location of the military camp: at the foot of Mt Nipur...line 78
D. Describing preparation for war...lines 79–82
E. Describing the difficulty of the journey...line 83-column v, line 7

---

89 Luckenbill, *Annals*, 64–66.
90 Luckenbill, *Annals*, 77.
91 Luckenbill, *Annals*, 71–72.
92 Grayson, *Sennacherib*, 178–179.
93 Grayson, *Sennacherib*, 222.

F. Defeating the enemy...line 8
G. Conquering and taking spoils from the cities of Nipur. Destroying, devastating and burning the cities ...lines 9–11a
H. In Ukku
    a. Describing the reason for the attack: King Maniye has not been submissive...lines 11b–14
    b. Describing the hardships of the journey... lines 15–22
    c. Maniye flees... lines 23–25
    d. Besieging and capturing the capital city, entering the palace and taking heavy booty from it...lines 26–28
I. Conquering 33 cities on the border of Maniye's district, carrying booty out of them and eventually devastating and burning them...lines 29–32
J. Conscripting soldiers from the prisoners...lines 33–40

3.7. The campaign against Cilicia in 696

Sources
The earliest account available is in the Heidel Prism, which was inscribed in 694.[94] In addition, part of the account of this campaign was inscribed in Bulls 2/3: 24[95] and Nebi-Yunus 17f.[96]

Episodes of the campaign
A. Introduction (in the eponymy of Šulmu-Bēl, the governor of Talmusu)...column iv, line 61
B. Mentioning the motive of the campaign:
    a. Kirūa, ruler of Illubru, a servant who belonged to Sennacherib, caused the men of Ḫilakku to rebel and prepare for battle...lines 62–65
    b. People of Ingirâ and Tarzu aligned themselves with him and seized a trade route through the land Que...lines 66–68
C. Itinerary formula (I sent against them)...lines 69–71
D. Defeating the population of Ḫilakku ...lines 72–74
E. Ingirâ and Tarzu are conquered and booty is taken...lines 75–76
F. Besieging the enemy king and conquering his city...lines 77–81

----

94 Grayson, *Sennacherib*, 135–136.
95 Luckenbill, *Annals*, 77.
96 Grayson, *Sennacherib*, 222.

G. Booty is brought with the enemy king to Nineveh...lines 82–85
H. The enemy king is flayed...line 86
I. Restoring Illubru and settling people in it...lines 87–89
J. Establishing a stele in the city...lines 90–91

3.8. The campaign against Tīl-Garimme in 695

Sources
Like the case of the campaign against Cilicia, the account of this campaign can be found in the Heidel Prism.[97] Additionally, the account of the campaign is in Bulls 2/3:24 f[98] and Nebi-Yunus: 19.[99]

Episodes of the campaign
A. Introduction (in the eponym of Aššur-bēl-uṣur, governor of the land of Kat-muḫu)...line 1
B. Itinerary formula (I sent my magnates against Tīl-Garimme, a city of Talmusu[100])...lines 2–3, 6
C. The motive of the campaign: Gurdî the king of Talmusu had mobilised his weapons at Tīl-Garimmu...lines 4–5
D. Besieging the city and conquering it ...lines 9–11
E. Booty is taken (people and gods)... line 12
F. Devastating the city and taking booty from it...lines 13–14
G. Conscripting soldiers from the prisoners...line 15–22

3.9. The campaign against Elam in 694–693

Sources
The earliest account of the campaign against Elam can be read in the Prism which was inscribed in 691. But the text contains only six brief lines about the campaign. Also, Bull 4 inscriptions only contain the beginning of the

---

97 Grayson, *Sennacherib*, 136–137.
98 Luckenbill, *Annals*, 77.
99 Grayson, *Sennacherib*, 222.
100 I am following Frahm's reading for the name of the city; Frahm, *Einleitung*, 88. Grayson reads it as Tabalu.

campaign.[101] For this reason, the text in the Chicago Prism, which was inscribed between 691 and 689, is used in this study. [102] Other inscriptions partially relating the account of this campaign are: Bull 2/3: 25–32;[103] Baltimore: 16–19;[104] Nebi-Yunus: 20–36;[105] and Ungnad/Winckler: 1'–5'.[106] Furthermore, in the non-royal inscriptions, the account is recorded in the Babylonian Chronicles[107] and some king lists.[108]

Episodes of the campaign

A. Introduction (on my sixth campaign)...column iv, line 32
B. The motive of the campaign: some people of Bīt-Yakīn escaped to Elam, a city of Nagītu...lines 33–36
C. Itinerary formula (I crossed the sea in boats)...line 37
D. The cities of Nagītu and Nagītu-di'bina together with three districts of Elam were conquered ...lines 38–39
E. The Bīt-Yakīn who were in Elam were brought to south Babylonia...lines 40–43
F. The cities in those districts were devastated...lines 45–46a
G. On the way back, Nergal-ušēzib, who made himself king of Babylon while Sennacherib was in Elam, is defeated...lines 46b–49
H. Nergal-ušēzib is captured and brought alive to Assyria...lines 50–51
I. The king of Elam, who came to the aid of Nergal-ušēzib, is defeated...lines 52–53

3.10. The second campaign against Elam in 693

Sources

The campaign is designated as the seventh campaign in the inscriptions. For the account of the campaign, Chicago Prism iv 54–v16 is, again, used in this study.[109]

---

101 Luckenbill, *Annals*, 73–76.
102 Grayson, *Sennacherib*, 179–180.
103 Luckenbill, *Annals*, 77–78.
104 Grayson, A.K., "The Walters Art Gallery Sennacherib Inscription", *AfO* 20 (1963), 88–91.
105 Grayson, *Sennacherib*, 222–223.
106 Grayson, *Sennacherib*, 229–230.
107 Grayson, *Chronicles*, 130–132.
108 Grayson, "Chroniken", 93:17; 101; 120:7–9; 122:2.
109 Grayson, *Sennacherib*, 180–181.

Additionally, the campaign is recorded in Baltimore: 19–44;[110] Nebi-Yunus 36–44;[111] Ungnad/Winckler: 16'–29';[112] and in the non-royal inscriptions, Babylonian Chronicles[113] and some king lists.[114]

Episodes of the campaign
A. Introduction (on my seventh campaign)...column iv, line 54
B. Itinerary formula (I marched to the land of Elam)...line 55
C. Two cities within the borders of Assyria were conquered, joined to Assyria and brought under the authority of Dēr...lines 56–61a
D. Many cities (with names mentioned) are surrounded, conquered, devastated and despoiled...lines 61b–81a
E. The Elamite king, Kudur-Naḫḫunte, leaves his city, Madaktu, and flees to another city in the district...line 81b-column v, line 5
F. Ordering a march to the royal city Madaktu...line 6
G. Explaining the setback and turning to Nineveh because of the weather...lines 7–11a
H. Reporting the death of the Elamite king...lines 11b–15

3.11. The third campaign against Babylonia in 692

Sources
Sennacherib's third campaign against the Babylonians was in 691, and it is called the eighth campaign. The full account is in the Chicago/Taylor Prism, which was inscribed in late 691, on which this study depends to display the episodes of the campaign. Other sources are: Baltimore: 11–16, 45–115;[115] Nebi-Yunus 44–55;[116] Ungnad/Winckler: 29'–52';[117] and Babylonian Chronicles.[118]

---

110 Grayson, "Walter", 90–91.
111 Grayson, *Sennacherib*, 223–224.
112 Grayson, *Sennacherib*, 230–231.
113 Grayson, *Chronicles*, 79.
114 Grayson, "Chroniken", 93:18; 101; 120:7–9; 122:3.
115 Grayson, "Walter", 88–95.
116 Grayson, *Sennacherib*, 223–224.
117 Grayson, *Sennacherib*, 231–232.
118 Grayson, *Chronicles*, 80.

Episodes of the campaign

A. Introduction (in my eighth campaign)...column v, line 17
B. The motive of the campaign: Mušēzib-Marduk had rebelled and gathered Arameans around him to support him...lines 18–24a
C. Sennacherib reacts: he besieges Mušēzib-Marduk ...line 24b
D. Reaction of Mušēzib-Marduk: he flees to Elam and comes back to Babylon... lines 25–30
E. The Babylonians bribe Elam to get their support...lines 31–37a
F. The king of Elam responds and gets other cities form a confederation with him...lines 37b–52a
G. The Elamite and Babylonian army goes to fight Sennacherib in Ḫalulê...lines 52b–62a
H. Sennacherib prays to the deities...lines 62b–67a
I. Sennacherib's military reaction and defeat of the enemy...line 67b-column vi, line 12
J. Receiving booty and capturing prisoners...lines 13–23
K. Fate of enemy kings...lines 24–35

3.12. The campaign against the Arabs in 690

Sources

A very short account of this campaign can be found in the Ungnad and Winckler inscriptions: 53'–59', dating between 690 and 689.[119]

Episodes of the campaign

A. Mentioning the name of the enemy queen (Te'elḫunu, Arab queen)...line 53'
B. Booty taken in the middle of the desert (thousands of camels)...lines 53'–54'
C. The ally of the Arabian queen (Haza'il)...line 54'
D. The retreat of the enemy (they left their tent and fled)...lines 54–56
E. Explaining the hardships in the desert...lines 57'–59'

---

119 Grayson, *Sennacherib*, 232.

3.13. The fourth campaign against Babylonia in 689[120]

Sources
An account of this expedition can be found in inscriptions that go back to 688, one year after the campaign. But the account available is very short, only 16 lines, and it narrates the destructive activity of Sennacherib.[121] Also, the Babylonian Chronicles relate the account of this campaign.[122] However, a fuller account of the story is narrated in the Bavian inscription, where more information is given about the campaign. Therefore, the basic source for the account will be the Bavian version.

Episodes of the campaign
A. Introduction (on my second campaign)...line 43[123]
B. Itinerary formula (against Babylon)...line 43
C. Besieging the city of Nit and killing the inhabitants...line 43
D. Taking the king (Mušēzib-Marduk) with his family as booty to Nineveh with the treasure of the city...line 43
E. Long explanation of removing the gods and taking them to Assyria...line 48
F. Destroying the city entirely and digging a canal in it...line 50
G. Establishing inscriptions on the board of the canal and making sculptures of gods and of his own...line 54.

4. Discussing the common motives and conventions of the campaigns

As is obvious, there is a certain policy in representing the campaigns. Despite the fact that Sennacherib did not have as many campaigns as his ancestors, the ones recorded have a particular rhetoric and they are orientated to take a certain shape. Close reading of the textual material indicates a pattern that the scribes used when they inscribed the events of the campaigns. In addition, from a quick reading of the episodes, it is noticeable that the military tactics used in defeating

---

120 The motive of the campaign is hatred and anger. Galter, H.D., "Die Zerstörung Babylons durch Sanherib", in *SO* 55 (1984), 161.
121 Grayson, *Sennacherib*, 203 – 206.
122 Grayson, *Chronicles*, 80.
123 Pognon, H., *L'inscription de Bavian: texte, traduction et un glassaire* (Paris, 1879 – 1880), 17 – 21.

the enemy and the economic outcome of the campaign are two essential themes in the inscriptions. Therefore, the discussion of these two themes will be longer than the discussion of other motifs within the rhetoric of each campaign. For the sake of convenience, this sub-section is divided into three parts. Firstly, the structure of the text and some themes like the motive of the campaigns and the fate of the enemy king are discussed. Secondly, the military strategy and Sennacherib's main targets are discussed. And thirdly, the economic exploitation of the campaigns is discussed. The conclusion demonstrates what the study of all the campaigns can tell us about the third campaign. However, before dealing with the themes, it is useful to give an overall view of the structure of the campaigns.

4.1. Structure and minor themes

4.1.1. Overall structure of the campaigns

Generally, the composition of each campaign account starts with the phrase *ina n gerrīya*, "on my n-th campaign"[124], as opposed to the inscriptions of the previous kings where the actions of war start with the regnal year *palû*. However, there are some exceptions that can be explained. The account of the "first campaign" begins not with *ina maḫrê gerrīya*, "on my first campaign", but with *ina rēš šarrūtīya*, which means "at the beginning of my reign." Frahm explains that the reason for this is "to count the campaigns when only one had taken place understandably seemed unsatisfactory to Sennacherib's scribes."[125] The two campaigns of the years 696 and 695, which were undertaken by the military officials of Sennacherib, open with *ina limmu PN*, "in the eponym of NP." If the king is not leading the campaign, the formulae *ina n gerrīya* does not make sense in the context. The other intriguing point is the campaign of 689 against Babylon, whose account opens with "on my second campaign." This can be attributed to the fact that the account of this campaign is related not in the annals with the other campaigns, but in another inscription, which is called the Bavian inscription. The only battle described in these inscriptions before relating the sacking of Babylon is Ḫalulê, a battle of the eighth campaign.[126] Thus, it is understandable that the eighth campaign in these inscriptions was considered the first campaign.

---

124 For more explanations about the difference between Sennacherib and his ancestors, see Frahm, *Einleitung*, 251.
125 Frahm, *Einleitung*, 251.
126 Grayson, "Walters", 84.

The introduction is usually followed by the itinerary formula, which indicates the geographical orientation of the campaign. The formula usually used is *ana...GN...allik*, "to the land of GN...I marched," or other alternative phrases that suit the context. For example, in the fifth campaign an expression that suits the mountainous place is used; in the two non-royal campaigns *uma"er*, "I sent", appears; and in the sixth campaign, when Sennacherib crossed the sea, the wording *ēbirūma*, "I crossed over", is used. In the eighth campaign, however, no itinerary formula is used. In general, the formula is used either immediately after the introduction "on my n-th campaign," or later after a short paragraph introducing the enemy or the motive of the campaign.

After narrating the account of the campaign, the text ends with a passage in which the scribe describes the successful outcome of the campaign by mentioning the booty and tribute the king got or by counting the captives whom Sennacherib would incorporate into his army. The last note about conscripting soldiers from the prisoners is added at the end of some campaign accounts starting from the third campaign.

Structurally, the individual episodes of each campaign are sandwiched between the introduction and the closing passage. The episodes in general explain common themes in all campaigns, but the style and language of these episodes differ according to each campaign. The major themes that dominate the episodes are: the motive of the campaign, the strategy and military technique used in the war, the reaction of the enemy, and the booty and tribute received at the end.[127] Therefore, it is worthwhile to go through the language and devices used in the rhetoric of the campaigns to know what makes a campaign or a victory in a campaign differ from the other campaigns. In what follows, I examine the episodes of the campaigns comparing the data given in the text of each campaign.

4.1.2. The motive of the campaign

Establishing the reason for launching a war is one of the prominent themes in the rhetoric of each campaign. The reason for this, as B. Oded aptly puts it, is that "the grounds for war constitute important elements in the royal inscriptions which were written for commemorative and propagandistic reasons, demonstrating that they had acquired their dominions justly."[128] Therefore, it is unsurpris-

---

127 See also Frahm, *Einleitung*, 251–255.
128 Oded, B., *War, Peace and Empire: Justifications for War in the Assyrian Royal Inscriptions* (Wiesbaden, 1992), 178.

ing that Sennacherib gave space to establish the motivation for his campaigns. The reasons varied from one campaign to another as follows:

- For the campaigns against Babylonia and Elam, the motivation is rather straightforward, except in the case of the fourth campaign. The motivation for the first campaign is the wicked nature of Merodach-Baladan, who was causing troubles for Assyria and therefore deserved to be punished by Sennacherib. No one is described as pejoratively as Merodach-Baladan is. In the sixth campaign, the text does not mention Merodach-Baladan, but the people of Bīt-Yakīn were causing trouble by seeking the aid of Elam. This alignment between Babylon and Elam was the motivation for the eighth campaign as well, which led to the final destruction of Babylon by Sennacherib, although he does not mention his motive for this last campaign. As for the fourth campaign, the text does not mention the motive of the campaign. Nevertheless, one can speculate about the motive based on the evidence given at the end of the text of the fourth campaign. Sennacherib places his son on the throne of Babylon instead of Bēl-ibni, whom he installed in his first campaign. This reveals that there was trouble in Babylonia and Bēl-ibni could not handle the situation, which is why Sennacherib removed him from the throne. There is no way to know for sure why the motive is not mentioned. However, one possible explanation is that Sennacherib did not want to show that his choice of Bēl-ibni was not successful. Similarly, the motive of the seventh campaign against Elam is not mentioned. However, the text of the sixth campaign gives hints of the motive of this campaign. Sennacherib mentions, in relation to the sixth campaign, that he defeated Nergal-ušēzib, who had taken the lordship of the land of Sumer and Akkad during the confusion. This means that Sennacherib's son, who was placed on the throne in the fourth campaign, was no longer king of Babylon. The question is: what does Sennacherib mean when he says there was "confusion in the land"? In his study of the events of the sixth and seventh campaigns Levine discusses this question in detail. By consulting other sources than the Assyrian inscriptions, Levine reconstructs the events of the two mentioned campaigns. His investigation leads him to conclude that while Sennacherib was in southern Elam (sixth campaign), the Elamite king took the opportunity to launch a counterattack against northern Babylonia, and take the appointed Babylonian king, Sennacherib's son, as a captive to Elam. This was the moment for Nergal-ušēzib to ascend to the throne of Babylon. Later on, Sennacherib's army moved from the far south to the centre of Babylon to defeat Nergal-ušēzib and his allies, the Elamites. After these events, while Sennacherib was still in the area, a revolt occurred in Elam. Sennacherib took this as an opportunity to launch a war against Elam, which in a sense was successful. The events of the last attack, however, are related in the text of the seventh campaign.[129]

In the light of these notes, we can explain why the motive is not mentioned in the seventh campaign. First of all, the text of the sixth campaign ends with the note about Nergal-ušēzib being defeated with his allies. No detail is given about his ascension or about the fate of the previous king, Sennacherib's son. It appears that Sennacherib is hiding a setback that he suffered while he was in the far south of Babylonia and that allowed the Elamites to take his son. Secondly, the attack against Elam, in the seventh campaign, came about as a result of unrest that happened in Elam very shortly after the events narrated in the sixth campaign. The real motive of the campaign was not any kind of evil or threatening action that the Elamites had taken against Assyria. Sennacherib just took the opportunity of unsettled conditions in the area and he attacked them. Justification for the attack is related later: restoring the two cities that were taken from Assyria during Sargon's reign. To sum up, not mentioning the motive in the text could be ascribed to other information that Sennacherib wanted to cover.

- Another motivation for a campaign is the non-submissive behaviour of other rulers. The people of the land of the Kassites and Yasubigallians were not submissive *lā kitnušū,* and neither were the Urartians in the north. But the text does not clarify explicitly what the "non-submissive" behaviour is.
- The motivation is not mentioned explicitly in the account of the third campaign against the west. Sennacherib does not state the reason for the campaign, but only explains when it comes to Ṣidqâ of Ashkelon that Ṣidqâ did not bow down to Sennacherib's yoke. But from the context and other sources we know that the motive was the withholding of the tribute by the kings of the Levant. Additionally, the third campaign had three phases: Phoenicia, Philistia and Judah. The motive of attacking each place does not seem to be the same. This could explain why Sennacherib did not mention the motive at the very beginning of his campaign.
- And finally, the motivation for the two non-royal campaigns is related in the text: the rulers of Cilicia and Tīl-Garimme incited others opponents to wage war against Sennacherib.

To conclude, the ways in which motivations are mentioned above uncover two facts. First, the Kassites and Yasubigallians, the kingdoms in the west, and the Urartians in the north did not pose a military threat to Assyria. The annals relate

---

129 Levine, "Sennacheirb's Southern Front", 41–48.

that they were not submissive, a fact which could have different meanings. In contrast, other states that were attacked, like Babylonia and Elam, formed a direct risk that threatened the Assyrian Empire by waging or preparing to wage war against Assyria. Secondly, the motive is not always mentioned in the texts because it does not serve the Assyrian ideology.

4.1.3. The fate of the enemy king or ruler

The survey of the episodes of the campaigns shows clearly Sennacherib's attitude towards the king or the ruler of the land he attacks. He never shows clemency to his main enemy. The enemy king cannot resist Sennacherib, and he is always depicted as being overwhelmed by the strength of Sennacherib. For example, from the very first campaign, the text relates that Merodach-Baladan, king of Babylon, fled from Sennacherib. So did Ispabāra, king of Ellipi, in the second campaign, Lulî, king of Sidon, in the third campaign, Mušēzib-Marduk the Chaldean, in the fourth campaign, Maniye, king of Ukku, in the fifth campaign, Kudur-Naḫḫunte, the Elamite king in the seventh campaign, and Ḫumban-menanu, king of Elam, along with the Babylonian king and Chaldean sheikh, in the eighth campaign.

Those who did not flee had to show submission to Sennacherib by coming out of their cities and offering tribute to the king. In the third campaign, eight kings of the west came out of their cities to meet Sennacherib in Ushu to kiss his feet. Those who did not show submissive behaviour were treated brutally. Ṣidqâ of Ashkelon was deported with the members of his family; Mušēzib-Marduk, the Babylonian, was taken to Nineveh in the last campaign; and Kirūa the ruler of Illubru was brought to Nineveh, where he was flayed.

There are, however, two kings whose fate does not fall under any of the above-mentioned categories. The text about the campaign of 695 against Gurdî, ruler of Talmusu, does not inform us about the fate of the ruler. It is not clear if he was deported with the prisoners or not. However, if he was deported, it would have been recorded in the text. Also, the text does not say that he fled. The other case is that of Hezekiah in the third campaign. He is the only king who did not come out of his city and show submissive behaviour, flee, or get taken from Jerusalem to Assyria. But the text relates that he sent his tribute from his city to Nineveh because he was overwhelmed by fear of the lordly brilliance of Sennacherib. No king in Sennacherib's inscriptions is treated like this. The explanation of this special treatment will be given in due course.

4.2. The military strategy used in the war

When relating the military tactics that Sennacherib used in war, the inscriptions relate different ways to defeat the enemy and achieve his goal. In what follows I investigate the language used to explain the military aspect of each campaign as narrated. Presently, the investigation is on the literary level. Historical issues will be discussed afterwards. For now, the literary conventions used to describe the military activities and the outcomes of the campaigns are the focus of the study.

The military tactics that Sennacherib used in his campaigns differ from one place to another, and from one campaign to another. However, it can be seen that Sennacherib's strategy was not only to weaken the land invaded, but also to establish a political condition that would serve Assyrian hegemony over that land. This was achieved mainly through besieging, conquering, carrying off spoils, and destroying, devastating, and setting cities on fire. Cities and other places that attracted Sennacherib's attention were capitals and fortresses, i.e. cities that were supposed to support the state politically and economically. It would be useful to examine the strategy for dealing with the cities.

In the first campaign, Sennacherib divided his army between Kish and Cutha. He himself fought in Cutha and sent another group to Kish. The annals are clear about the fate of Cutha; after slaughtering the warriors, he took possession (ṣabātu) of the walled city and brought heavy tribute out of it. At Kish, Sennacherib defeated the enemy and seized what was abandoned as booty. Then he entered the capital city, Babylon, took charge of the possessions and property of the palace and established a puppet on the throne of Babylon. After dealing with the main trouble-causing cities, Sennacherib turned to other cities and settlements. The text relates that 88 fortified cities and 820 small settlements were besieged, conquered, and their spoils carried off. Moreover, these cities and settlements were destroyed, devastated, and set on fire. There is no more explanation about the technique used in conquering these cities. The annals are interested only in clarifying that they were taken and controlled by Sennacherib. Two other cities are mentioned in the first campaign: Hararatu and Hirimmu. The first city just paid a tribute without military involvement, while the other city suffered as Sennacherib killed a large number of the population and rearranged the district.

It is obvious that the focus in representing the campaign is on showing the huge army that was defeated and the extensive booty and tribute Sennacherib received. This is obvious from the space which was given for naming the cities and the items of the booty and tribute. Not much is mentioned about the military tactics that Sennacherib used in this campaign.

As for the second campaign, although the text starts with the land of the Kassites and the Yasubigallians, no detail is given about military activity in this area.[130] Only a description of the way there is given. When Sennacherib enters the mountains, three names are mentioned: Bīt-Kilamzaḫ, Ḫardišpu and Bīt-Kubatti. The strong walled cities of these three places were besieged (*lamû*) and conquered (*kašādu*). People and animals were removed and brought back as booty (*šalālu*). The small cities were destroyed (*napālu*), devastated (*naqāru*), and turned into ruins and the tents were set on fire (*qamû*). But the three cities did not share the same fate. Bīt-Kilamzaḫ was made a fortress; its walls were made stronger, and along with Ḫardišpu and Bīt-Kubatti it was added to Arrapḫa, the Assyrian city, where a stele was set up.

Then Sennacherib went to the land of Ellipi. The two royal cities Mar'ubištu and Akkuddu along with 34 small cities were besieged (*lamû*), conquered (*kašādu*), destroyed (*napālu*), devastated (*naqāru*), and burned with fire (*qamû*). He took people and animals and items as spoil (*šalālu*). Ṣiṣirtu and Kummaḫlum along with their small cities and the province of Bīt-Barrû were cut off and added to the territory of Assyria. Sennacherib turned Elenzaš into a royal city and called it Kār-Sennachrib, then handing it over to the governor of Ḫarḫar. On his way back he received (*maḫāru*) tribute (*mandatum*) from the Medes.

Again, the annals do not explain the strategy used to conquer the cities in this campaign. More attention is given to the policy of rearranging the land.

Sennacherib's third campaign had three phases: Phoenicia, Philistia and Judah. In the first phase, the text relates that the enemy was overwhelmed by the lordly brilliance of Sennacherib. It is not known if there was a battle or not. The king, Lulî, escaped and Sennacherib established another puppet on the throne. Next, the text mentions Ashkelon. Again, no military engagement between the people of Ashkelon and Sennacherib is mentioned. The king and his family were taken to Assyria, so one assumes that Sennacherib entered the city without resistance; therefore, the city was intact, with no destruction and no devastation. Only the king was changed. Four cities of Ṣidqâ – Bīth-Daganna, Joppa, Banayabarqa, and Azuru – which did not bow in submission were besieged (*lamû*) and conquered (*kašādu*), and their people and animals were removed and brought home as booty (*šalālu*).

In the second phase, Sennacherib's policy was different. When he turned to Ekron, he waged a battle in Eltekeh and defeated the Egyptian princes and the forces of the Nubian king (*aštakan tahtašu*). Eltekeh and Tamnâ were besieged (*lamû*) and conquered (*kašādu*), and their spoils were taken as booty (*šalālu*).

---

130 See also Levine, L.D., "The Second Campaign of Sennacherib", *JNES* 32 (1973), 312–317.

As for Ekron, he drew near to the city and slew the rebels and sinners, but forgave the others who were not sinners. The city was left intact and there was no devastation. Its king, Padî, was brought back from Jerusalem and Sennacherib imposed kingly tribute (*mandatum*) on him.

In Judah, Sennacherib's policy was different: 46 of Hezekiah's strong walled cities were besieged (*lamû*) and conquered (*kašādu*), and booty, people and animals were taken as spoils (*šalālu*). Hezekiah was shut up (*esēru*) in Jerusalem and a fortress (*ḫalṣu*) was constructed against him (*rakāsu*), with no one being allowed to leave the city. The cities which were taken from him were given to other kings, thus diminishing the extent of his lands (*ṣeḫēru*). The three kings to whom the cities of Hezekiah were given had to grant "in addition to their former annual tribute...additional presents due to Sennacherib as overlord". Then the text turns again to Hezekiah and gives a long list of the items that Hezekiah sent to Nineveh to pay tribute; Hezekiah sent his messengers to offer (*epēšu*) his servitude (*wardūtu*).

It is obvious that Sennacherib was engaged in military activities in the last two phases, but not in the first one. According to the annals, in the first phase Sennacherib did not destroy, devastate or set cities on fire. He reduced the kingdom of Hezekiah and established puppets in Sidon and Ashkelon, but left Hezekiah on the throne. He had control of the main cities Sidon and Ashkelon, and set a blockade around Jerusalem without entering it.

The fourth campaign seems to have been conducted to defeat Merodach-Baladan. There was no serious military involvement in this campaign as the enemy king fled, and Sennacherib took booty out of Bīt-Yakīn. In a brief note, the text relates that Sennacherib destroyed, devastated and ruined his cities. Then he placed his son on the throne of Babylon. It is obvious that the campaign was not meant to be destructive, but was launched to solve the trouble caused by the rebel Merodach-Baladan, and probably the inability of Bēl-ibni to run the state.

In the account of the fifth campaign, there is a long description of the mountainous path Sennacherib had to walk. Seven cities were conquered, plundered, destroyed, devastated and burned. But the text does not relate how this happened and what strategy Sennacherib used in the war. When Sennacherib turned to Ukku, the city of the king, he besieged, conquered and plundered the city after the king fled. Moreover, 33 cities were conquered on the border of Urartu, plundered, destroyed, devastated and burned.

In the campaign against Cilicia, the population of Ḫilakku was defeated and two cities were conquered and plundered. The king was besieged (*lamû*) in his city and defeated by means of siege engines; the city was seized and the king was taken to Assyria. Afterwards, the city of Illubru was reorganised. The weapon of Aššur was publicly installed with the stele in front of it.

In the campaign against Til-Garimme, the city was besieged and taken. After being plundered, the city was destroyed and devastated.

In the sixth campaign, some districts of Elam were conquered (kašādu): Nagītu-di'bina, Ḫilmu, Pillatu and Ḫupapanu. The people of Bīt-Yakīn were again carried out from Elam and brought to Assyria. Cities in the mentioned districts were destroyed, devastated and burned.

In the seventh campaign, two cities on the border of Assyria with Elam were conquered, plundered and brought back into Assyria. Twenty-two cities with another 12 cities and small cities were besieged (lamû), conquered (kašādu), taken as spoils (šalālu), destroyed (napālu), devastated (naqāru), and burned (qamû). Sennacherib intended to march to the Elamite capital city Madaktu, but he was prevented by the cold weather.

In the account of the eighth campaign, there is a long description of the enemy's preparation for war. The battle in Ḫalulê is explained in highly poetic language. Although narration of the campaign starts in line 7, the actual combat and encounter with the enemy only starts to be related in line 74. In line 79, the text communicates the defeat and turning back of the enemy. Afterwards, some details about the battle in Ḫalulê are given. The military technique in this campaign was different. The only actions narrated are the brutal slaughter of the enemy soldiers and the taking of booty from the battlefield. There is no note about besieging, conquering, devastating or destroying any city.

In the last campaign against Babylonia, the city of Nit was besieged and the inhabitants were killed. The king and his family were taken to Nineveh. Next, the entire city was destroyed.

To conclude the discussion about the policy of relating the military activity of the campaigns, one can safely say that the targets that attracted Sennacherib were the capital cities and the fortresses and strong cities of the lands invaded. Many important cities were besieged and conquered, and booty was taken out of them; subsequently, some cities were destroyed, devastated and set on fire. The chart below shows the cities that were affected by Sennacherib in his campaigns:

The campaign	State	Cities	Military action
First	Babylon	City of Cutha	ṭīb šamri aškunuma
		Kish, the king ran away	I made a savage assault
		Babylon: enter the palace	
		75 strong walled cities + 420	alme, akšud, ašlula
		small cities of the Chaldeans	

Continued

The campaign	State	Cities	Military action
		18 tribes of the Aramaeans who were not submissive	*alme, akšud, ašlula, appul, aqqur, aqmu*
Second	Zagros region Land of the Kassites and Yasubigallians	Three main cities	*alme, akšud, ašlula*
		Their small numberless cities	*appul, aqqur, ušēme* (turned into ruins)
	Ellipi (vassal became rebel)	Two royal cities + 34 small cities	*alme, akšud, ašlula,*
		Two main cities + strong cities	*appul, aqqur, aqmu* Annexed to Assyria
Third	West	Four cities of Philistia which did not submit quickly	*alme, akšud, ašlula*
		Eltekeh and Timna	*alme, akšud, ašlula*
		Judah: 46 strong and fortified cities	*alme, akšud, ašlula*
Fourth	Babylon	Cities of Bīt-Yakīn	*appul, ušēme* (turned into ruins)
Fifth	Urartu	Their cities which were not submissive	*alme, akšud, ašlula appul, aqqur, aqmu*
696	Illubru	Two cities	*akšud, ašlula*
695	Tabal	One city: Tīl-Garimme	*alme, isbat, appul, aqqur, aslula* (turned into ruins)
Sixth	Babylon	Bīt-Yakīn	*akašād*
		Cities of these province	*appul, aqqur, aqmu, ušēme*
Seventh	Elam	Two cities	*akšud, ašlula* (and they were restored to Assyria)
		56 cities	*alme, akšud, ašlula appul, aqqur, aqmu*
Eighth		Ḫalulê	

From the table one can see that the texts indicate a pattern in explaining the military activity, which can be summarised as follows:

- There are two prominent formulae that Sennacherib likes to repeat in describing his military action. One formula is "I besieged" (*alme*), "I conquered" (*akšud*), and "I carried off their spoils" (*ašlula*). The other one is "I destroyed" (*appul*), "I devastated" (*aqqur*), and "I set on fire" (*aqmu*). As is clear in the table, in his campaign to the Levant, the campaign against Cilicia, and his eighth campaign, the second formula is not used. One can ask a question: does not using the second (more aggressive) formula mean that Sennacherib intended to be less aggressive in these three campaigns, and decided to treat the enemy kings mildly? The answer cannot be positive about all the three cases (the Levant, Cilicia and Ḫalulê). As for the campaign against Cilicia, the annals record that the enemy king was brought to Nineveh and he was flayed. So, not using the aggressive formula (I destroyed, I devastated, I set on fire) does not mean that harsh treatment was not intended. As for Ḫalulê, not using the aggressive formula is understandable because the battle was in Ḫalulê and Sennacherib did not penetrate into the land of the enemy to destroy its cities. As for the third campaign, it is not clear why the scribe did not use the second formula. Did Sennacherib intend not to be aggressive in this campaign, and thus, treat the enemy king mildly? At this stage of the study, it is not wise to give a definitive answer to this question. For now, we can conclude that the language used in describing the military strategy against the Levant shows Sennacherib's less aggressive treatment of the west.
- In two campaigns Sennacherib annexed cities to Assyria: in his second campaign, he seized two main cities with their strong cities, which were in the land of Ellipi; and in his campaign against Elam, he restored two cities as well. Apart from that, Sennacherib did not expand the empire of Assyria. His time apparently was not one of extending the empire, as it had been with his ancestors.[131]
- Sennacherib had different plans for different cities even within the same campaign. In the same region, some cities were conquered and others were devastated. It seems that his policy was to weaken these regions and leave them powerless in order to guarantee his hegemony over the region.
- Accordingly, it seems that the main object of the war was not the destruction or elimination of the enemy but the destruction of its opposition to Assyria.

---

131 Liverani, M., "The Age of Sennacherib", in C. Lippolis (ed.), *The Sennacherib Wall Reliefs at Nineveh* (Mesopotamia 15; Firenze, 2011), 2.

As C. Crouch argues, "if an opponent could be relieved of its identification with chaos via a non-violent transfer of affiliation, this was sufficient to satisfy the Assyrian ideological requirements."[132]

4.3. Economic exploitation

4.3.1. Introduction

Although gaining booty and tribute was not the only reason for the Assyrian kings' campaigns, one can safely assert that it was one of the important reasons which motivated their military actions. In his article, Levine aptly describes the economic aspect of the campaigns: "they were necessary to maintain the empire and the economic base which it encompassed, and they often produced immediate booty and the longer range prospect of continuing tribute from the newly conquered areas".[133] This, indeed, is obvious if we look at the inscriptions and notice the occasional references to the booty and tribute that the Assyrian kings carried off from the countries they conquered and subjugated. This is not surprising given the fact that Assyria had successfully spread its domination all over the world not only by a successful internal system, but also by controlling the economy of the surrounding nations. One way of achieving this control was a systematic collection of tribute through bureaucratic machinery,[134] which was imposed over the subjugated states. Any complacency in paying the tribute in due time was a reasonable occasion for launching a war against that country.[135]

Sennacherib was no different in his policy; he adopted the same strategy with the controlled and subjugated countries around Assyria. As is obvious in the inscriptions, recording of booty and tribute took up a remarkable amount of space in the reports of the campaigns. For Sennacherib, mention of the spoils taken during the campaign was an occasion for boasting and showing suprem-

---

132 Crouch, C., *War and Ethics in the Ancient Near East: Military Violence in the Light of Cosmology and History* (BZAW 407; Berlin, 2009), 47.
133 Levine, "Sennacherib's Southern Front", 54.
134 Jankowska, N.B., "Some Problems of the Economy of the Assyrian Empire", in I.M. Diakonoff (ed.), *Ancient Mesopotamia. Socio-Economic History* (Moscow, 1969), 255–256.
135 More studies on booty and tribute are: Martin, W.J, *Tribut und Tributleistungen bei den Assyrern* (SO 8/1; Helsinki 1936); Postgate, J.N., *Taxation and Conscription in the Assyrian Empire* (StPol 3; Rome, 1974); Bär, J., *Der assyrissche Tribut und seine Darstellung: Eine Untersuchung zur imperialen Ideologie im neuassyrischen Reich* (AOAT 243; Neukirchen-Vluyn, 1996).

acy and domination.[136] As was the case with his forefathers,[137] recording of the economic exploitation was documented not only in written sources but also in iconographic sources which have survived. In the next few pages, therefore, the economic exploitation and its technique in Sennacherib's campaigns will be examined.

Before we come to the details of Sennacherib's policy of economic exploitation, it is worthwhile to provide an outline of the occasions of plundering and receiving tributes in his military activities. All the campaigns will be mentioned, comprising the royal ones and those that were led by his magnates.

4.3.2. The occasions of plundering and receiving tribute

The occasions attested in the annals are arranged in chronological order:

1) The campaign against the Kulummeans in 704. The sources which report this campaign do not mention any booty or tribute taking[138].
2) The "first campaign"[139] against Babylonia in 704.
   a) First occasion
      i. After taking the city of Cutha, booty was taken (*šallatiš amnu*).
      ii. Items of booty: horses and people (the bowmen of the Elamites, Aramaeans, and Chaldeans; centurions of the Elamites; Nergal-nāṣir, and the wrongdoer citizens).
   b) Second occasion
      i. In the city of Kish, after the battle.
      ii. Items of booty: people (Adinu, nephew of Merodach-Baladan, and Basqānu, the brother of Iati'e, queen of Arabia, with his soldiers) and war equipment (chariots, wagons, horses, mules, donkeys, camels and Bactrian camels).
   c) Third occasion
      i. After entering the capital city, Babylon, Sennacherib entered the palace (*šallatiš amnu*).

---

136 Streck, M. (ed.), *Assurbanipal und die letzten assyrischen Könige bis zum Untergange Ninivehs* (VB 7; Leipzig, 1916), 12 I- 116.

137 Yamada, S., *The Construction of the Assyrian Empire. A Historical Study of the Inscriptions of Shalmaneser III (859–824) Relating to His Campaigns to the West* (CHANE 3; Leiden, 2000), 225.

138 Millard, *Eponym*, 84.

139 We use the quotation marks for some campaigns because this is the way they were described in the annals.

ii. Items of booty: precious goods (gold, silver, implements of gold and silver, precious stones, beds, chairs with a back, rickshaws, royal paraphernalia with inlays of gold and silver, all kinds of property and goods, abundant treasure), and people (his wife, his palace women, female stewards, eunuchs, *tiru*-courtiers, *mazzaz-pani*-courtiers, male singers and female singers, the palace servants and all the *ummânu* experts).

d) Fourth occasion

    i. After trying to catch Merodach-Baladan, horses and wagons were gathered (*mitḫariš upaḫḫir*).

e) Fifth occasion

    i. In the course of his campaign, Sennacherib took booty from the tribal areas and the major cities after their siege and conquest (the note of this occasion is repeated later in the same text) (*ašlula šallassun*).

    ii. The items of the booty: people (auxiliary forces of Aramaeans and Chaldeans who were in Uruk, Nippur, Kish, and Hursagkalama). No goods are mentioned.

f) Sixth occasion

    i. In the course of the campaign, a tribute was received from Nabû-bēl-šumāti, the governor of Ḫararatu (*mandatu...amḫur*)

    ii. Items of tribute: goods (gold, silver, and great *musukkannu*-trees) and animals (donkeys, camels, oxen and sheep).

g) Seventh occasion

    i. Tribute was established for all time in Ḫirimmu after cutting down the subjects of the city (*dārišam*).

    ii. Items of tribute: animals (one ox and 10 sheep) and goods (10 homers of wine and 20 homers of dates).

h) Eighth occasion

    i. On his way to Assyria, Sennacherib carried off huge spoils (*ašlula*).

    ii. Items of the booty: people (208,000 men) and animals (7,200 horses and mules, 11,073 asses, 5,230 camels, 80,050 cattle, 800,100 oxen, and 800,100 sheep).

3) The "second campaign", against the land of Kissates and the land of Yasubigallians.

a) First occasion

    i. In the city of Bīt-Kilamzaḫ, after its siege and conquest (*šallatiš amnu*).

    ii. Items of booty: people and animals (horses, mules, asses, oxen, cattle and sheep).

b) Second occasion

       i.   After conquering and destroying the cities of Ellipi, booty was carried off (*ašlula*).

      ii.   Items of booty: people and animals (horses, mules, donkeys, oxen, and cattle and sheep).

  c) Third occasion

       i.   A tribute was received from the Medes (*mandatu....amḫur*).

      ii.   The items of the tribute are not mentioned.

4) The "third campaign", against the west.

  a) First occasion

       i.   After Lulî, king of Sidon, fled, his cities submitted to Sennacherib. Tribute and taxes were imposed, to be paid annually without interruption (*biltu mandattu bēlūteya šattišam lā baṭlu*).

      ii.   The items of the tribute are not mentioned.

  b) Second occasion

       i.   Eight western kings brought fourfold gifts to Sennacherib in Ushu (*igisê*). Frahm translates the Akkadian word as tribute.

      ii.   The items of the gifts are not mentioned.

  c) Third occasion

       i.   From Ashkelon, the city of King Ṣidqâ , Sennacherib deported and led items and people to Assyria.

      ii.   Items of the booty: gods of his (Ṣidqâ 's) father, himself, his wife, his sons, his daughters, his brothers, and the offspring of his father.[140]

  d) Fourth occasion

      i.   A tribute was imposed on Šarru-lū-dāri, the new puppet of Ashkelon (*bilat*).

      ii.   The items of the tribute are not mentioned.

  e) Fifth occasion

       i.   Booty was taken from four cities of Ṣidqâ after their siege and conquest (*ašlula šallassun*).

      ii.   The items of the booty are not mentioned.

  f) Sixth occasion

       i.   Booty was taken after a battle in the vicinity of Eltekeh.

      ii.   Items of the booty: chariots and sons of the Egyptian kings and the chariot commander of the king of Meluḫḫa.

  g) Seventh occasion

       i.   Booty was taken from the cities Eltekeh and Tamnâ after their siege and conquest (*ašlula šallassun*).

---

140 No Akkadian word for booty is mentioned in this occasion.

ii. Items of booty are not mentioned.
h) Eighth occasion
   i. Booty was taken from Ekron after killing the officials and the rulers.
   ii. Items of booty: people of the city who had committed crime.
i) Ninth occasion
   i. Tribute was imposed on Padî after replacing him (*mandattu*).
   ii. Items of tribute are not mentioned.
j) Tenth occasion
   i. Booty was taken from 46 cities of Judah after their siege and conquest (*šallatiš amnu*).
   ii. Items of the booty: 200,150 people, small and big, horses, wild asses, donkeys, camels, oxen and sheep.
k) Eleventh occasion
   i. Tribute and gifts were imposed on the kings of Ashdod, Ekron, and Gaza.
   ii. Items of tribute are not mentioned.
l) Twelfth occasion
   i. Tribute was paid and sent by Hezekiah to Sennacherib in Nineveh (*mandatti*).
   ii. Items of tribute: ambushers, selected troops, 30 talents of gold, 800 talents of silver, choice antimony, large blocks of carnelian, beds with ivory, armchairs with ivory, elephant hide, ivory, ebony, boxwood, garments with multi-coloured trim, linen garments, blue-purple wool, red-purple wool, utensils of copper, iron, bronze, tin and iron, chariots, shields, lance, coats of mail, swords on belts, bows and arrows, tillu-equipment, and instruments of war without number along with Hezekiah's daughters, palace women, and singers.
5) The "fourth campaign", against Babylon
  a) First occasion
   i. Booty was taken after attacking Bīt-Yakīn (*šallatiš amnu*)
   ii. Items of booty: Merodach-Baladan's brothers along with the rest of the people of Bīt-Yakīn.
6) The "fifth campaign", against the north – Mount Nipur and the city of Ukku
  a) First occasion
   i. Booty was taken from cities in Mt Nipur after their siege and conquest (*ašlula šallassun*).
   ii. The items of booty are not mentioned.
  b) Second occasion
   i. Booty was taken from Ukku after its siege and conquest (*ašlula šallassun*).

      ii. Items of booty: all kinds of goods and merchandise, the treasure of Ukku's palace.
- c) Third occasion
  - i. Booty was taken from 33 cities after capturing them (*ašlula*).
  - ii. Items of the booty: people, asses, cattle and sheep.
7) The campaign against Cilicia
   - a) First occasion
     - i. Booty was taken after taking two cities, Ingirâ and Tarzu (*šalālum*).
     - ii. Items of booty are not mentioned.
   - b) Second occasion
     - i. Booty was taken from Illubru after its siege and conquest, and the booty was brought to Nineveh.
     - ii. Items of booty: Kirūa, the city ruler, the spoil of his cities, people of Ḫilakku who had come to his aid, asses, cattle and sheep.
8) The campaign against Tīl-Garimme
   - a) First occasion
     - i. Booty was taken from the city Tīl-Garimme after its capture (*šallatiš amnu*).
     - ii. Items of booty: people with their gods of that city.
9) The "sixth campaign" against Elam

It is surprising that, in the Chicago Prism, the account of this campaign does not report any occasion of plundering or taking booty. It only relates that after conquering the Elamite cities, garrisons, men of Chaldeans, all gods of Bīt-Yakīn with their goods, and the Elamites' wagons, mules and asses were brought to Babylonia. But it does not say explicitly that they were taken as booty.

10) The "seventh campaign", against Elam
    - a) First occasion
      - i. Booty was taken from Bit-Ha'iri and Rasha, cities on the border of Assyria, after their conquest (*ašlula šallassun*).
      - ii. Items of booty are not mentioned.
    - b) Second occasion
      - i. Booty was taken from 52 cities after their siege and conquest (*ašlula šallašunu*).
      - ii. Items of booty are not mentioned.
11) The "eighth campaign", against the coalition of Babylonia and Elam
    - a) First occasion
      - i. Booty was taken in the battlefield in Ḫalulê (*amḫur*).

      ii. Items of booty: bracelets, slings of gold, silver from the arms of the enemies, gold and silver belt-daggers, the living, wagons, mules, chariots and horses, camps and royal tents.

12) The campaign against the Arabs was to prevent them supporting the Babylonians

    a) First occasion

      i. Booty was taken in the midst of the desert after the battle (*šalālu*).

      ii. Items of booty: thousands of camels, precious stones and scents of all kinds.

    b) Second occasion

      i. Tribute was received (*mandattu... amḫur*).

      ii. Items of tribute are not mentioned.

13) The campaign against Babylonia and its destruction

    a) First occasion

      i. Booty was taken from Babylon after its attack.

      ii. Items of booty: Mušēzib-Marduk, king of Babylonia, his family, and his nobles, with the wealth of the city: silver, gold, precious stones, property and goods.

Having presented the occasions and items of booty and tribute that Sennacherib received from his campaigns, it is time to investigate Sennacherib's strategy in collecting booty and receiving tribute as it is demonstrated in the textual materials. There are 36 occasions of plundering, taking booty and receiving tribute. The discussion will be divided into two parts. In the first part I discuss booty and in the second part I discuss the tribute and its occasions.

4.3.3. Booty

The table above shows that Sennacherib's annals report 26 occasions of booty-taking during the military expeditions which he conducted during his reign. From the way the scribes recorded these occasions, one can divide the booty into four categories according to the circumstances:

1) Booty taken from cities after their conquest (2.a.i; 2.c.i; 2.e.i; 3.a.i; 3.b.i; 4.c.i; 4.e.i; 4.g.i; 4.h.i; 4.j.i; 5.a.i; 6.a.i; 6.b.i; 6.c.i; 7.a.i; 7.b.i; 8.a.i; 10.a.i; 10.b.i; 12.a.i; 13.a.i)

2) Booty taken after open field battles (2.b.i; 4.f.i; 11.a.i)

3) Booty taken after the pursuit of enemies (2.d.i)

4) Booty taken on Sennacherib's way to Assyria (2.h.i)

As is obvious from the table above, in each of these categories, different sorts of goods were gained, and certain expressions were used to describe the spoiling. Below each of these categories will be explained.

4.3.3.1. Booty taken from cities after their conquest

Out of 26 occasions of booty-taking, the annals record 20 occasions which belong to this category. Although there are some occasions where the items of booty are not listed, the occasions where the items of the booty taken are listed demonstrate that this kind of booty was a good source of valuable items which enriched the Assyrian economy (see specially 2.c.i and 4.j.i). From the 18 occasions where the items are listed, one can notice that the items pursued by Sennacherib were mainly people, members of royal families, war equipment, domestic animals, and on some occasions the gods of the state. It is obvious that these items had a good impact on the Assyrian economy in many ways.

As is usual in the Assyrian inscriptions, the standard verb used for booty-taking is *šalālu*, "to plunder, to take as booty".[141] Often, the verb is used without enumerating the specific items of the booty—it is only on two occasions that the items are counted (2.h.i and 14.j.i). This could be problematic in measuring the size of the booty, as one cannot tell how many animals or people were taken as booty.

It is noticeable that other verbs are used to explain booty-taking. In his campaign to the west, Sennacherib describes what he takes from Ashkelon as "leading" the people of the palace. The verb *šalālu* is not used, but it is obvious from the context that the king, his gods and his people were taken as booty to Assyria. The other occasion is in the account of the campaign against Cilicia, which was not led by Sennacherib. The booty was brought (*ublūni*) to him in Nineveh.

4.3.3.2. Booty taken after battle

Three occasions of booty-taking after a battle are attested in Sennacherib's inscriptions. From the table above, it is obvious that this kind of booty consists of people, military equipment and goods taken from the enemies. The verbs used to explain this kind of booty-taking are *maḫāru* and *kašādu* with the subject *qātāya*, "my hands".

---

141 *CAD*, Š Part I, *šalālu*, 196, 200.

4.3.3.3. Booty taken after the pursuit of the enemy
The only occasion where this kind of booty-taking is recorded is in the campaign against the south in 704, when Sennacherib tried to catch Merodach-Baladan. The expression used is *miṭḫariš upaḫḫir*, "to gather together".

4.3.3.4. Booty taken by Sennacherib on his way to Assyria
Only one occasion is recorded for this kind of booty (2.h.i). The amount is so large that one can conclude that it was the booty that Sennacherib got from all the cities and settlements he conquered.

4.3.4. Tribute
Ten occasions of receiving and imposing tribute are attested in the annals of Sennacherib. As in the case of the booty, tributes can be divided into categories as is demonstrated in the table above. The matter, however, is not straightforward. It is generally understood that the booty is taken by force —it comes in the context of war or military activity. Tribute, on the other hand, is not. It could be given, received or taken by force after an attack. Scholars differ on how to categorise tribute.[142] The division that could be applicable to the Sennacherib corpus is that which is suggested by S. Yamada, who categorises tributes into two sorts: "spot tributes" and "annual tributes".[143] In this discussion I follow this division.

4.3.4.1. Spot tribute
Before dealing with the occasions of this kind of tribute, it is important to clarify what is meant by spot tribute in this study. Spot tribute is considered to be a tribute Sennacherib received or took while he was in the land he invaded. Kings usually came out of their cities to present their tribute, or Sennacherib himself went to the city and received tribute from the king of that city. In this regard, four occasions of tribute-receiving belong to this category. They are usually formulated in one of the following forms: *mandattašu(nu)...amḫur*, "I received his/their tribute" (2.f.i; 3.c.i; 12.b.i), or other terms as in the case of the eight western kings

---

142 Elat categorised tribute into two sorts: "tribute of surrender" and "annual tribute". Elat, M., "The Impact of Tribute and Booty on Countries and People within the Assyrian Empire", in *AfO Beiheft* 19 (1982), 244–251. Liverani, however, divides tributes into three sorts: "spot tribute", "annual tribute" and "tribute from afar". Liverani, M., *Studies on the Annals of Ashurnasirpal II. 2: Topographical Analysis* (Rome, 1992), 155–156.
143 Yamada, *Construction*, 236–241.

(4.b.i): *kališunu igisê šadlūti tāmartašunu...iššûnimma*, "all of them, gifts and tributes they brought..."

It is not easy to determine the circumstances in which this kind of tribute was given. On the first occasion, Sennacherib received tribute from the governor of Ḫararatu; there does not seem to have been a military confrontation. So one can safely infer that the tribute was offered by the governor without any preceding struggle; it was the kind of tribute offered to show loyalty to the Assyrian overlord and could be considered "audience tribute".[144] The second occasion when tribute was received from the Medes is not clear in terms of the tribute since the reason for the campaign against Ellipi and Media is obscure.[145] There is no mention of a military confrontation with the Medes; the only fact Sennacherib mentions about them is that he made them submit to the yoke of his rule. On the other hand, if the Medes submitted for the first time, it is unlikely that they offered the tribute to show their loyalty. So, one can conclude that the tribute was not "audience tribute" but "surrender tribute".[146] The same can be said about the tribute received from the Arabs. The tribute was received after the campaign that Sennacherib launched; it is clear, therefore, that the tribute was a "surrender tribute".

The fourth occasion is rather ambiguous in describing the sort of tribute offered to Sennacherib in the first phase of his campaign to the west. On the one hand the tribute was offered in the context of military activity. After the escape of Lulî, king of Sidon, eight cities submitted to Sennacherib. The names of eight kings, who carried their tributes and came to Sennacherib in Ushu, are listed. So one would expect the word used for tribute to be *maddattu*, especially if we note that these states were vassals to Assyria whose due tribute was withheld because of the unrest that Assyria experienced after the death of Sargon II.[147] The way Sennacherib describes this event in the annals, however, is rather unclear:

> *šarrāni māt Amurri kališunu igisê šadlūti tāmartašunu kabittu adi erbšêu ana maḫriya iššûnimma iššiqū šēpīya*

> All of them, the kings of the Westland, carried before me numerous presents, their heavy gifts fourfold and kissed my feet.

---

144 See Yamada, *Construction*, 237.
145 Levine, "Sennacherib's Southern Front", 39.
146 Levine, depending on other sources, concludes that there was a military attack on the Medes. Levine, "Sennacherib's Southern Front", 39.
147 Gallagher, *Sennacherib's Campaign*, 106.

Two words for what was offered are used in the text: *igisû* and *tāmartu*. As for the second word, *tāmartu*, when it is used in the royal inscriptions, it could refer to something received (*maḫāru*)[148] or imposed (*šakānu, kânu*). It could also be in reference to something that is withheld[149]. This means that it was compulsory.[150] The other word *igisû*, however, means gift or offering.[151] It does not have a compulsory sense as is the case with *tāmartu*. The verb which is used to describe the act of the eight kings, *iššûnimma*, is also worth mentioning. It comes from the root *našû*; when this verb comes to be used in the context of delivering tribute, it is used with the words *biltu* and *maddattu*, and very rarely with *tāmartu*, but it is never used with *igisû*. So it seems that the context implicitly is concerned with the tribute more than voluntary gifts. What was carried by the eight kings was due tribute that had to be paid to the king. One could ask why Sennacherib uses the word *igisû* instead of *maddattu*, which is apt in this context. In his solution to the problem, Gallagher thinks that Sennacherib wanted to obscure the fact that these were tribute payments. He accepted the payments as gifts, as a sign of forgiveness offered to those kings, instead of explicitly mentioning his forgiveness, which might later lead others to abuse it. This conclusion could be strengthened by the fact that Sennacherib on other occasions is also shown to forgive his enemies. In his eighth campaign, the text demonstrates this clearly.[152] However, the solution proposed by Gallagher bears discussion. It is true that the text of the eighth campaign relates the fact that Sennacherib let his enemy kings escape, whether or not this is a historical fact.[153] But it is possible that Sennacherib, in the text of the third campaign, wanted to depict the kings presenting gifts rather than compulsory tribute to create a positive portrayal of himself, to whom the vassal kings came voluntarily to show their loyalty.

4.3.4.2. Annual tribute

Five occasions of annual tribute are attested in Sennacherib's annals (2.g.i; 4.a.i; 4.d.i; 4.i.i; 4.k.i). The terminology used is *ukīn* and *aškun*, which mean "I estab-

---

148 Luckenbill, *Annals*, 57.
149 Lie, A.G, *The Inscriptions of Sargon II, King of Assyria* (Paris 1929), 42.
150 See also Gallagher, *Sennacherib's Campapign*, 106.
151 *CAD*, I-J, *igisû*, 41 – 42.
152 Grayson, "Walters", 95.
153 Not all scholars agree that this event (Sennacherib's forgiving his enemies in the eighth campaign) is historically accurate, because the Babylonian Chronicles relate the story of this campaign in a different way. Frahm, however, questions the matter—Sennacherib set siege on the city of Babylon after one year; if he was defeated in Ḫalulê, how could he have set that siege? Frahm, "Sîn-aḫḫê-erîba", 1125.

lish" and "I impose". The occasions when tribute is imposed are not informative. The only occasion when the items of the tribute are mentioned is when it was imposed on Ḫirimmu: one ox, 10 sheep, 10 homers of wine and 20 homers of dates. We do not know much about the economic situation of Ḫirimmu, but it seems that the amount of tribute imposed on it is relatively small. The other occasions when tribute is imposed (on Sidon and its cities, Ekron and Ashkelon), specific items are not mentioned. It is important to mention that these cities were already vassals to Assyria and Sennacherib's imposition of tribute was not something that happened for the first time. Maybe this is why the amount of the tribute is not recorded.

4.3.4.3. Hezekiah's tribute

Hezekiah's tribute presents a unique kind of tribute paid to Sennacherib as it differs from other occasions of paying tribute. It cannot be categorised as either of the two sorts mentioned above. Therefore, it is discussed on its own in this subsection of the study.

The way this tribute was delivered is rather obscure; the text does not say that it was imposed, nor does it say it was sent as a gift. One cannot decide from the context if it was surrender tribute,[154] annual tribute, or even peace-time tribute. In order to understand what kind of tribute Hezekiah paid, we need to examine the circumstances in which the tribute was paid.

After Sennacherib attacked Judah, conquering most of its cities, Hezekiah sent his tribute to Sennacherib in Nineveh. Four important aspects are noted about Hezekiah's tribute:

- The motive for paying the tribute: from the text we know that what made Hezekiah pay tribute was the fact that he was overwhelmed by the royal quality and "lordly brilliance" of Sennacherib. Usually, being overwhelmed caused kings to escape and flee, as in the case of Lulî, king of Sidon. Hezekiah, however, did not flee but sent his tribute.
- Place of paying tribute: it was sent to Nineveh, after Sennacherib. This means that Sennacherib went to Nineveh, and then Hezekiah paid his tribute.
- The amount of tribute: it is the second largest tribute that Sennacherib received in all of his campaigns. Moreover, it contained members of the royal family.

---

154 If it were a surrender tribute, Hezekiah would have gone to Sennacherib and given him the tribute.

- The goal of paying the tribute: the text is clear about the aim of Hezekiah's tribute. The text relates ...*ušebilamma ana nadān maddatti u epēš ardūti iš-pura rakbūšu*, which means "he sent and in order to deliver tribute and to do obedience as a slave, he sent his messengers". It is obvious that this act was not only the sending of tribute, but also had the purpose of showing himself as a slave to Sennacherib. The verb *epēšu* with the object *urdūtu*[155] is used to recognise a person as one's master by a symbolic gesture or act. However, every time this expression is mentioned in the Assyrian inscriptions, it requires the presence of the enemy king himself who is making the act of obedience, like kissing the feet of the Assyrian king.[156] However, in our case, Hezekiah is not involved himself, but rather it is his messengers.

A tribute with such features is not attested in Sennacherib's inscriptions. It is the only time in the Assyrian inscriptions that a vassal king sent his tribute to an Assyrian king in such circumsatnces. From the data given about Hezekiah's tribute one can assume certain points. Since Hezekiah did not humiliate himself and go to Sennacherib—he kept his position as a king and did not share the unfortunate fate of the other kings—this means that Hezekiah was not in the weak position of other kings. And it was up to him to choose the way he paid the tribute. Could this be a sign of Hezekiah's victory? On the other hand, the tribute was paid out of fear, which means that Hezekiah was obliged to pay the tribute, i.e. the military risk was still present and the campaign, even if Sennacherib had gone back to Nineveh, was not over. This assumption can be supplemented by evidence from Sennacherib's annals. When Sennacherib mentions the motivation for paying the tribute, he says: "*šū Ḫazaqiyu pulḫi melamme bēlūteya isḫupušuma,*" which means: "as for Hezekiah, the terror of the fearsome radiance of my lordship overwhelmed him." In explaining this sentence, S.Z. Aster is of great help.[157] In his study, Aster investigates the Akkadian word *Melammu* and the context in which it usually occurs. When it is followed by the word *bēlūteya*, the expression refers to "royal power" (exercised against foreign kings).[158] However, when the word *melammu* follows the word *pulḫi*, which means "terror," the expression usually refers "to the force that causes people in one land to submit to the king, while the king is in another land. Although the king is not physically present, his powerful reputation causes the inhabitatnts of particular area to

---

155 *Urdūtu* (*urduttu*) is related to *wardu*, "slave, servant". See *CAD*, A part II, *ardu*, 243.
156 *CAD*, E, *epēšu*, 203.
157 Aster, S.Z., *The Unbearable Light. Melammu and Its Biblical Parallels* (AOAT 384; Munster 2012).
158 Aster, *Unbearable*, 86.

submit to him."[159] If what Aster explains about the expression *pulḫi melamme* is correct, then we can conclude that Sennacherib gives another piece of evidence to emphasize the fact that Hezekiah paid tribute in Nineveh. Moreover, it supplements the assumption that Hezekiah was still threatened after Sennacherib went back to Nineveh. Hezekiah wanted to appease Sennacherib by sending him such large tribute and showing his submission. Apparently, the tribute which was taken from Hezekiah was the biggest of all tributes received from the west. It included all kinds of goods, people, gold and silver. The tribute was oddly large. One can conclude that Hezekiah's tribute was more than a surrender tribute. This conclusion is strengthened by the note about Hezekiah sending his daughters to the Assyrian court with the items of the tribute, which deserves consideration.

Sending members of the defeated king's royal family to the Assyrian court was a common custom in the ancient Near East. Usually, these members were called hostages. Although the Akkadian word for hostage, *līṭu*, is not used in Sennacherib's inscriptions, the status of Hezekiah's daughters seems to be very similar to that of hostages. In his article, S. Zawadzki discusses the status of hostages in the Assyrian royal inscriptions.[160] His discussion will help our understanding of Hezekiah's tribute. Reading the Assyrian inscriptions, Zawadski concludes that hostages were not only taken by the Assyrian kings, but also sent by the kings who had been defeated. This custom of taking hostages guaranteed obedience to the Assyrian king, and also ensured the regular fulfilment of the imposed obligations. Zawadski concludes his discussion with a statement that is worth quoting.[161] He states: "The sending of hostages was manifestation of a new kind of relationship with Assyria; a recognition of its sovereignty and an acceptance of the new relationship between Assyria and vassal state. That relationship was best expressed by the word *ardūtu* or the idiom *ana epēš ardūti*."[162]

If we look at Hezekiah's tribute in the light of these notes, things seems clearer. Obviously, the context of the tribute was military. This means that, despite the fact that Sennacherib was in Nineveh, the military atmosphere was

---

159 Aster, *Unbearable*, 86.
160 Zawadzki, S., "Hostages in Assyrian Royal Inscriptions", in K. van Lerberghe and A. Schoors (eds.), *Immigration and Emigration within the Ancient Near East. Festschrift E. Lipiński* (OLA 65; Leuven 1995), 449–458. See also, Radner, K., "After Eltekeh: Royal Hostages from Egypt at the Assyrian Court", in H.D. Baker *et al.* (eds.), *Stories of Long Ago. Festschrift für Michael D. Roaf* (AOAT 397; Münster, 2012), 471–480.
161 Zawadzki, "Hostages", 455–457.
162 Zawadzki, "Hostages", 458.

still present in Jerusalem. Sending tribute with hostages does not mean that Hezekiah was forgiven; rather, he was avoiding a conflict with Sennacherib, who had already gone back to Nineveh. Also, Hezekiah aimed to start a new relationship with Sennacherib by sending his daughters. This is clear from the expression (*epēš ardūti*) used to describe Hezekiah's tribute, which is used on other occasions of sending hostages in the Assyrian inscriptions.

To conclude the discussion about the nature of Hezekiah's tribute, it was not paid after the war was over as a sign of gratitude on Hezekiah's side. Nor was it paid to Sennacherib to make him return to Nineveh. However, it was paid to Sennacherib to convince him to withdraw the forces that Sennacherib might have left around Jerusalem.

4.3.5. Conclusion

Before summarising and concluding on the discussion above, I shall provide a table which summarises the information relayed thus far, focusing on the occasions of booty-taking and tribute-receiving:

Campaign	Against	What was taken	Recording of items
A campaign	Kulummeans 704, Gurdî		
First	Babylonia 704–702, Marduk-apla-iddina	Cutha—·—·—booty	
		Kish—·—·—booty	
		Babylon—·—·—booty	Items recorded
		After tracing enemy—·——·—booty	
		Tribes and cities—·—·—· booty	Items recorded
		Ḫararatu—·—·—tribute	Items recorded
		Ḫirimmu—·—·—tribute	
		The whole amount of booty	
Second	Zagros 702	Bīt-Kilamzaḫ—·—·—booty	Items recorded
		Cities of Ellipi—·—·— booty	
		Medes—·—·—tribute	Items recorded

Continued

Campaign	Against	What was taken	Recording of items
Third	West 701	Sidon—·—·—imposed tribute	Items not recorded
		Western kings—received tribute	Items not recorded
		Ashkelon—·—·—booty	Items recorded
		Ashkelon—·—·—imposed tribute	Items not recorded
		Cities of Ashkelon—·—·— booty	Items not recorded
		Near Eltekeh—·—·—booty	Items recorded
		Eltekeh and tImna—·—·—booty	Items not recorded
		Ekron—·—·—booty	Items recorded
		Ekron—·—·—imposed tribute	Items not recorded
		Cities of Judah—·—·—booty	Items recorded
		Ashdod, Ekron, Gaza—·—·—imposed tribute	Items not recorded
		Jerusalem—·—·—imposed tribute	Items recorded
Fourth	Babylonia 700	Bīt-Yakīn—·—·—booty	Items recorded
Fifth	Mount Nipur and Ukku 697	Cities in Mt Nipur—·—·— booty	Items not recorded
		Ukku—·—·—booty	Items recorded
		33 cities—·—·—booty	Items recorded
A campaign	Cilicia 696, Kirūa, Assyrian official	2 cities—·—·—booty	Items not recorded
		Illubru—·—·—booty	Items recorded
A campaign	Tīl-Garimme 695, Gurdî , king of a vassal city	Til-Garimmu—·—·—booty	Items recorded
		All the land—·—·—booty	Items recorded
Sixth Maritime	Elam 694, Subsequent military clashes in Babylonia 693		
Seventh	Elam 693	2 cities—·—·—booty	Items not recorded
		52 cities—·—·—booty	

Continued

Campaign	Against	What was taken	Recording of items
			Items not recorded
Eighth	Ḫalulê 691	Ḫalulê—·—·—booty	Items recorded
A campaign	Arabs 690	Desert—·—·—booty	Items recorded
	Te'elhunu, Arab queen and priestess		Items not
		???? —·—·—received trib-ute	recorded
A campaign 689	Babylon Destruction	Babylon—·—·—booty	Items recorded

1) It is very noticeable that gaining valuable goods from the attacked countries was one of the prominent goals of Sennacherib's campaigns. It seems that, in doing so, Sennacherib was simulating the actions of Assyrian kings before him, as such forcible acquisition was attested in the Assyrian records of the Assyrian campaigns from the middle Assyrian period onwards.

2) Compared to the number of booty-taking occasions (26), the number of tribute-receiving occasions is rather small (only 10). This could tell us something about Sennacherib's policy in his economic exploitation; he depended on plundering and preying more than receiving tribute. [163]

3) Apparently his treatment of the west was different and special. Of the ten occasions of receiving tribute in all his campaigns, six occasions occurred in his campaign to the west. It is safe to say that the most revenue Sennacherib obtained in his campaigns was from the west.

4) Apart from the booty he took from Babylon in his first campaign, the tribute he received from Hezekiah is the biggest one in all his campaigns. Sennacherib (according to the text) was concerned about the tribute more than about Hezekiah as a rebel.

5) It is clear that the west was a significant source of tribute and payments that guaranteed annual profits for the Assyrian kingdom. Destroying it was not

---

[163] Sennacherib had a smaller number of tribute-receiving occasions than the other well-known Assyrian kings who ruled before him. While he had 10 such occasions, the other kings had the following numbers: Ashurnasirpal II 49; Shalmanessar III 17; Tiglath-pileser III 23; Sargon II 25; Esarhaddon 13; and Ashurbanipal 14. Bär, *Der assyrissche Tribut*, 29–56.

for the benefit of the kingdom. The tribute that Hezekiah paid shows how prosperous that state was under the leadership of Hezekiah.

6) Sennacherib is always the subject of the verbs which explain taking or receiving the booty or the tribute. Moreover, Sennacherib always receives the tribute either in the city of the enemy king, or in a city in the land invaded. The enemy has to present the tribute himself as a sign of submission. However, this is not the case with Hezekiah. In the third campaign, Sennacherib did not receive the tribute from Hezekiah personally. The discussion above showed that Hezekiah's tribute is more than a surrender tribute. First of all, this tribute did not make Sennacherib return to Nineveh. Something else made him go back to his land, and only then did Hezekiah pay his tribute to appease Sennacherib and make him either withdraw his forces from Jerusalem, or prevent him from launching another military campaign against him.

5. Conclusion to chapter two

Having read thoroughly the textual materials of Sennacherib's campaigns as narrated in the inscriptions, some points can be concluded about Sennacherib's policy in general and his policy in the third campaign in particular. The survey and the discussion showed that narrating and representing the military activities followed certain forms and literary conventions that the scribes used to present the event woven together with the Assyrian ideology. The literary reading of the texts showed that Sennacherib's attention in his campaigns was directed to the main cities of the land invaded and its king or ruler. The enemy king was obliged to show submission to Sennacherib or to flee, being overwhelmed by the lordly radiance of Sennacherib. The only two kings who did not behave in this way were Hezekiah, king of Judah, and Gurdî , the city ruler of Talmusu in the land of Tabal. In the third campaign, Hezekiah did not flee, and he did not come out of his city to show submission to Sennacherib like other kings. In the account of the campaign of 695, the text does not say anything about Gurdî , and his fate is not known.

Also, one can easily notice that the inscriptions avoid presenting some data about the campaign when they do not serve the Assyrian ideology. The motive of the fourth campaign is not recorded because showing that Bēl-ibni was unable to control Babylon would undermine Sennacherib's policy in choosing the governors to rule the states.

Moreover, the language used to express the military strategy used to defeat the enemy and weaken the land invaded showed that the scribe usually used aggressive terminology to depict Sennacherib's policy. The phrase "I destroyed, I devastated, I set on fire" came to be said repeatedly of all campaigns apart from the third, the campaign against Cilicia, and the eighth. As for the campaign against Cilicia, not using the aggressive formula does not mean that Sennacherib treated the enemy king mildly, as he was brought to Nineveh and was flayed. Also, the city of the enemy king was besieged and the Assyrian entered into the city to get the enemy king out of it. As for the eighth campaign, one can understand why the phrase is not used. As is clear in the text of the campaign, it was the Babylonians along with the Elamites who launched a war against Sennacherib and started the attack in Ḫalulê. This campaign was mainly a reaction on the part of Sennacherib to the enemy's attack. Also, historically, it is not known if Sennacherib won the battle or not. The text in the annals is different in narrating the event from the text in the Babylonian Chronicles. So one can conclude that the outcome of the campaign was not as satisfying as that of other campaigns. As for the third campaign, however, there is no explanation of the absence of the aggressive phrase in the annals. Scholars concluded that Sennacherib did not intend to be destructive in his third campaign, which is why he did not use the aggressive language. However, such a conclusion seems too hasty; therefore, we defer the discussion for later.

The other noticeable point in the literature narrating the campaigns is the place dedicated to the booty and tribute Sennacherib received from the lands he invaded. What is obvious in the scenario of the campaigns is the amount of goods and tribute that Sennacherib gained from the west. While the largest amount of booty he acquired was from plundering other states, especially Babylonia, the largest amount of tribute he received was from the west. Hezekiah's tribute was the largest that Sennacherib received from all the kings of the lands he attacked. But the text does not inform us why Sennacherib received Hezekiah's tribute in Nineveh. Additionally, the amount of the tribute and its content (including Hezekiah's daughters) marks Hezekiah's tribute with special criteria that make it difficult to decide if it was a surrender tribute.

To sum up, a survey of the campaigns showed that the literary representation of Sennacherib's third campaign displays a kind of special treatment of Hezekiah and Jerusalem. Not dethroning Hezekiah, the acceptance of tribute in Nineveh, and not destroying the land demonstrate that Sennacherib either was not able to achieve full victory in his campaign or treated Hezekiah mildly deliberately.

Having reached this stage in our investigation, we have to remind ourselves that so far we have been dealing with the written text. Therefore, it might be too early to draw conclusions about the outcome of the third campaign and Sennacherib's treatment of Hezekiah. Other issues have to be discussed before coming to conclusions. There are still other sources to be consulted, which could shed light on other sides of the campaign.

Chapter Three: Sennacherib's Conquest of Lachish in the Reliefs and the Archaeological Evidence

1. Introduction

In the previous chapter, the written accounts of Sennacherib's campaign against Judah have been discussed in the context of all the other campaigns that Sennacherib launched in his lifetime against the neighbouring states. This helped us to gain an idea of how Sennacherib presented himself in his written narratives. The study demonstrated that the language that the Assyrian scribe used does not express an aggressive or violent attitude on Sennacherib's part towards the western states in general, and the Judean kingdom in particular. Another part of the study dealt with the economic exploitation of Sennacherib's campaign and it showed that the invader gained a great amount of booty and tribute from his third campaign. Now, before deriving any conclusion from this fact, another essential source from the campaign should be considered so that we may gain a wider picture of this campaign. This other source is the reliefs of the conquest of the city of Lachish in Sennacherib's south-west palace at Nineveh (now in the British Museum).

Assyria employed mural art to depict certain scenes that expressed different themes with different styles.[164] Obviously, the Assyrians realised that the visual presentation was a noteworthy means to convey the awe and admiration in the beholder that the written text could not achieve. Reade states the aim of this work at the very beginning of his article, which was meant to show "how the Assyrians viewed themselves and their relationship with the outside world, and how they wished the outside world to view them."[165] In this respect Sennacherib was no exception. Many reliefs, most of them with military scenes, decorated the walls of his famous palace in Kouyunjik (Nineveh). He also employed this kind of art to present his deeds as one of the elites whom Assyrians knew. Studying the sculptures, therefore (the reliefs in our case), is significant as they contain some details that Sennacherib found appropriate to express in reliefs rather

---

164 Concerning the style, see Albenda, P., "Assyrian Wall Reliefs: a Study of Compositional Styles", in H. Waetzoldt and H. Hauptmann (eds.), *Assyrien im Wandel der Zeiten, XXXIXe Rencontre Assyriologique Internationale, Heidelberg 6 – 10 Juli 1992* (Heidelberg, 1992), 223 – 226.
165 Reade, "Ideology", 329.

than in the written text; these visual features present a different view of the campaign that cannot be seen in the inscriptions.

In this section of the research, my focus will be on the reliefs and what they tell us about Sennacherib's military activity. Methodologically, the aim of this chapter is first, to go through all the slabs that narrate the event of the conquest of Lachish in Room XXXVI. The subject matter of the reliefs will be tackled systematically so as to gain an idea of how they narrate the event. The goal of this is to demonstrate what the reliefs really depict. Secondly, the question why Lachish is not mentioned in the annals of Sennacherib will be discussed. Scholars have reached conclusions about this issue without examining Sennacherib's policy in mentioning cities conquered in his annals. Their conclusions, therefore, are somewhat speculative and lacking basic grounds. Thirdly, the relation between the annals and the reliefs will be discussed, and if it is appropriate the reliefs will be compared with the written sources so as to trace the consistency between the texts and the visual features. The investigation of this matter will help us to decide if it is plausible to depend on the two sources to know about the aim of the campaign. In this task, the archaeological data will be consulted to support our conclusion concerning what happened in Lachish at the end of the eighth century. This will help us to gain a clearer idea of how to use the results of different sources when they are dealt with separately. In other words, it is important to distinguish between what the reliefs include and what the excavations yield, keeping in mind that it is misleading to study the reliefs with presuppositions influenced by the archaeological findings or vice versa.

2. Subject matter of the reliefs

Although many studies have been made on the Lachish reliefs, a systematic study that combines all the features of these reliefs has not yet been undertaken. The present work will examine the different aspects of the reliefs and try to deal with them as a whole to explain what the Assyrian sculptors were trying to tell the beholder about the events of 701. Close scrutiny of the conventions shown in the reliefs helps to achieve that aim.

Needless to say, in looking at the whole dado of the reliefs, we immediately notice that there is one prominent theme dominating the whole story from the beginning to the end: the presence of the Assyrian soldiers in every single register of each slab, from the beginning in Slab 1 to Slab 12.[166] The immediate con-

---

166 See the depictions of the slabs at the end of this research.

clusion that comes to mind is that these reliefs are concerned with the military strategy used against a city. The artist wanted to show how strong and fortified the city was, and yet the Assyrians conquered it. Different features are used in order to present this theme. Therefore, in the next part of the work, I shall shed light on the different devices the Assyrian artist used to depict this event. Apparently, there are three predominant aspects that are emphasised in the dado:

- The architecture of the city attacked;
- The military strategy and tactics applied depending on the geographical region;
- The progressive narration.

Below, these three aspects are going to be considered with a detailed explanation. However, before that, it is worth mentioning that, so far, the major reliable studies of all the slabs that depict the conquest of the city of Lachish are those by D. Ussishkin[167] and R.D. Barnett (*et al.*).[168] Ussishkin provides the reader with a detailed description of each slab, while Barnett includes all the reliefs of Sennacherib's palace, which enables us to look at the reliefs of Lachish in their larger context. This section, therefore, will draw a great deal on these two sources so far as it concerns the whole dado of the reliefs.

2.1. The architecture of Lachish

The Assyrians apparently had certain ideas about Lachish to convey. This is obvious from what is depicted of Lachish. Few features are shown but they are rich in details. Geographically, Lachish is depicted as a rocky place; the whole series is characterised with a scale armour background,[169] probably to indicate the rocky area. The vegetation carved on the background of the slabs shows three kinds of trees, which can be seen in other reliefs as well.[170] Architecturally, the walls of the city are emphasised. The artist uses the full extent of three slabs to depict the walls. First, they are in the right-hand portion of Slab 2,

---

167 Ussishkin, D., *Conquest of Lachish by Sennacherib* (Tel Aviv, 1982).
168 Barnett, R.D. *et al.*, *Sculptures from the Southwest Palace of Sennacherib at Nineveh* (London, 1998).
169 Ussishkin, *Conquest*, 94.
170 Interestingly, two kinds of the trees (grape vines and fig trees) presented in the reliefs are mentioned by the Rabshakeh in his speech to the Judeans at the walls of Jerusalem (2 Kgs 18:31)

then in the left-hand of Slab 3, where the city gate is seen isolated from the walls, and finally in the left-hand of Slab 4. In all the slabs the structure has the same architectural features. It is important to notice that the upper parts of the three slabs (2, 3 and 4) are missing; this suggests that there were fortifications depicted in these parts (see Figure 1 in the Appendix).[171] One can conclude that the artist devoted a reasonable amount of space to the walls in order to emphasise the strength of the fortifications of the city.

A closer look at the walls helps us to grasp the architectural details the Assyrian artist drew to show how those walls were constructed to protect the city. Despite the fact that the walls are shown from a distance, some lines can be identified. The first features to be seen are the towers, with projecting rooms, which were meant to strengthen the walls. The windows of the rooms from where the Judean soldiers could monitor the enemy are clearly shown. Other details are shown like the balconies, shields and the beams of the fortifications. Further, to show the height of the walls, the city is depicted on a higher level than that of the Assyrian soldiers; the steep slope is emphasised by the line which comes from below the walls and goes down to the ramps. Apparently the artist made an effort to show the high quality of those walls more than anything else. Nothing inside the city is shown; there are neither houses nor inner structures in the scenes. In the reliefs of other campaigns, some scenes from inside a city are shown (Figure 2). This means that the artist was mainly interested in the fortifications of the city and their technique.

2.2. Assyrian military strategy

Having discussed how Lachish was depicted, it is now appropriate to discuss the military tactics that the Assyrians applied in their battle, in a way that suited the environment of Lachish. Sennacherib's attack on Lachish was carried out in the Shephelah, and the city is shown on a mound, not on a high mountain.[172] Accordingly, a certain strategy had to be used.

---

171 Uehlinger, C., "Clio in a World of Pictures—Another Look at the Lachish Reliefs from Sennacherib's Southwest Palace at Nineveh", in L.L. Grabbe (ed.), *'Like a Bird in a Cage': The Invasion of Sennacherib in 701 B.C.E.* (JSOTSup 363; London, 2003), 269.

172 Despite the fact that mountains are depicted in the upper parts of the slabs, these do not indicate a high mountainous place. Jeffers argues that the mountains are depicted only as a distant background to the primary action in the plains; Jeffers, J., "Fifth-Campaign Reliefs in Sennacherib's Palace 'Palace without Rival' at Nineveh", Iraq LXXIII (2011), 102.

As in the case of the walls of Lachish, the battle at its height is depicted in three slabs (2, 3 and 4). There the military strategy is portrayed in fine detail. The first thing that attracts the attention is the ramps on which the assailants with their armament kit are jauntily drawn. It is obvious that the artificial ramps were the main technique that the Assyrians used in this war. This makes perfect sense if the geography of Lachish is taken into consideration, as the construction of the artificial ramps in order to gain the top of the city walls, and to employ the battering rams, would not have required the huge effort that would have been necessary in mountainous places. This tactic would not have suited other places such as the mountainous city shown in the reliefs of Alammu and Ukku. In both cases a different strategy and armament kit are employed.[173]

The Akkadian word for making a ramp is *šukbusu*, which means "to make a road or ramp by compressing and stamping the soil."[174] The Assyrians therefore used these ramps to get into the city as a means to overcome the artificial obstacle they found on their way to conquer the city instead of using ladders, which the Assyrians would have needed a big number of as well as many soldiers to climb up. These ramps, however, were not the last step of the battle. In his monograph, W. Mayer explains systematically the tactic of besieging a city. The walls of the city attacked were the main difficulty for the Assyrians, so the best way to overcome this difficulty was to make holes or gaps within those walls. To achieve this wall-breakers and battering rams were used in order to dig into the walls. The ramps would have been erected to a certain height in order to allow the battering rams to reach the walls.[175] I. Epha'al provides us with further details about the features of the siege ramps. He draws attention to their width which could be around 25 meters. These were used to support the soldiers and the battering rams that were supposed to breach the walls of Lachish and allow the Assyrian soldiers to enter the city.[176]

It is obvious then that the artist focused on the military tactics that had been used in order to show the Assyrian aptitude for choosing the right strategy for the right geographical circumstances. The number of ramps and the geometrical

---

173 In the city of Alammu, ladders are used to reach the top of the walls. And in the city of Ukku the walls are not depicted despite the fact that Sennacherib mentions in his annals that he besieged the city. For more about Alammu and Ukku, see Nadali, D., "Sennacherib's Siege, Assault, and Conquest of Alammu", in *SAAB* 14 (2002–2005), 113–128; and Jeffers, "Fifth-Campaign", 78–116.
174 See *CAD*, K, *kabāsu*, 10–11.
175 Mayer, W., *Politik und Kriegskunst der Assyrer* (Münster, 1995), 472–475.
176 Eph'al, I., *The City Besieged. Siege and Its Manifestations in the Ancient Near East* (CHANE 36; Leiden, 2009), 93.

way they are arranged, the number of the infantry and auxiliary soldiers support-ing the ramps all support the assertion that the aim is to show that the campaign was planned and studied beforehand, by foreseeing the number of the troops, the functional corps for the expedition and the necessary weapons for battle. Also, the Assyrian artist wanted to create a certain reality and a sense of awe and respect in the beholder and so make him/her feel like part of the events.

2.3. The narrative progression

One can easily notice that the narration of the conquest in the reliefs is generally progressive, moving from left to right. From a *structural* point of view, there are two focal points: the scene of the battle (Slabs 2, 3, and 4) and that of the king receiving the booty of Lachish (Slab 8). These two scenes break the direction of the movement: in the scene of the direct attack the Assyrian soldiers are por-trayed countering each other; likewise the movement of the soldiers guiding the deportees and the soldiers in the Assyrian camp are both in the direction of the throne of the king. The emphasis on these two points is also shown by their position in Room XXXVI. On the one hand, the section depicting the storm-ing of the city was placed in the centre of the rear wall, opposite the entrance;[177] on the other hand, the section showing Sennacherib receiving the booty was placed in the centre of the right wall of the room, which was probably the place where the throne of the king was positioned (Figure 3).

From the *narration* point of view, there are 12 slabs arranged in consecutive order. As for the missing slabs in the left wall of the room, the only way to know the content of these slabs is the hint from Layard which Ussishkin cites: "the re-serve consisted of large bodies of horsemen and charioteers."[178] This could be very similar to the reliefs of the city of Alammu in Room XIV, where the early slabs show the ranks of the Assyrian army in motionless positions (Figure 4).[179] It seems that the first slabs of the reliefs were dedicated to depicting the different ranks participating in the war.

The first slab and the left side of the second slab show three columns of three different sets of Assyrian infantry approaching the city;[180] in all three col-umns the soldiers are in a position of attack. The archers are shooting their ar-rows in a high direction, and the slingers are whirling their slings around their

177 Ussishkin, *Conquest*, 71.
178 Ussishkin, *Conquest*, 71.
179 Nadali, "Alammu", 118.
180 A reason for the different sets is to avoid repetition. See Albenda, "Assyrian", 225.

heads with stones in their left hands. The direction of the three columns is toward Lachish. Ussishkin describes the condition of these soldiers as approaching the city of Lachish,[181] but if we consider their position, we realise that the soldiers are actually attacking the city. They were probably protecting the soldiers who were on the ramps and those who were using the battering rams below the wall.[182] The three arrows on the shield of the Assyrian soldier in the second slab demonstrate that these soldiers were attacking too. So one can conclude that what is focused on here is the action.

In the section about the storming of the city, the Assyrian attackers are depicted as being extremely active and as prevailing. The condition of the ramps is emphasised; despite the fact that the ramps were very steep, the soldiers on them are shown with great control. The position of their feet and legs and the way they handle their weapons is very well demonstrated.

What is interesting in this section is the fact that the ramps are depicted in a special way. There are ten ramps; seven of them are leaning on the walls of the city towards the right and the other three are leaning in the opposite direction, towards the left, as if the city is surrounded by ramps. This pincer condition is not new in the reliefs of Sennacherib; D. Nadali in his article draws attention to the pincer movement of the Assyrian soldiers in the attack on Alammu.[183] So the pincer movement of the army in Alammu is substituted by the pincer condition of the ramps in Lachish reliefs. In both cases, the aim seems to be an attempt to show the enemy's structure engulfed by the Assyrian attack.

What makes this even more intense is the way the storming section is portrayed. Usually the slabs are divided into registers; the battle section, however, is not divided, and yet it shows more than one feature: the walls, the Assyrian army attacking and the deportees leaving Lachish at the bottom of slabs 3 and 4. J.M. Russell draws attention to this device and asserts aptly, "the vertical expansion of the picture is to give opportunity to say as much as possible about the battle and the density of the attack."[184]

After the battle section, the movement goes back to its normal direction, from left to right, towards the king. Again we have the pincer movement but now the king is at the centre; everything is directed towards him: the soldiers with the booty, the exiled Judeans and his retinue. The attention of the beholder

---

181 Ussishkin, *Conquest*, 94.
182 See also Mayer, *Politik*, 472.
183 Nadali, "Alammu", 118.
184 Russell, J.M., *Sennacherib's "Palace without Rival": A Programmatic Study of Texts and Images in a Late Assyrian Palace* (Pennsylvania, 1990), 237.

is now changed from the battle to the king. After showing the king on his throne, the scenes are motionless; the horses and the men are still.

Before finishing this part, there is one significant point worth mentioning. In slabs 4 and 5 the Assyrian soldiers are depicted carrying items looted from the city. These items are swords, shields, lances, a chariot and incense stands. From this, one can safely assume that the Assyrians entered the city and sacked some important centres like the palace of the governor. Strangely enough, the artist has no interest in showing the sacking of the city or depicting the Assyrian army inside the city as is done in some other reliefs. The whole battle is shown outside the city at the walls; no houses are depicted and no looting is shown. The main focus of the artist was the battle and the military strategy at the walls of the city.

2.4. Conclusion on the subject matter of the reliefs

Having discussed the reliefs, one can safely conclude that they focus on the walls of Lachish and the versatility of the Assyrian army. The strength of the fortifications, the emphasis on the Assyrian tactics applied in the battle, and the way the story is visually narrated could all prove that the main aim of depicting Lachish in this way was to show that the Assyrians considered their victory against Lachish a great military achievement. However, this does not mean that the victory at Lachish is considered by the Assyrians to be the high point in their campaign against the west;[185] the destroyed reliefs and the fragmentary nature of many of them make it difficult to know if there were other cities depicted or not. Therefore it is better, for the moment, to adhere to what the reliefs show.

3. The absence of Lachish in the annals

Another question about Lachish worth discussing is: if Lachish was so important, why did Sennacherib not mention its name in his annals? In his article, C. Uehlinger deals with this question, calling it "an often-raised dilemma"; he puts the question like this:

> If the victorious conquest of Lachish really did matter that much to Sennacherib, why are his inscriptions absolutely silent about this crucial event concentrating instead on Heze-

---

185 Uehlinger, "Clio", 305.

kiah's surrender at Jerusalem? And since the latter episode is presented by the annals as the ultimate climax of Sennacherib's Western campaign, why should the subjugation of Jerusalem be absent from the pictorial record of Sennacherib's palace sculptures?[186]

Obviously, Uehlinger is not asking one but two questions: one about Lachish and the other about Jerusalem. However, the answer he gives to the dilemma is only about the second part of the question —why is Jerusalem not depicted in the reliefs? He does not offer an answer to the question why Lachish is not mentioned in the annals of Sennacherib.[187] He argues that Jerusalem was probably depicted, and the reliefs in the Throne Room (I) Slabs 1 to 28 show the walls of Jerusalem, with the figure of Hezekiah standing alone (imprisoned like a bird) in one of the towers (Figure 5). It is beyond the aim of this work to discuss his opinion about the depiction of Jerusalem. More pertinently, whether we accept this argument or not, the question why Lachish is not mentioned in the annals is unanswered. It seems that the two questions are not related to each other, and that it is important to differentiate between them and deal with each separately.

Another possible answer to the question regarding Lachish is that Sennacherib in fact wanted to compensate for his failure to take Jerusalem, and this is why he made the most of the reliefs to show publicly that he did not lose the battle.[188] This answer seems to be hypothetical and stems from dealing with the matter in an incomprehensive way, considering it an isolated case. In fact, Lachish is not the only city depicted in the reliefs. If we deal with this issue as part of a larger picture, other conclusions could be more reasonable. It is the task of this part of the work to answer this question thoroughly, using both the reliefs and the annals together so that the answer might be adequate.

First of all, we have to note that Lachish is not the only conquered city depicted in the reliefs whose name is not mentioned in the annals. If we consider this matter in a wider context, we realise that there are other names of cities or settlements found in the reliefs of Sennacherib's palace that are not mentioned in the annals. In his updated version of the edition of Sennacherib's epigraphs, Russell presents 16 names of cities and place(s);[189] those which are legible include: Dilbat, Ukku, Kasusi, Aranziash, Balatai, Alammu, Lachish, Bit-Kubatti,

---

186 Uehlinger, "Clio", 293.
187 Uehlinger, "Clio", 293–302.
188 Mazar, A., "The Divided Monarchy: Comments on Some Archaeological Issues", in I. Finkelstein and A. Mazar (B. B. Schmidt, ed.), *The Quest for the Historical Israel. Debating Archaeology and the History of Early Israel* (SBL 17; Atlanta, 2007), 173
189 Russell, J.M., *Writing on the Wall. Studies in the Architectural Context of Late Assyrian Palace Inscriptions.* (MC 9; Winona Lake, 1999). Prior to this, Russell published *Sennacherib's Palace without Rival* (Chicago, 1991), but he updated his version of the epigraphs in *Writing on the Wall.*

Sahrina and Mt Lebanon.[190] Russell asserts that of these names "only three – Balatai, Bit-Kubatti and Sahrina – are definitely included in his [Sennacherib's] annals."[191] Actually, there are two other names that are mentioned in the annals of Sennacherib: Ukku, of which Russell is aware,[192] and Dilbat.[193] So there are five names mentioned in the annals, and five which are not.

Being aware of this lack of overlaps between the epigraphs and the annals, Russell states three reasons to explain it:
1. The visual narratives and their accompanying epigraphs could have been compiled at a different time, presumably earlier, than the written annals.
2. Different people compiled the epigraphs (visual) and annalistic (verbal) records.
3. Types of records were conceived for different purposes or with different emphases.[194]

These three reasons might give a clue as to why Lachish is not mentioned in the annals; nevertheless, they require some discussion. As for the first reason, it is known (almost for sure) that the report of the third campaign was written as early as 700, only one year after the campaign, at least the first copy of the inscription.[195] In this case, one can soundly assume that there was not a huge temporal gap between the writing of the annals and the carving of the reliefs, given the fact that Sennacherib commenced the construction of his palace early in his reign.[196] So, one can conclude safely that the explanation involving the different time is not applicable in our case. As for the second reason, it is also not quite convincing, because in any case the king is the one who administered the whole work and the writing and carving should have been accomplished as he ordered it to be. In other words, the project of recording the events was very well monitored and controlled. So we cannot assume that such important tasks like writing the annals and carving the reliefs were undertaken by two different groups of people who did not know what the other part was doing. As for the third reason, it is truly tempting to think that the pictures and words were

---

190 Russell, *Writing*, 283–292.
191 Russell, *Writing*, 140.
192 Russell, *Writing*, 135, 284.
193 Sennacherib mentions the name of the city of Dilbat among other cities in his "*First Campaign*" *Inscriptions*. Russell, however, in his *Writing on the Wall*, is depending on Luckenbill's *The Annals of Sennacherib*, where Dilbat is not found.
194 Russell, *Writing*, 141–143.
195 Frahm, *Einleitung*, 252.
196 Russell, *Writing*, 135.

independent realms and had different aims. However, Russell does not answer the question why some cities are mentioned in the annals while others are not. This brings us again to our question: why is Lachish not mentioned in the annals?

One good way to answer this question is to consider the name of Lachish among other names. In other words, the other cities should also be considered. To do so, I am presenting in the tables below all the names of lands and cities mentioned in the annals of Sennacherib.

Campaign	Territory	City	Events
1st campaign	Babylonia	Uruk, Larsa, Ur, Eridu, Kulaba, Kissik, Nemed-Laguda	
		Bit-Iakin, Bit-Amukkani, Bit-Asilani, Bit-Sa'alli, Bit-Dakkuri Tu'muna, Rihihu, Iadaqqu, Gibre, Malihu Gurumu, Ubulu, Damunu, Gambulu, Hindaru, Ru'u'a, Puqudu, Hamranu, Hagaranu, Nabatu, Lita'u	They were all gathered by Merodach-Baladan against Sennacherib
		Nippur, Dilbat, Marad, Kish, Hursagkalam, Babylon, Borsippa, Cutha	
		Kish, Cutha..................................	Battle
		Babylon...	Royal city: plundered
		Amattu, Haua'e, Supapu, (Nuqabu), Bit-Sannabi, Qudayyin, Qidrina, Dur-Ladini, Bitati, Banitu, Guzummanu, Dur-Iansuri, Dur-Abiyata', Dur-Rudumme, Bit-Rahe, Hapisa, Sadi-AN, Hurudu, Sahrina, Iltuk, Allallu, Sab/phanu, Kar-Nergal, Apak, Bit-Dannaya, Bit-Abdaya, Bahir, Marira, Marad, Iaqimuna, Kub/pruna, Bit-Kudurri, and Suqa-Marusi	Cities of Bit-Dakkuri + 250 cities: captured
		Dur-Appe, Dur-Tanne, Dur-Sama, Sarrabatu, Salahatu, Dur-Abdaya, Sappihimari, Sibtu-sa-Makka-me,	Cities of Bit-Sa'alli + 120 cities: captured
		Sapia, Sarrabanu, Larak, Parakmarri, Bit-ilu-bani, Ahudu, Alu-sa-issur-Adad, Saharratu Manahhu, Alu-sa-amele, Dur-Akkia, Nagītu, Nur-abinu, Har-Suarra, Dur-Ruqbi,	Cities of Bit-Amukkani + 350 cities

Continued

Campaign	Territory	City	Events
		Danda-Hulla, Dur-Bir-Dada, Bit-re'e, Dur-Ugurri, Ginda'ina, Dur-Uwayt, Dur-Taura, Sabhuna, Puharru, Harbat-Iddina, Harbat-Kalbi, Sabarre, Bit-Bani-ilu'a, Suladu, Bit-Iltam-sama', Bit-Dini-ilu, Daqalu, Hamesa, BE(Til)-la-a, Ta'iru, Kibranu, Iltaratu, Akamasakina, Sagabatu-saMardukia.	
		Bit-Zabidia, Larsa, Kulaba, Eridu, Kissik, Nemed-Laguda, Dur-Iakin, Kar-Nabu	Cities of Bit-Iakin + 100 cities
		Uruk, Nippur, Kish, Hursagkalama	Sinners were brought out as spoils
		Tu'muna, Rihihu, Iadaqqu, Ubudu, Gibre, Malihu	Cities captured
		Gurumu, Ubulu, Damunu, Gambulu, Hindaru, Ru'u'a, Puqudu, Hamranu, Hagaranu, Nabatu, Lita'u	
		Hararatu	Tribute
		Hirimmu	district reorganised
2nd campaign	Land of Kassites + land of Yasubigallians	Bit-Kilamzah	Stronghold: captured, and then turned into a fortress and settlement for people
		Numberless small cities	Devastated
		Hardišpu + Bit-Kubatti[197]	Settlement of people and annexation to Assyria
	Ellipi	Mar'ubištu + Akkuddu + 34 strong cities	Two royal residences: both devastated
		Šiširtu + Kummahlum + small cities + district of Bit-Barrû	All added to the territory of Assyria
		Elenzaš	Turned into a stronghold city and its name changed
		Medes	Tribute
3rd campaign	Hitti	Sidon	Royal city: its king ran away

---

197 In the Rassam Edition, which was published one year later, the name of Bit-Kubatti appears with two other cities which were captured.

Continued

Campaign	Territory	City	Events
		Great Sidon, small Sidon, Bit-Zitti, Zaribtu, Mahalliba, Ushu, Akzib, Akku	Overwhelmed by the weapons of Ashur and they submitted
		Samsimur, Sidon, Arbad, Gublu, Ashdod, Bit-Ammon, Moab, Edom, Amuru	Cities and lands whose kings brought tribute
		Ashkelon	Royal city: the house sacked
		Bīth-Daganna, Joppa, Banayabar-qa, Azuru	Captured
		Eltekeh + Tamnâ	Battle and both captured
		Ekron	Royal city
		Jerusalem	Royal city: its king imprisoned
		46 strong cities	Besieged and spoils taken
4th campaign	Babylonia	Bittūtu	Royal residence: Its king was overthrown
		Bit-Iakin..	Royal city captured and royal family taken as booty
5th campaign	Urartu	Tunurru, Sharum, Ezama, Kibshu, Halgidda, Kua, Kana	The warriors were fought, and their cities were devastated
		Ukku	Royal city captured
		+ 33 cities	Devastated
Camp.696	Tabal	Ingirâ and Tarzu	The cities which aligned with the enemy king
		Illubru	The fortified city of the enemy king and his royal residence
Camp.695	Tabal	Tīl-Garimme	City where the battle happened
6th campaign	Babylonia	Nagītu, Nagītu-di'bina, Ḫilmu, Pillatu and Ḫupapanu	The first two are cities, and the others are districts in Elam: conquered.
		Babylon	Capital city
7th campaign	Elam	Bit-Ha'iri, Rasa	Cities on the border of Assyria were joined to Assyria
		Bube, Dunni-Shamash, Bit-Risia, Bit-ahlame, Duru, Kaltesulai, Shilibtu, Bit-Asusi, Kar-Zer-ikisha, Bit-Gissi, Bit-Katpalani, Bit-Imbia, Dimtu-sha-Sulai, Dimtu-sha-Mar-Biti-etir, Harri-ashlaki, Rabbai,	All these cities were devastated

Continued

Campaign	Territory	City	Events
		Rasu, Akkabarina Tel-Uhuri, Ham-ranu, Naditu	
		+ cities of Bit-Bunaki, Tel-Humbi, Dimtu-asha-Dume-ilu, Bit-Ubia, Balti-lishir, Tagab-lishir, Shanaki-date, the lower Masutu, Sar-hudiri, Alum-sha-belit-biti, Bit-ahe-iddina, Ilte-uba,	
		+ 34 cities	
		Madaktu	Royal city, not conquered because of the snow
8th campaign	Babylon and Elam	Ḫalulê	Battle

Using the chart above, I shall discuss the way Sennacherib mentions the names of the cities in his annals and the reason for doing so. This will lead us to some conclusions about the city of Lachish.

Generally speaking, the table reveals that Sennacherib had a certain reason for naming places. The mechanism of mentioning the names is as follows:

1) The name of the capital city or royal residence is mentioned in almost all the campaigns. Apparently, the royal city was considered a politically significant city to enter or conquer.

2) Cities which are "besieged, conquered and plundered", or "destroyed, devastated and set on fire" are usually recorded in groups. There is no mention of an individual city (apart from a royal city) being conquered or devastated.

3) If one or two names of places are mentioned, this means that:

   a. The place was either paying tribute or was reorganised, as was the case in the first campaign.

   b. The city was captured and then turned into a fortress in which people were settled, like the case of Bīt-Kilamzaḫ at the beginning of the second campaign.

   c. The city was annexed to Assyria and became part of the empire, like the two cities of Ḫardišpu and Bīt-Kubatti in the second campaign.

   d. The city presents a place where an open battle was launched in a plain, like the cases of Kish in the first campaign, Eltekeh in the third campaign, Tīl-Garimme in the non-royal campaign of 695, and Ḫalulê in the eighth campaign.

e. The people of the city aligned themselves with the enemy king as the case in the cities of Ingirâ and Tarzu in the non-royal campaign of 696.

If we consider the four cities—Dilbat, Sahrina, Bīt-Kubatti, and Ukku—mentioned in both sources (the annals and the reliefs) and those which are not mentioned in the annals, keeping in mind the points presented above, we might create a synthesis.[198]

As for the cities depicted in the reliefs and mentioned in the annals:

- Dilbat and Sahrina are among a group of named cities: Sahrina is one of the cities belonging to the tribe of Bīt-Dakkuri which were conquered; and Dilbat is one of the cities whose people Merodach-Baladan has gathered in coalition against Sennacherib. One, therefore, would not be surprised to see the names of these two cities in the annals. But in the second edition of the first campaign in the "Bellino Cylinder",[199] the two names—Dilbat and Sahrina—are not mentioned, as the groups in which they are recorded in the first edition are missing too.
- The city of Bīt-Kubatti[200] is mentioned in the first version as one of the two cities in which Sennacherib settled people.[201] In the later edition, however, the name of the city comes in a group of (three) cities that were conquered[202] —a fact that is not mentioned in the first edition of the account.
- The city of Ukku is a royal and capital city; one would expect it to be in the annals.

As for the cities that are not mentioned in the annals:

- The city of Kasusi is unattested in the Assyrian inscriptions; one therefore cannot draw any conclusion about the city, as its location cannot be identified easily. The slab which contains the name of the city is in a sequence of slabs that show the Assyrian army attacking a city (Room V, Slabs 10 – 23).[203] The slabs are so fragmentary that the landscape of the city cannot be recognised.

---

198 We leave the name "Balatai" because the name is not recorded in the context of war. The city was not an enemy city when Sennacherib launched an attack.

199 Grayson, *Sennacherib*, 51.

200 The reliefs of this city are in one of the rooms which are described but not illustrated. Russell, *Sennacherib's*, 117.

201 Grayson, *Sennacherib*, 52.

202 Luckenbill, *Annals*, 26, 67.

203 Russell, J.M., *The Final Sack of Nineveh. The Discovery, Documentation, and Destruction of King Sennacherib's Throne Room at Nineveh, Iraq* (New Haven, 1998), 142 – 160.

- The city of Aranziash is in reliefs that depict the Assyrian army launching a battle against a mountainous city. According to the inscriptions where this name is attested, its location is in the mountains of Ellipi.[204] So one can assume that the city was one of the cities captured in the second campaign.
- The city of Alammu is depicted in the reliefs in Room XIV. It is commonly held that the city was conquered in the second campaign.[205]

To sum up, having these points in mind, we can conclude that focusing on certain cities in a relief programme does not mean that Sennacherib was hiding a near-failure or compensating for the fact that he could not conquer another city. Aranziash and Alammu were conquered in the second campaign, and yet they are not mentioned in the annals. On the other hand, there is no sign that Sennacherib lost the war in his second campaign, so what failure would he have hidden by depicting Aranziah and Alammu in the reliefs and not mentioning them in the annals?

All this leads us to conclude that any assumption about Lachish's depiction should be made carefully. Whether or not Sennacherib failed in his third campaign should not be mixed with the issue of the depiction of Lachish. The assumption that Sennacherib depicted Lachish in order to hide the fact that he failed to conquer Jerusalem needs more explanation. The first question we need to answer is: was he intending to besiege Jerusalem just as he did with Lachish or not? The textual material does not support an affirmative answer to this question. The military tactics he used with Jerusalem were not the same as with the other cities. While the 46 cities were besieged, conquered and plundered, Jerusalem was blockaded. So if he were to depict a scene for propagandistic reasons, he would not choose Jerusalem, which he did not besiege. Rather, he would choose a city that was besieged and conquered. And as for the question why Lachish is not in the annals, our study has led us to conclude that the name of the city is not mentioned because it does not meet the criteria that the other mentioned cities have. Lachish is one of the 46 cities that were besieged and conquered; it was not a royal city; it was not annexed to Assyria; Sennacherib did not resettle people in it; and a battle did not take place in it. This is why it is not mentioned in the annals.

---

204 Parpola, S., *Neo-Assyrian Toponym* (AOAT 6; Kevelaer, 1970), 23.
205 Nadali, "Alammu", 114.

4. Textual material and the reliefs

Our investigation above shows us that consulting the textual materials is very helpful in comprehending the reliefs and, accordingly, Sennacherib's policy in presenting his ideology. In this regard, the discussion can be extended to examine how far the textual materials match the visual art in conveying Sennacherib's strategy in his dealing with the west, and especially with Hezekiah and Jerusalem.

I start my investigation of this matter by discussing a reasonably recent opinion about the relation between the reliefs and the written text. In a 2011 article, J. Jeffers discussed the reliefs of the fifth and third campaigns, and how they agree with the annals. I shall briefly present his hypothesis and then discuss it. The main task of his article is to identify other fifth-campaign relief programmes in the palace of Sennacherib that were previously assigned to the third campaign to the west. To achieve this, the author differentiates among the various distinct military campaigns to identify the Assyrian artistic conventions at work in the different depictions. In doing so, he comes to the following conclusions concerning the Lachish reliefs: (1) examining the annals that narrate the events of third campaign, he concludes that the language used does not make any reference to extensive devastation of the cities conquered in the west; and (2) examining the reliefs, he concludes that they correspond to the annals, as they do not make reference to devastation or setting the city ablaze; the reliefs of Lachish do not show the city set on fire, as is the case in the reliefs that depict the conquest of the city of Ukku. Then he makes this statement concerning the reliefs: "These relief programmes present the style of warfare that matches the *goal* of Sennacherib's third campaign from the annals, and can safely be identified as part of his invasion of Palestine."[206] Since according to the statement of Jeffers the annals and the reliefs do not show any sign of devastation, one can conclude that historically Sennacherib's aim was not to destroy the Judean cities in general and Lachish in particular. This is obvious from the way he phrases his conclusion about Lachish: "despite the fact that there is much conflict in these scenes, the cities themselves remain intact, being neither devastated nor set ablaze."[207]

Needless to say, there is some original insight in this conclusion. In any case, the reliefs and the written text were both produced to serve the Assyrian ideology and the Assyrian king authorised both of them. Therefore, it is not surprising to find an agreement between the two sources. Our investigation in the second and

---

206 Jeffers, "Fifth-Campaign", 88–90. The emphasis is mine.
207 Jeffers, "Fifth-Campaign", 89.

third chapters, so far, has shown us that Jeffers' statement has some validity. Nevertheless, to assume that the aim of Sennacherib's third campaign can be known by consulting only the reliefs and the annals needs more solid grounds. In my opinion, the matter bears more discussion.

First of all, it is not enough to speak about the goal of the campaign using only the annals and the reliefs. The reliefs were made after the campaign for a certain aim, as mentioned above in the introduction to this section. The mural art had been meant to commemorate the king's acts and his victory. Of course it is not impossible to derive certain conclusions from the reliefs about the aim, but it is more appropriate to do so with the aid of other sources like the archaeological data and the wider context of the reliefs of Sennacherib's campaigns. Doing so will help us to know how much the textual materials and the reliefs agree with or depart from archaeology. Only then will our conclusions about the textual materials and the reliefs be more probable. In this regard, two points are discussed. The first is on consulting other reliefs, and the second involves archaeological data about Judah after Sennacherib's attack.

4.1. Consulting other reliefs

Surprisingly, Jeffers did not consider other reliefs that were related to the matter. As is known from the reliefs found in the palace, names of ten cities (or settlements) are mentioned in the epigraphs.[208] Although the reliefs are fragmentary and accordingly, it is difficult to grasp the theme of the reliefs in certain rooms, there are, however, reliefs of the conquest of the city of Alammu in Room XIV which could be helpful in the present discussion. Despite the fact that the name of the city is completely absent from the annals,[209] the city has been identified as one of the cities conquered by Sennacherib in his second campaign to the east near the Zagros Mountains.[210] In representing the second campaign in the annals, Sennacherib repeats twice that he "destroyed, devastated... and set on fire" some of the cities and settlements in that area. These included the cities in the land of the Kassites and of the Ellipi that were attacked during the second campaign. The text informs the reader that those cities were devastated and set on fire. The reliefs of Alammu in Room XIV, however, do not clearly show this; they do not show any sign of a burnt city.[211] Moreover, Nadali has con-

---

208 Russell, *Writing*, 140.
209 Grayson, *Sennacherib*, 52–53.
210 Nadali, "Alammu", 115.
211 Barnett, *Sculptures*, 158–182.

sidered the reliefs of the city of Alammu and draws attention to some significant issues within the reliefs. Having scrutinised the architecture, the landscape and the military strategies, he argues persuasively that the visual presentation is concerned with showing the versatility of the Assyrians in planning and preparing for war in advance.[212]

If we were to follow Jeffers' methodology, it would be difficult to conclude about the aim of the second campaign, because the relief programmes do not apparently agree with the annals. Therefore, it seems that we ought not to rely solely on the reliefs. Seemingly, Sennacherib is focuing on the versatility of the military strategy the Assyrians applied in their attack. The artist wanted to show how the Assyrians considered the different geographical nature of the city and the environment to plan accordingly the military tactic that should be used to achieve their aim. The condition of Alammu is very similar to that of Ukku. They are both in mountainous territory; in both cases Sennacherib mentions in his inscriptions that he burned the cities. However, the depictions of them in the reliefs are different.

It is safe now to conclude that if the reliefs do not show the action of destruction inside the city of Lachish, this does not mean that there was not any destruction undertaken by Sennacherib. The reliefs of Lachish show the priority that the city acquired in Sennacherib's mind after winning the battle. This is why the artist focused on the military strategy and its results as is shown above in this study; what happened inside the city, and whether it was destroyed or not, apparently did not matter to the artist.

4.2. Archaeological data

There is much to say about archaeology and the third campaign. But, for now, we confine our discussion to what is related to this point of our study. In other words, the impact of Sennacherib's military tactics in the city of Lachish will be the main focus in this part, i.e., what happened to the city in the light of archaeology.

As for the city of Lachish, strangely enough, Jeffers does not consider the results of the excavations at the site of Lachish. One cannot close one's eyes on those results and simply conclude that the attack was only against the walls of the city. The extensive excavation work of Ussishkin and others has yielded results concerning the city of Lachish at the end of eighth century. In his 2006

---

212 Nadali, "Alammu", 117.

article, he asserts that "the Assyrian army forced its way into the city (Level III) and burned it to the ground...The population was driven out and deported, and Lachish remained abandoned for many years."[213] This can be supported by the other studies made of the Judean Shephelah, which demonstrate a shrinkage in the size and importance of some cities at the end of eighth century and the beginning of seventh century; one of those cities is Lachish.[214]

It is obvious that the city was deliberately weakened extensively for certain reasons. If we consider the historical background we might understand the motive. In this case the archaeological data are a great help as well: first of all, the city of Lachish was prosperous and economically successful since the Late Bronze age in the 12th century, but it was abandoned because of the destruction and resettled afterward. It started to function as a royal fortified city between the 9th and 8th centuries. A fire consumed all the buildings at the end of the 8th century, which the majority of archaeologists assign to the destruction of Sennacherib in 701. After being resettled, the last destruction is assigned to the Babylonian king, Nebuchadnezzar II, in 587/6.[215] It is clear that the city was from the beginning a significant place, which any attacker would consider when coming to Judah. Secondly, from a commercial point of view, Lachish had a strategic position. There were two important longitudinal routes in the Judean Shephelah. One of them was from Egypt directly to Lachish. From Lachish this road appears to have continued through the heart of the Judean Shephelah, on the one hand, and from Lachish to Jerusalem on the other.[216] This road represented a way for Judean diplomats, messengers, and merchants to reach the coastal highway to Egypt without passing through Philistia. This means that Lachish was a strategic point. It provided independence for Judah from Philistia. And thirdly, the reliefs show that Lachish had a military significance. This is clear from the items depicted; the soldiers are carrying war kit. From the way the Judeans are depicted Uehlinger concludes: "the depiction of unarmed natives leaving the town indicates that the Assyrians correctly perceived the double status of Lachish as a civilian

---

213 Ussishkin, "Sennacherib's Campaign to Philistia and Judah: Ekron, Lachish, and Jerusalem", in Y. Amit *et al.* (eds.), *Essay on Ancient Israel in Its Near Eastern Context: A Tribute to Nadav Na'aman* (Winona Lake, 2006), 345; see also Ussishkin, *Conquest*, 26; and Grabbe, L.L., *Like a Bird in a Cage. The Invasion of Sennacherib in 701 BCE* (JSOTS 363; London, 2003), 7–8.
214 Vaughn, A.G., *Theology, History, and Archaeology in the Chronicler's Account of Hezekiah* (ABS 4; Atlanta, 1999), 32.
215 Ussishkin, D., *The Renewed Archaeological Excavations at Lachish (1973–1994)*, Vol. I (Ms 22; Tel Aviv, 2004), 44; Ussishkin, *Conquest*, 26.
216 Dorsey, D., *The Roads and Highways of Ancient Israel* (Baltimore, 1991), 69, 154.

city and a major, well-armed Judahite military garrison." And from the depiction of the weapons he concludes that the Assyrian "recognition that Judahite weapons was quite developed and posed a serious threat to Assyria."[217] This means that Lachish was one of the focal places on which Sennacherib directed his attention to weaken Judah.

To sum up the evidence of the textual materials and the reliefs, we can conclude that concerning the military tactics that Sennacherib used in his campaigns, the textual materials do not necessarily show the same military strategy. This does not mean that they contradict each other. Rather, each source has its own way of depicting a particular reality. The reliefs showed that the main focal point in depicting the campaigns was the military strategy and tactics employed by the Assyrians in the war. For the Assyrians, the conquest of Lachish was a great achievement that needed to be honoured and remembered. So one can say that the reliefs present a propagandistic work to explain the power and versatility of Sennacherib. The architect, the way of narration and the presentation of the Assyrian army all direct the attention to two focal points: the storming of the city and the king's receipt of the tribute. The textual materials focus on the same aspects but from a different angle.

Moreover, if the two sources, the textual materials and the reliefs, agree about presenting certain aspects of a campaign this does not mean that they reveal the aim of the campaign. In this respect, the archaeological data served our study in two ways: first, consulting other reliefs, our investigation led us to conclude that the textual materials do not always show the same details that the reliefs do. Secondly, the archaeological data show that Lachish was destroyed and abandoned for many years after the third campaign. Here the written texts depart from the archaeology; as we noticed, the inscriptions do not express violence or dramatic destruction in Judah, while the archaeology shows a different reality in Lachish.

5. Conclusion to chapter three

The aim of this section was to examine another source of the third campaign, i.e., the reliefs of Lachish. The main issues that have been discussed were: the subject matter of the reliefs and the way one of the events of the third campaign is represented; the absence of Lachish in the annals; and the relation between the written sources and the reliefs, i.e., how much they agree about Sennacher-

---

217 Uehlinger, "Clio", 283.

ib's policy in his dealing with Judah, and if they really reveal the aim of the third campaign.

Having studied the subject matter of the reliefs, one can conclude that the main focus of representing the attack against Lachish was on showing the Assyrian militaristic greatness and its ideology of conquest. This is obvious from what is depicted. All the slabs from beginning to end focus on the army's size, its weapons, its units, the military tactics, the heights of Lachish's walls, the fall of the city and the presentation of the tribute to Sennacherib at the end. What happened inside the city is not depicted and, apparently, Sennacherib was not interested in telling viewers that the city was devastated. The strategy he used to overcome the main obstacle, the high walls, was the real victory that Sennacherib wanted to be depicted.

The discussion about the absence of Lachish in the annals aimed to answer the question: if the victory in Lachish was so great, why did Sennacherib not mention it in his annals? Studying the matter in a wider context helped us to draw conclusions about this point. Having examined all the cities mentioned in the annals and the reliefs, we noticed that there was a policy in mentioning the conquered cities in the annals. First of all, there are cities that are depicted in the reliefs but are not mentioned in the annals. Additionally, there is a pattern in mentioning cities conquered during the campaigns. Cities are usually mentioned in a group of three cities or more. The name of a city is mentioned if the city is the capital or the city where battle was launched, or if the city is annexed to the Assyrian Empire. Lachish is not any of these, which is why it is not mentioned in the annals.

As for the relation between the textual materials and the reliefs, our study showed us that the representation of the third campaign in mural art agrees to some extent with the written texts. The reliefs focused on attacking the walls of the city and not on destroying the city from the inside. In other words, the conclusions from studying the reliefs strengthened the assumption that Sennacherib was not aggressive in his third campaign. Thus, the textual material and the reliefs indicate that there is no reason to assume that Sennacherib failed in his campaign, because he came for a certain aim, i.e., to quell the rebel and receive the tribute. That is why he went back without conquering or entering Jerusalem. When the archaeological evidence was consulted, however, we realised that the written texts and the reliefs do not exactly show all the facts of that campaign.[218] Archaeologically, many sites in Judah were destroyed and

---

218 See Dalley, S., "The Language of Destruction and Its Interpretation," *BM* 36 (2005), 275 – 285.

Lachish was burned and devastated. This leads us to conclude that if the written text and the reliefs do not show Sennacherib's aggressive treatment in his third campaign, this does not mean that he was not aggressive or he did not intend to be destructive. More importantly, the discussion led us to conclude that we cannot depend on the textual materials and the reliefs to know the aim of Sennacherib in his third campaign.

So instead of trying to reconcile the textual evidence and the depiction of reality in the reliefs, one can ask another question: why does Sennacherib use less aggressive language in the annals, when he had destroyed some cities like Lachish? There is no way to get a satisfying answer to this question. There is always a big difference between what Sennacherib intended of his campaign, what he actually did and the way he represented the campaign.[219] What we can safely assume is that neither the textual materials nor the reliefs seemed to reveal the whole reality of the campaign. In this case, the assumption based on the non-aggressive language of the annals and the reliefs that Sennacherib intended to treat Hezekiah mildly, and not enter Jerusalem or punish Hezekiah, the rebel, is not valid. Before deriving a conclusion about the outcome of the campaign, one more point needs to be discussed.

---

219 Galil, G., review of F.M. Fales, *Guerre et Paix en assyrie: Religion et imperialism. Les Conférences de l'école Pratique des Hautes études* (Paris, 2010), 3.

Chapter Four: The Blockade of Jerusalem in the Context of Other Blockaded Cities

1. Introduction

In the previous sections the investigation led us to conclude that the representation of the third campaign in the annals and the depiction of Lachish in the reliefs do not necessarily convey the reality of what happened in 701. We noticed that the textual materials and archaeology depart from each other concerning the military strategy that Sennacherib used to subdue Judah. More evidence about the outcome of the campaign, then, is needed to understand Sennacherib's behaviour toward Judah in general and Jerusalem in particular. The comparison we applied in the first section on the campaigns of Sennacherib helped us to conclude that Sennacherib's treatment of Jerusalem was different from his treatment of other cities. However, the investigation did not provide us with enough material to establish the reason for this treatment: was it because Sennacherib did not intend to enter Jerusalem or because he could not? One good way to answer this question is to examine the attack against Jerusalem in the wider context of other cities that suffered a similar treatment. So what happened to Jerusalem and Hezekiah in 701 will be compared with other cases where cities were blockaded and their kings were enclosed in their cities. In other words, the military tactic which was employed against Jerusalem and Hezekiah will be focused on in this chapter. By so doing we will have the opportunity to view Sennacherib's behaviour in its wider context, and accordingly more reasonable conclusions will be derived. The archaeological findings will be used when their use supplements the discussion. The main goal of this chapter is to identify the kind of language used in the Assyrian royal inscriptions to describe a blockaded city, and accordingly recognise (if there is any) the pattern used to designate a successful and unsuccessful blockade. This will help us decide whether or not the blockade of Jerusalem was successful, and whether Sennacherib did not enter Jerusalem (and dethrone Hezekiah) because that was not in his plan, or because something prevented him from doing so.

Methodologically, after reading the Assyrian account of the attack on Jerusalem, and presenting the scholarly opinions about it, terminology used to describe the attack will be scrutinised. This helps us to understand how to describe the military attack on Jerusalem, and accordingly choose similar cases in the Assyrian inscriptions. Discussing these cases will provide the study with the data needed to decide if the strategy used was successful or not.

2. Identifying the problem

To start our discussion in this section it is important to identify the problem with which we are going to deal. A good way to achieve that is to read the Assyrian account of Sennacherib's attack against Jerusalem, and see what is odd in the account that calls for explanation. This helps us to limit our study and focus on one main question.

The Assyrian account in the Rassam Cylinder relates:

[49](As for) Hezekiah of the land of Judah, I surrounded and conquered forty-six of his fortified walled cities and small(er) settlements in their environs, which were without number, (50) by having ramps trodden down and battering rams brought up, the assault of foot soldiers, sapping, breaching, and siege engines. I brought out of them 200,150 people, young (and) old, male and female, horses, mules, donkeys, camels, oxen and sheep and goats, which were without number, and I counted (them) as booty.

As for him (Hezekiah), I confined him inside the city Jerusalem, his royal city, like a bird in a cage. I set up blockades against him and made him dread exiting his city gate. I detached from his land the cities of his that I had plundered and I gave (them) to Mitinti, the king of the city Ashdod, and Padî, the king of the city Ekron, (and) Ṣilli-Bēl, the king of the land Gaza, (and thereby) made his land smaller. To the former tribute, their annual giving, I added the payment (of) gifts (in recognition) of my overlordship and imposed (it) upon them.

As for him, Hezekiah, fear of my lordly brilliance overwhelmed him and, after my (departure), he had the auxiliary forces (and) his elite troops whom he had brought inside to strengthen the city Jerusalem, his royal city, and who had provided support, (along with) 30 talents of gold, 800 talents of silver, choice antimony, large blocks of..., ivory beds, armchairs of ivory, elephant hide(s), elephant ivory, ebony, boxwood, garments with multi-coloured trim, linen garments, blue-purple wool, red-purple wool, utensils of bronze, iron, copper, tin (and) iron, chariots, shields, lances, armour, iron belt-daggers, bows and uṣṣu-arrows, equipment, (and) implements of war (all of) which were without number, together with his daughters, his palace women, and male singers, (and) female singers brought into Nineveh, my capital city, and he sent a mounted messenger of his to me to deliver (this) payment and to do obedience.[220]

Sennacherib's description of his action in Judah is apparently divided into three sections[221]:

–   In the first section, he describes the military action employed in the attack to subjugate the Judean cities.

---

220 I am depending on Grayson concerning the translation of the account from the Akkadian language into English. Grayson, *Sennacherib*, 65 – 66.
221 For detailed interpretation of the text see Gallagher, *Sennacherib's Campapign*, 132 – 142.

- In the second section, he describes the military tactics used against Hezekiah and Jerusalem.
- In the third section, he describes what happened to Hezekiah: overwhelmed with fear of Sennacherib, he paid the tribute and showed his servitude by sending his messengers to Nineveh.

In every section, Sennacherib relates his action and the result of that action. First he besieged and conquered the cities, and then he brought out the booty. In the second section, he imprisoned Hezekiah, and then cut off the cities that he had despoiled and gave them to other kings. In the third section, Sennacherib does not explain explicitly the military action against Hezekiah. He relates that the fear of his radiant splendour overwhelmed Hezekiah, and the consequence was that Hezekiah sent him heavy tribute and showed his servitude.

The text clearly does not show the chronological arrangement of these three parts. It is not clear if Sennacherib conquered the cities first and then imprisoned Hezekiah, or if he conquered the cities while Hezekiah was imprisoned; and the time when Hezekiah paid the tribute is not precisely narrated either. The three sections start with the three words referring to Hezekiah, *ša* (of, concerning), *šâšu* (him) and *šū* (he), which indicate the beginning of a new paragraph, but they do not specify which event happened first. The message of the text, nevertheless, is clear to some extent: Hezekiah rebelled[222] and that act called for military action from the Assyrian side, his kingdom was reduced, and he paid a heavy tribute. But is that what the text is really saying? Can this campaign be described as successful after all?

Apart from the problematic chronology, if some facts which are narrated in the texts are called into question, the text will show some embarrassment that makes the fact of accepting the text difficult. For example, why was Hezekiah imprisoned in his city? Was this part of the military strategy employed by Sennacherib, or was the latter obliged to do so because he could not enter Jerusalem? Is not entering Jerusalem part of the plan, or a sign of failure? Who won the battle at the end, Hezekiah or Sennacherib? If it was Hezekiah, why did he send such a heavy tribute to Nineveh? If Sennacherib won the battle, why did not he receive the tribute before he went to Nineveh?

It is obvious that one cannot avoid questioning the Assyrian text when it is read critically. The history of research in this matter extends for more than a century and a half since the discovery of the Assyrian inscriptions in the second half of the nineteenth century. Therefore, in order to start systematically, and avoid

---

222 For the reasons why Hezekiah rebelled, see Gallagher, *Sennacherib's Campaign*, 263–274.

repeating others' work, it is important to confine our study to Sennacherib's statement about Jerusalem and Hezekiah as it is narrated in the inscriptions.

Before we start our journey, it is important to mention that this is not the first time Sennacherib's statement is going to be considered. The issue has been discussed before, but the way the case of Jerusalem was dealt with was usually by treating it as an isolated case,[223] whereas the method of isolating a city was not employed only for Jerusalem. There are other examples where a city was isolated to cut it off from supplies of food and war materials. If these cases are taken into consideration, some illuminating insights might come to shed more light on the case this section is investigating.

3. Scholarly opinions about what happened to Jerusalem

Having read the text and focused on the main points that will be discussed in this section, we move to the next step of investigating what Sennacherib did to Jerusalem and Hezekiah. Apparently, Sennacherib used two tactics in his attack: besieging the cities and erecting a *ḫalṣu* against Jerusalem. This means that Jerusalem is not counted among the besieged cities; there was another strategy employed against it. Before dealing with Sennacherib's military strategy against Jerusalem, it is important to present the views of some scholars who have dealt with this matter. Some of the opinions are quite illuminating. In the next paragraphs, I present some opinions and then discuss them and make some observations.

The statement of Sennacherib about imprisoning Hezekiah "like a bird in a cage" has been taken literally by some Assyriologists, as they assert that Jerusalem was besieged. In this view the siege was not successful and Sennacherib was obliged to withdraw for a certain reason, which differs from one Assyriologist to another. While Luckenbill[224] suggests that the Assyrian army was exhausted because of its battle with the Phoenician and Philistine cities, which brought Sennacherib to a standstill, Frahm[225] suggests that there was a sudden epidemic which spread within the Assyrian army which caused Sennacherib to withdraw from Jerusalem. Laato[226], on the other hand, although he agrees with Luckenbill and Frahm that there was a siege, does not give a reason for the withdrawal.

---

223 Gallagher, *Sennacherib's Campaign*, 133–134; and Millard, "Hezekiah", compare Jerusalem with other cities; their conclusions will be discussed.
224 Luckenbill, *Annals*, 15.
225 Frahm, *Einleitung*, 47–61.
226 Laato, "Falsification", 198–226.

However, he draws attention to the points in which Sennacherib's siege cannot be considered successful.[227]

Mayer, looking at the event in the light of Assyrian military logic, comes to a similar conclusion about Sennacherib. This view from the opposing camp suggests a different interpretation of events. Starting with the assertion that the campaign was well planned, the author explains the tactics used by Sennacherib to achieve his aims: splitting the troops up into divisions; positioning them at points close to the enemies' territory; and using certain cities like Lachish as headquarters to leave the enemy powerless. In addition, Mayer suggests some solutions concerning certain questionable points. He considers the translation of the Akkadian word ḫalṣu as "siege walls" to be an anachronism; rather it indicates forts built around the territory of the city of Jerusalem. This outpost system involved Assyrian units being stationed in frontier areas. The destruction of Lachish was the warning which made Hezekiah surrender and Jerusalem return to its vassal status intact. [228] Very similarly, Dalley asserts that there was no Assyrian royal camp at Jerusalem. In her opinion, the meaning of the Akkadian word ḫalṣu does not imply an aggressive siege, but rather a "fort" by means of which "the Assyrians blockaded Jerusalem in a passive way without attempting to besiege it in an active way." [229] Thus there was no intention to capture the city. The attack was rather a kind of punishment intended to keep Judah's vassal status intact. As soon as Hezekiah admitted he was a sinner, Sennacherib withdrew from Judah and went back to Nineveh. In E.A. Knauf's opinion, the oddity in the text is caused by the geographical account rather than the chronological narrative that was deliberately spun by the Assyrian scribes to add glory to the achievements of Sennacherib. In Knauf's view, Sidon and Ashkelon were the first to be conquered, then the cities of Hezekiah were taken, and finally Hezekiah was obliged to surrender. After Sennacherib finished with Hezekiah, the Egyptian

---

227 He asserts that Sennacherib did not achieve his goal, but had to abandon the siege. He drew his conclusion after studying the particular literary and stylistic devices used in the inscriptions when military setbacks are being concealed: hiding the reason for the sudden withdrawal to Nineveh; mentioning Hezekiah's paying of the tribute to give the impression that his campaign to Judah had been successful, even though the main rebel had not been dethroned; not destroying Jerusalem; and exaggerating the number of deportees to bolster his campaign. These coded statements prompt Laato to conclude that the siege was not successful.
228 Mayer, W., "Sennacherib's Campapign of 701 BCE", in L.L. Grabbe (ed.), 'Like a Bird in a Cage': The Invasion of Sennacherib in 701 BCE (JSOTSup 363; London, 2003), 179–181.
229 Dalley, "Recent", 392.

army stepped in to outflank the Assyrian army. By this point the Assyrian army must have been diminished. The three parties, therefore, came to terms. [230]

4. Discussion and observations

The question whether there was or was not a siege set against Jerusalem is one of the main problems to be examined whenever the event of 701 is discussed. As has been shown above, there are two viewpoints concerning this issue: those who assert that there was a siege that was abandoned by Sennacherib, and others who assert that there was no siege. However, both of these positions need to be questioned. Each solution given to the problem raises another question that needs to be answered seriously. If the siege was not successful, why did Hezekiah pay such a heavy tribute? If there was no siege and the campaign was only to punish the rebels, why did Hezekiah remain on the throne? If he was forgiven, why did Sennacherib surround Jerusalem?

The other obvious point is the fact that there is confusion in dealing with this matter. Not annexing Judah to Assyria is not necessarily connected with Sennacherib's entrance into Jerusalem, and entering into Jerusalem would not have affected Sennacherib's relations with Egypt. He did not annex Edom or Moab, which were Judah's neighbours, and yet, he managed to have them come to him personally and present their tribute. The oddity in Sennacherib's behaviour lies in the fact that he neither entered Jerusalem nor had Hezekiah seize his feet as the other kings did. Rather he accepted Hezekiah's tribute in Nineveh, not in the royal city Jerusalem or any other Judean city. Hezekiah's surrender (as Mayer suggests), the family relationship (as Dalley suggests), and the agreement of the three parties—Sennacherib, Hezekiah and the Egyptians—(as Knauf suggests) all might be reasonable. However, they do not clarify why Sennacherib did not enter Jerusalem and receive the tribute there.

Apparently, these conclusions about the campaign were derived from studies that focused on one aspect of the campaign. There is a need to tackle the event from a much wider context in order to have a better picture of what Sennacherib meant in his statement about imprisoning Hezekiah in Jerusalem. The task of the present section, therefore, is to deal with Sennacherib's statement in a different way. In our discussion the above contributions will be dealt with in a more detailed way, each in turn.

---

230 Knauf, E.A., "Sennacherib at the Berezina", in L.L. Grabbe, (ed.), *'Like a Bird in a Cage': The Invasion of Sennacherib in 701 BCE* (JSOTSup 363; London, 2003), 141–149.

5. Terminological problem

To start appropriately, definitions of some of the terms being used in the inscriptions are necessary. As is noticeable, in the earlier research presented above different words such as "siege", "fortification", and "blockade" have all been used to translate the expression that the Assyrian scribe used: $^{uru}hal\text{-}su^{meš}$. Clarification, therefore, is in order to remove the obstacles to understanding the event in a better way. This term, apparently, occurs more than once in the Assyrian inscriptions with more than one meaning. According to *CAD*, originally, the word came from the verb *halāṣu*, which means "to press, to squeeze out or to clean by combing".[231] The word *halṣu* could be an adjective meaning "pressed out" or it could be a noun with the following two meanings:[232]

1. A "fort or fortress", as is mentioned in Sargon's annals when he states that he conquered 55 strong walled cities of the enemy's eight provinces, together with 11 inaccessible forts ($^{uru}hal\text{-}su^{meš}$).[233] Since the words "walled cities" and "inaccessible forts" are the objects of the verb "conquered", one can conclude that $^{uru}hal\text{-}su^{meš}$ in this context means a "fortress" like a city, town or settlement.

2. A "fortification", which is also attested in Sargon's annals: "I dammed up (the river) with earth and reeds and built two fortification walls ($^{uru}hal\text{-}su^{meš}$) side by side..."[234]

Another word which is relevant to our discussion is *birtu*. According to *CAD*, the term also has three different meanings: it could mean a "citadel or castle as part of the city." Or it could mean a "fort" as is attested in Sargon's annals: "I established 10 strong forts around it."[235] Or it could mean a "land protected by fortified outposts around a city".[236]

Moreover, it is important to differentiate the expression $^{uru}hal\text{-}su^{meš}$ from the verb *lamû*, which means "to besiege". As observed, the verb usually occurs with two other verbs: *kašādu* "to conquer", and *šalālu* "to plunder". The verb means to surround or to encircle a city. It does not necessarily mean building a structure

---

231 *CAD*, Ḫ, *halāṣu*, 40.
232 *CAD*, Ḫ, *halṣu*, 51–52.
233 Winckler, H., *Die Keilschrifttexte Sargons, nach den Papierabklatschen und Originalen*. Band II (Leipzig, 1888), no. 66:43.
234 Lie, *Sargon*, 48.
235 Lie, *Sargon*, 37:216.
236 *CAD*, B, *birtu*, 262–263.

around the city, but rather could be limited to setting a number of soldiers and chariots in certain outposts around the city.[237]

With these definitions, it is possible now to provide our discussion with some enlightening explanation. As noted, the terms discussed above could be similar in a way that makes it hard to distinguish between one and another. The context in which they are used, however, sheds light on some vital nuances. As for $^{uru}ḫalṣu^{meš}$, one can safely conclude from the context that it refers to physical construction (city, fort, fortification, dam) being established, erected or built. It is not a military unit that contained a number of soldiers only, but rather an erected structure. Similarly, the word is attested in Assurbanipal's annals as a structure constructed around the city of Tyre.[238]

Obviously, Sennacherib's statement concerns the second meaning of the word ḫalṣu. According to his annals, he erected a structure around Jerusalem and forbade anyone to leave the city gate. It is not clear what kind of structure this was and how big it was. Was it a huge structure like a wall, or was it only some scattered military camps arranged in a way that allowed military units consisting of the Assyrian soldiers to remain? In this sense the word ḫalṣu can be interchanged with birtu, which is apparently similar to the former in the sense that both could mean "fort". Nevertheless, from the context one can discern that the word birtu is a simpler structure and less sophisticated, as it could be limited to military outposts around a city. In this regard, the word ālu is significant in this discussion. It could mean "fort, military strong point."[239] The word seems to mean a physical construction erected for military reasons. In this matter, one might expect that the archaeological data would be of great help, but we will leave this issue for the next paragraph. The three words (ḫalṣu, birtu and ālu) should be distinguished from the verb lamû, which is, seemingly, associated with an active direct assault. As mentioned above, it occurs in the sequence "I besieged, I conquered and I took as spoils", as if the word is used to explain the first step of an intended attack. It is used in the annals of Sennacherib, not against Jerusalem though, but rather against the other (46) cities. So, one can safely exclude this word from the discussion and assert that Jerusalem was not directly besieged in the sense that there was no immediate attack. Having said that, it is convenient to declare that we position ourselves with Mayer fol-

---

237 *CAD*, L, *lamû*, 73.
238 Borger, R., *Beiträge zum Inschriftenwerk Assurbanipals* (Wiesbaden, 1996) BII44–66 (28; translation, 216, B.15).
239 *CAD*, A Part I, *ālu*, 387.

lowed by Gallagher[240], who understands the word ḫalṣu as a blockade and not an active direct siege.

Before moving from this discussion about terminology, one last term is worth considering. Although it does not indicate any physical structure, the verb esēru has been used in the context of a blockaded city more than once. The verb could mean "to shut in, to enclose, to confine."[241] And when it is used in a military context, it indicates a condition in which the enemy king is blockaded inside his city.[242] Considering it in our discussion is, therefore, significant.

It is crucial to mention that, regrettably, the archaeological data do not help much in our discussion. So far, there is no archaeological evidence for an erected ḫalṣu around a city. Fairly recently Ussishkin concluded, "there is no archaeological evidence indicating that a battle, siege, or conquest ever took place here. On the contrary, the archaeological data indicate a continuation of settlement until the Babylonian destruction in 586 B.C.E".[243] The absence of such evidence makes the question of what ḫalṣu is very problematic. Another important point to be mentioned is the fact that archaeology is silent not only about Jerusalem, but also about other occasions when a ḫalṣu was erected around a city. A ḫalṣu was erected twice in the famous city of Tyre, one by Esarhaddon and the second by his son Assurbanipal, [244] yet there is no archaeological evidence for those events. This lack of archaeological evidence for the ḫalṣu of Jerusalem and Tyre leads us to think that ḫalṣu seems to be a kind of structure which was set for a certain goal, which could be removed once the mission was over. This leads us to conclude that it is not surprising if there are no archaeological data to prove the ḫalṣu against Jerusalem; and secondly, one should not expect a huge structure like a wall or fortifications, but a military outpost with a certain structure set to guard the city and blockade it. Thirdly and importantly, one cannot pass over the matter quickly and assert that nothing happened or Sennacherib did not pay attention to Jerusalem as he did to the other cities; the blockade does not imply the absence of an intended attack. Having set up the ḫalṣu, this

---

240 Gallagher, *Sennacherib's Campaign*, 134–135.

241 *CAD*, E, *esēru*, 334.

242 Nadali, D., "Sieges and Similes of Sieges in the Royal Annals: The Conquest of Damascus by Tiglath-pileser III", *Kaskal: Rivista di storia, ambienti e culture del Vicino Oriente Antico* 6 (2009), 137.

243 Ussishkin, "Ekron", 352–353; see also Faust A., "Settlement and Demography in Seventh-Century Judah and the Extent and Intensity of Sennacherib's Campaign," *PEQ* 140, 3 (2008), 184.

244 Katzenstein, H.J., *The History of Tyre: From the Beginning of the Second Millennium E. until the Fall of the Neo-Babylonian Empire in 538 B.C.E.* (Jerusalem, 1973), 291.

means that Jerusalem was targeted; however, one cannot tell if the blockade was intended only to isolate Jerusalem and Hezekiah while conquering other cities, or Sennacherib intended to attack Jerusalem at a certain point. In my opinion, it is not impossible to know about this matter if we learn more about Assyrian blockade tactics.

At this stage of the study, having discussed the problem of terminology, and clarified why we accept the fact that Jerusalem was blockaded, we move to the next stage. This deals with the technique of a blockade, what it demanded as a military tactic, and its consequences. Was it after all a military strategy or a forced action that the Assyrian king had to use?

6. What was the tactic of a blockade?

The military tactic of blockading a city seems to have been used at least as far back as King Adad-nirari II (911–891). The way this blockade was carried out differed from one king to another. To define a blockade, therefore, is not straightforward. Eph'al gives a definition of the blockade saying:

> The imposition of a blockade on a city is intended to cut it off from supplies of food, water and war material (weapons, ammunition, fortification materials, medical supplies and the like), as well as to prevent the entrance of reinforcements and relief and the evacuation of the non-combatant population, whose presence in the city hampers its ability to withstand attack. The effect of a blockade is cumulative, so it must be continuous and generally extended in time...[245]

One can understand from this definition that the blockade could be a first stage of a long strategic process to conquer a city. But does it always have the same result? Is it always successful? In order to answer these questions, some examples of blockaded cities in Assyrian royal inscriptions will be presented below to have a clearer idea of what the blockade is and how it functions. The aim of this task is to read closely the representation of blockading cities, and accordingly, to be able to distinguish if there is any pattern in expressing the technique of the blockade. The different stages of a blockade will be considered in order to be able to determine whether a blockade was successful or not.

---

245 Eph'al, *The City Besieged*, 35.

This study deals with the cases when there is direct mention of one of the four words (*ḫalṣu, birtu, ālu,* and *esēru*), which indicate a blockade of a city. The presentation of the blockaded cities will be chronological. [246]

In his sixth campaign against the land of Hanigalbat, Adad-nirari II explains how he confined the enemy king in his city Naṣibina:[247]

> "I confined (*ēsiršu*) Nūr-Adad, the Temannu, in the city Naṣibina (and) established seven redoubts (*ālāni*) around it.[248]

The Assyrian king continues to explain what he did after confining the enemy king. After laying his army around the moat dug by the enemy, he entered the city. And then he continues to describe what he did within the city; he carried off a great booty from the city; he brought back into his presence Nūr-Adad, the enemy king, together with his extensive troops as hostages; he granted cities with people to Assyria and counted them; then he brought him into Nineveh. [249]

A very similar tactic was used by Shalmaneser III (858–824), who imprisoned Hazael, king of Damascus, in his city in 841. The text says:

> "To save his life, he ran away but I pursued him. I imprisoned (*ēsiršu*) him in Damascus, his royal city, and cut down his gardens."[250]

The only fact mentioned against the enemy king is that he was imprisoned in his city. Nothing is mentioned about what happened afterwards: no booty or tribute is taken from Hazael. But the Assyrian king said that he marched to other cities and destroyed them. The way the enemy king was imprisoned is not mentioned either; nothing was erected or placed around the city.

Adad-nirari III (810–783) also later confined the king of Damascus, Mari, in Damascus in 796.[251] But the action seems to be different this time:

> I marched to Damascus. Mari, king of Damascus, I confined (*ēsiršu*) in Damascus, his royal city. The awesome brilliance of Aššur, my lord, overwhelmed him, he submitted to me, and

---

246 English translations of the Akkadian texts are taken from the sources from which the citation is taken.
247 Naṣibina is a city in the Urartian territories.
248 Grayson, A.K., *Assyrian Rulers of the Early First Millennium BC I (1114–859)* (Toronto, 1996), 151: 63.
249 Grayson, *Rulers I*, 151:63, 66, 68, 79, 81.
250 Grayson, A.K., *Assyrian Rulers of the Early First Millennium BC II (858–745)* (Toronto, 1996), 60: 25–26.
251 Athas, G., *The Tel Dan Inscription: A Reappraisal and a New Introduction* (JSOTSup 12; London, 2003), 264.

became my vassal. I received 2,300 talents of silver, 20 talents of gold, 3,000 talents of bronze, 5,000 talents of iron, linen...within his palace in Damascus, his royal city."[252]

Unlike Hazael, Mari submitted to the Assyrian king. The latter entered the city and received heavy payment; it is not clear from the text whether the payment was a gift, booty or tribute. Again, the way the enemy king was confined within the city is not expressed, nor is the way the Assyrian king entered the city. The only facts related are that the enemy king was overwhelmed by the brilliance of Aššur and the Assyrian king received the payment inside the royal city of the enemy king.

The blockade tactic continued to be used by Tiglath-pileser III (744–727), who also confined the king of Damascus, Rezin, in his city in 733:

> That king of Damascus, in order to save his life, fled alone, and entered the gate of his city [like] a mongoose. His chief ministers I impaled alive and had his country behold them. For 45 days my camp I set up around his city, and I cooped (*ēsiršu*) him up like a bird in a cage. His gardens...orchards without number I cut down; I did not leave a single one.[253]

Just as in the case of Hazael, the Assyrian king does not mention any attack being directed against the city of Damascus. There was a camp around the city, but apparently, the attacker could not enter the city. Accordingly, no booty or tribute was received from the enemy king.

There are two other occasions when Tiglath-pileser III enclosed an enemy king. The first one was against the Urartian Sarduri II in 735:

> "Sarduri, the Urartian, revolted against me, and with Mati'il he schemed (against me)... I enclosed (*ēsiršu*) him in Turushpa, his city, and inflicted a great defeat upon him before his city gate."[254]

And the second one was against Mukin-zeri of Bit-Amukkani in Sapiya in 731:

> "I enclosed (*ēsiršu*) Mukīn-zēri of Bit-Amukkani in Sapiya, his royal city. I inflicted a heavy defeat upon him before his gate."[255]

---

252 Grayson, *Rulers* II, 213 15–21.
253 Tadmor, H., *The Inscriptions of Tiglath-pileser III King of Assyria. Critical Edition, with Introductions, Translations and Commentary* (IASH; Jerusalem, 1994), 78–79.
254 Tadmor, *Tiglath-pileser*, 124: 23.
255 Tadmor, *Tiglath-pileser*, 163:23–25.

In both cases, the city remained intact, and the Assyrian king did not enter it. Again, the text is very unclear why he did not enter the city. There was a battle. However, the king remained on the throne and he was not punished. He did not pay tribute, and booty was not taken either.

Sargon II (722–705) used another kind of blockade in his campaign against Babylonia in 710:

> "the Tubliash River, the river of their confidence, with heaps of earth and reeds I dammed, and two fortresses (birāti), one opposite the other, I constructed, and distress I caused to come over them. ...and they came and seized my feet."[256]

Apparently, the tactic was effective. The enemy came to Sargon and showed their submission. Also, hostages were taken and then tribute was imposed on them.

Esarhaddon (681–669) used the same policy with Tyre when he targeted it in 671:

> "In the course of my campaign, I set up fortifications (ḫalṣu) against Ba'alu, the king of Tyre, who trusted in his friend Taaharga, the king of Kush...I cut off the supply of food and water that sustained their lives."[257]

Despite the fact that Esarhaddon is boasting in his inscription, the campaign does not seem to have been successful. The supply of food and water was cut off, yet he did not enter the city, nor did Ba'al pay tribute. We do not know what made Esarhaddon withdraw from Tyre; the text does not mention any reason for this.

The same king, however, changed his policy with Assurbanipal (668–627) when the latter set a blockade on Tyre in his third campaign:

> I threw up earthworks (ḫalṣu) against him, by sea and land I seized his approaches. I pressed them (sorely and) made their lives miserable. I made them submit to my yoke. A daughter, the offspring of his loins and the daughters of his brothers he brought into my presence, to serve as my concubines. Iahi-miliki, his son, who had never crossed the sea, he had (them) bring (to me), for the first time, to render me service. His daughter and his brothers'

---

256 Lie, *Sargon*, 48. See also, Fuchs, A., *Die Inschriften Sargon II aus Khorsabad* (Göttingen, 1994), 146.
257 Leichty, E., *The Royal Inscriptions of Esarhaddon, King of Assyria* (680–669) (RINAP 4; Winona Lake, 2011), 87:12–14.

daughters I received from him, with large dowries. I had mercy upon him and gave him back his son, the offspring of his loins. [258]

This is actually the last time the strategy of blockade is mentioned in the Assyrian inscriptions; and also, one can safely say, it is a very particular one. The city was blockaded and roads were blocked. The enemy king submitted and came out of his city to show loyalty to the Assyrian king. Then the latter forgave his enemy and received a heavy tribute from him. This is the only case where tribute (*mandatu*) was paid after blockading a city. The Assyrian king did not enter the city of Tyre; rather he received the tribute apparently not in Tyre or in Nineveh but from afar, because the text says that he went back to Nineveh safe and sound. So before entering Tyre, Ba'al submitted and came to the Assyrian king with his heavy tribute.

Having presented these nine cases, discussion about how the blockade functions is in order.

7. Discussion and conclusions about the blockade tactic

As is obvious, the results of blockades were not always the same. At the same time it is not straightforward to decide whether or not a blockade was successful. But, by examining the nine cases presented above, we realise that there were certain motives and actions that the scribe focused on. The notable items of interest most mentioned are the fate of the enemy king, the attitude of the Assyrian king (if he entered the city or not), and the tribute (if it was paid or not). These topoi, which can be recognised in the written documents, will help us understand the blockades in general and the blockade of Jerusalem in particular. Therefore, in the next stage of our study, the circumstances of each case will be discussed.

The first observation is that in four out of nine cases the result of the blockade is related: the Assyrian king entered the enemy city after the blockade and received booty or tribute, or the enemy king came out of his city to show submission. However, in five cases the fate of the city or its king is not mentioned in the inscriptions. These cities seem to have resisted the blockade strategy. Damascus resisted the blockade of Shalmaneser III in 841 and Tiglath-pileser III in 733; the two cities Turushpa and Sapiya also resisted the blockade of Tiglath-pileser III;

---

258 Luckenbill, D.D., *Ancient Records of Assyria and Babylonia.* Vol. 2: *Historical Records of Assyria from Sargon to the End* (Chicago, 1927), 296; for the Akkadian text, see Borger, *Assurbanipals*, BII 44–66.

and Tyre resisted the blockade of Esarhaddon. Yet, we cannot decide if that means that the blockade was not necessarily an effective process. Consideration of some issues relating to the cities that survived the blockade might be helpful. Before doing so, it is important to mention that, regrettably, archaeology does not supply us with much information about these cities during the Iron Age: their walls, their fortresses, and the area they comprised. So, our investigation will depend on the written sources which narrate the events related to these cities.

As for Damascus, as mentioned above, it survived two blockades, in 841 and in 733. This means that the city was noticeably capable of defending itself. Studies demonstrate that by the mid-ninth century, Damascus was so powerful that it became the leading state of a coalition against the military expansion of Assyria.[259] This can be confirmed by the fact that Shalmaneser III, in 841, had to fight Aram-Damascus alone.[260] As for the circumstances of Shalmaneser's blockade, we learn from the inscriptions that Hazael was defeated in the battlefield where he mustered his army to encounter Shalmaneser III. Therefore, the former fled to his city Damascus, and Shalmaneser III enclosed him there. Meanwhile, Shalmaneser III continued his military activity to destroy a countless number of towns and plunder them. The question that arises at once is: why did Shalmaneser III not enter Damascus and punish Hazael? This leads us to another question: what was the aim of the blockade? Did Shalmaneser III intend to blockade Damascus just to enclose Hazael in his city and cut him off from the other cities which he was conquering? Or did he blockade Damascus to attack it using military forces? The only source that can help us answer this question is the text. The inscriptions do not indicate any prolonged siege or military action around the city. One can assume that the blockade was not meant to be a first step of an attack, but it was set to separate Hazael from his cities. The fact that he fought Hazael, defeated him, and then pursued him means that Shalmaneser III wanted indeed to get rid of Hazael. Imprisoning him inside Damascus means that something prevented him from entering the city. One can safely state that Shalmaneser III did not defeat Hazael because the latter remained intact and his city was not conquered. Accordingly, this kind of blockade was not a choice, but rather an enforced solution the Assyrian king had to make because something prevented him from entering into the city.[261]

---

259 Pitard, W.T., *Ancient Damascus. A Historical Study of the Syrian City-State from Earliest Times until its Fall to the Assyrians in 732 BCE.* (Winona Lake, 1987), 99.
260 Pitard, *Damascus*, 146–147.
261 Nadali, "Similes", 145.

On Tiglath-pileser III's campaign against Damascus in 733, the text relates the events in a way similar to that of the blockade of Shalmaneser III. But the different note we have in this case is that Tiglath-pileser III set up his camp for 45 days around Damascus. However, there is no description of a direct assault or indication that Tiglath-pileser III had his army fight the Damascenes. Before drawing any conclusion about this event, it would be very helpful to look at it in its wider context. In this regard, Dubovsky's reconstruction of Tiglath-pileser III's campaigns in 734–732 is of great help. In his 2006 article, he reconstructs the course of the campaigns and investigates their logistics.[262] As this part of Dubovsky's article is highly relevant to our discussion, a summary of this reconstruction will be useful. The campaign against Damascus and its blockade is an event that took place while Tiglath-pileser III was in the Levant during the period 734–732. Dubovsky divides the military activities into three phases: first, against the coastal cities; secondly, against Damascus and Transjordan; and thirdly, against Israel and Damascus.[263] So, after attacking the coastal cities, Tiglath-pileser III turned to Damascus. He fought the Damascenes and won the battle in the field, but Rezin escaped into Damascus, and Tiglath-pileser III enclosed him there. Meanwhile, he destroyed the orchards and isolated Rezin. Then Tiglath-pileser III continued his military actions and attacked the Arabian queen, Samsi, and received tribute from the kingdoms of Transjordan. Next, he moved to Israel and conquered cities there, and eventually, he turned again to Damascus in 732, by now weakened because of the previous attack and being separated from food supply. Damascus fell and that was the end of Tiglath-pileser III's campaigns against the Levant.[264]

In the light of this reconstruction, we can look at the blockade of Damascus in 733. It is obvious that the camp that the Assyrian king set up around Damascus for 45 days did not enable him to conquer the city. Therefore, he chose to follow another strategy, leaving Damascus for a while and coming back to it in due course. Obviously, he left some troops around Damascus to guard the city; a year later, he came back. The question that arises from this explanation of the event is: why would he wait a year to conquer Damascus? Why would he starve the city? The probable answer is that Tiglath-pileser III chose not to assault the city directly to save a large amount of military effort and resources. In other words, Tiglath-pileser III could not enter the city easily to get the rebel immediately, because something prevented him from doing so, possibly the walls

---

262 Dubovsky, P., "Tiglath-pileser III's Campaigns in 734–732: Historical Background of Is 7; 2 Kgs 15–16 and 2 Chr 27–28", *Bib* 87 (2006), 153–170.
263 Dubovsky, "Tiglath-pileser", 158–161.
264 Dubovsky, "Tiglath-pileser", 162–164.

of the city. The city had to be weakened from within so that it might be conquered. Accordingly, we can conclude that the blockade of 733 was not successful because the king remained safe in his city and the city was not captured. Moreover, not entering the city and choosing the strategy of starving people inside the city indicates that the city was well fortified and the walls prevented both kings, Shalmaneser III and Tiglath-pileser III from entering the city.

The campaign against Turupsha was launched in the 11th *palû* of Tiglath-pileser III, in 735. Despite the fact that this was the second campaign of Tiglath-pileser III against Urartu, it was the first time the Assyrian army reached the Urartian capital.[265] The course of the event as it is related in the summary inscription is as follows: the Urartian king, Sarduri II, was defeated in a battle, and then he fled to his capital city Turupsha. Next, Tiglath-pileser III enclosed the enemy king in his city. Afterwards, he continued his military activities to conquer and annex some Urartian cities. The text, however, does not describe the military action against the city Turupsha. The Akkadian verb used in the inscriptions is *ēsiršu*, but this does not explain if there was a direct assault, or if it was only a blockade to isolate Sarduri II. Whatever the explanation is, the fact that neither the fate of the enemy king nor entry into the city is mentioned means that the Assyrian king could not get the enemy or conquer the city. Like the other two cases mentioned above, there was something that prevented Tiglath-pileser III from entering the city.[266]

As for the city of Sapiya, Tiglath-pileser III attacked it in his 15th *palû*, in 731. In the summary inscription, the text relates that Mukin-zeri was enclosed in his royal city, Sapiya, and the Assyrian king inflicted a heavy defeat on him at the gate of the city. Then he continued with his military activities to conquer other cities, after destroying the orchards of Sapiya. To understand the course of the event, F.M. Fales is of great help, as he reconstructs the events of 731–729 using the available sources and especially the Nimrud letters.[267] He reconstructs the events as follows. As a result of a revolt by the Chaldean king Mukin-zeri,

---

265 Tadmor, *Tiglath-pileser*, 125.

266 Zimansky argues that Sarduri was defeated. But Zimansky depends on the statement of Tiglath-pileser in his inscriptions. Zimansky, P.E, *Ecology and Empire. The Structure of the Urartian State* (SAOC 41; Chicago, 1985), 59.

267 Fales, F.M., "Moving around Babylon: On the Aramean and Chaldean Presence in Southern Mesopotamia", in E. Cancik-Kirschbaum et al (eds.), *Babylon: Wissenskultur in Orient und Okzident* (TBSAW 1; Berlin, 2011)", 91–111. See also, Fales, F.M., "Tiglat-pileser III tra annalistica reale ed epistolgrafia quotidiana", in F.P. Daddi and M.C. Guidotto (eds.), *Narrare gli Eventi. Atti del Convengo degli Egittologi e degli Orientalisti Italiani in Margine alla Mostra "La Battaglia di Qadesh"* (SA 3; Roma, 2005), 163–191.

Tiglath-pileser III launched a war against Babylonia and set up a siege against Sapiya in 731. Other Chaldean chiefs paid homage. The siege was lifted for an unknown reason. There were three years of hostilities. Tiglath-pileser III set up another siege by which he conquered Sapiya and defeated the rebel. Among the actions that the official inscriptions of Tiglath-pileser III do not mention is the negotiation between Tiglath-pileser III and the enemy king.[268] If the reconstruction of Fales is accepted, then again, we realise that Tiglath-pileser III had difficulties entering the enemy city, because of which he returned without conquering the city or punishing the rebel. However, he came back to the city and achieved his aim after having made some effort to weaken it. Again, we can conclude that Tiglath-pileser III's attack (and blockade) in 731 was not successful.

The last case to discuss is that of the blockade of Tyre by Esarhaddon in his tenth campaign. Initially, it is important to say, the campaign was not mainly directed at Tyre, but rather against Egypt. Esarhaddon decided to attack Tyre because Ba'al had violated the treaty with Esarhaddon and allied himself with Tirhakah, king of Egypt.[269] Esarhaddon, therefore, first directed his attention to Tyre before he went to Egypt. The military strategy that Esarhaddon applied was setting up a siege (ḫalṣu) around Tyre to cut off its food supply. As in the three cases discussed above, the text does not mention any direct attack against the city of Tyre. The fate of the city and the enemy king is not mentioned either. Therefore, it is unlikely that the city submitted; otherwise there is no explanation why Esarhaddon did not use it as an opportunity for boasting about.[270] It is most likely that Esarhaddon left troops around Tyre to cut off its food supply, but he left because the Egyptian war required his presence.[271]

From the five cases discussed above, one can draw some conclusions about the blockade strategy and decide whether it is successful or not.

The first thing to notice is that the Assyrian army had a greater opportunity to win a battle in a field than to assault a walled city. After being defeated in the battlefield, Hazael, Rezin and Sarduri II escaped to their cities, where the Assyr-

268 Fales, "Moving", 100–110.
269 Boardman, J., *The Cambridge Ancient History, III part 2, The Assyrian and Babylonian Empires and other States of the Near East, from the Eighth to Sixth Century* (Cambridge, 1991), 126.
270 Radner mentions in her article where she discusses the route of Esarhaddon's tenth campaign that although the text does not mention it explicitly, the blockade against Tyre was successful. Radner, K., "Esarhaddon's Expedition from Palestine to Egypt in 671E: A Trek to Negev and Sinai", in D. Bonatz, *et al.* (eds.), *Fundstellen Gesammelte Schriften zur Archäologie und Geschichte Altvorderasiens ad Honorem Hartmut Kühne* (Wiebaden, 2008), 307.
271 Rawlinson, G., *Phoenicia* (London, 1889), 142.

ian kings could not get them. Therefore, one can assume that there was a great possibility of failure, despite the fact that the Assyrian inscriptions do not explain it in this way. In his 2008 article, A. Fuchs directed attention to the difficulty and risk which a blockade could involve. The blockade of a big city, he asserts, could endure for a long time and might bring misery and misfortune to the attacker, especially if the blockaded city had impressive defensive walls. In addition, blockading a city needed the presence of the king himself, and a huge amount of supplements to the camp. An unsuccessful blockade could result in enormous loss and humiliation for the Assyrians.[272] Consequently blockading a city did not always end up with a satisfactory result.

Secondly, in the four cases when the blockade was successful, certain events took place as a continuation of the blockade:

a. *As for the fate of the enemy king:*
    i.   Adad-nirari II brought Nur-Adad together with his extensive troops as hostages to Nineveh.[273]
    ii. Mari, king of Damascus, submitted to Adad-nirari III and paid a heavy payment (tribute)[274] to the Assyrian king within the former's palace.
    iii. The chiefs of the cities destroyed by the dam came and seized the feet of Sargon.[275]
    iv. Ba'al, king of Tyre, came out of his city and submitted to Assurbanipal. The latter forgave him and received tribute.

In all four cases, the enemy kings were not replaced; they remained on the throne after making submission to the Assyrian king. Despite the fact that Nur-Adad was brought to Nineveh as a captive, there is no evidence that he remained there and did not go back to his throne. From this one can conclude that showing surrender was an important result of a successful blockade. The enemy king was not necessarily removed from his throne; he could stay as long as he showed obedience to the Assyrian king. But it is noteworthy that the Assyrian king did not go back to his city before solving the problem with the enemy king.

b. *As for the city and paying tribute:*
    i. Adad-nirari II entered the city of Nur-Adad and plundered it.
    ii. Adad-nirari III entered Damascus and received tribute from Mari in his palace.

---

272 Fuchs, A., "Über den Wert von Befestigungsanlagen", *ZA* 98 (2008), 61.
273 Grayson, *Rulers, I* 151: 75 – 79.
274 Kuan, J.K., *Neo-Assyrian Historical Inscriptions and Syria-Palestine* (Hong Kong, 1995), 87.
275 Lie, *Sargon*, 48 – 49.

iii. Sargon attacked a number of cities and he dammed a river nearby to destroy them. In this case, the Assyrian king was not expected to enter the cities.

iv. Assurbanipal did not enter Tyre, but he received a heavy tribute from Ba'al outside Tyre, from afar.

From this one can conclude that receiving tribute was a crucial element for the Assyrian king, as a sign of submission; entering the city and plundering it happened when the enemy king did not show submission.

Thirdly, when the blockade was not successful in the five cases mentioned above, neither of the two aspects which are noticed in the successful blockades are narrated in the inscriptions. No king in the five cases came out of his city to show submission or pay tribute; the Assyrian king did not enter the city or plunder it; and the city remained intact in the five cases. One aspect that is found here is the emphasis on cutting off the gardens and damaging the environment of the city blockaded.

Fourthly, there was the possibility that the Assyrian king could forgive an enemy king, as was the case with Assurbanipal and Ba'al, the king of Tyre.[276] But the text is clear about this "forgiveness". While Tyre was blockaded, Ba'al came out of his city with his tribute to meet Assurbanipal and to show submission to him; only then was Ba'al forgiven. King Assurbanipal's forgiveness was not for nothing; it was because Ba'al surrendered before Assurbanipal went to Nineveh.

Having discussed the blockade strategy, and decided which blockades were successful and which were not, we may now turn to the blockade of Jerusalem.

8. Where are we to place the Jerusalem blockade?

Are we to place Jerusalem among the cities in which the blockade was successful or among those in which it was unsuccessful? Actually Jerusalem shares aspects of both. On the one hand, Sennacherib did not enter the city; he did not plunder Jerusalem; Hezekiah did not leave his city to show submission and seize the feet of Sennacherib; and the latter went back to Nineveh without solving his problem with the enemy king. So far, these aspects show signs of an unsuccessful blockade. On the other hand, Hezekiah eventually paid a heavy tribute, showing the kind of behaviour that the kings in successful blockades showed, which might

---

276 See Millard, "Hezekiah", 69–71; see also Gallagher, *Sennacherib's Campaign*, 134.

lead us to conclude that Jerusalem was captured after the blockade, as some Assyriologists think.[277] Nevertheless, he did not pay the tribute in one of the cities of Judah, but sent it to Nineveh.[278] which raises a question about the success of the blockade.

If we go back to the text, we realise that Sennacherib is explicit in describing his tactic in Judah: mainly besieging the cities and blockading the capital.[279] If Jerusalem was blockaded, it means that a direct immediate attack was not intended. Sennacherib planned to separate Hezekiah and Jerusalem and leave them in isolation for the right moment to attack. Jerusalem was a huge city in Hezekiah's time (as it expanded during his reign probably to absorb refugees from the north). Attacking such a big city, therefore, would have cost Sennacherib an enormous amount of war supplements. Fuchs aptly directs attention to the fact that a direct attack was a big risk that one would employ for small cities or poorly defended settlements. In the case of big cities, hunger was preferable.[280] A long-term blockade then was apparently intended, and Sennacherib blockaded Jerusalem to isolate the main centre of the region from the other cities. Imprisoning Hezekiah was a strategy rather than a compulsory solution that Sennacherib had to choose in the end. One can safely conclude that the conquest of 46 cities took place simultaneously with the blockading of Jerusalem.

As for Hezekiah, it is not clear if he remained in Jerusalem because Sennacherib imprisoned him or he chose to stay in his city. The Assyrian scribe relates the fact as if Hezekiah had no other choice but to stay in his city. This, however, might be questioned if Hezekiah's action is compared to actions of other kings in the inscriptions. Before him, Hazael and Razin survived the blockades imposed by Shalmaneser III and Tiglath-pileser III while they were in Damascus. So it seems that a well-fortified city was a better choice for kings to stay in. Maybe this is why Hezekiah preferred to stay in Jerusalem and take refuge inside the city, rather than run away from the city to another place.

This leads us to conclude that what is related in the annals about Hezekiah being confined in Jerusalem is part of a negative picture that the Assyrian scribe

---

277 Nadali, D., "Assyrian Open Field Battles. An Attempt at Reconstruction and Analysis", in J. Vidal (ed.), *Studies on War in the Ancient Near East. Collected Essays on Military History* (Münster, 2010), 130.

278 It is important here to notice that Hezekiah paid tribute and not booty as Gallagher and Millard would translate the Akkadian word *mandatu*. Booty is what is taken by the attacker after conquering a city, while tribute is what is given by the one who lost the war, mainly to show submission to the king who won the war.

279 See also Nadali "Similes", 143.

280 Fuchs, "Wert" 59.

used to characterise the enemy's weak condition.[281] So far things seem to be understandable. The oddity, however, lies in the third part of the narrative relating the attack on Judah. Sennacherib relates that Hezekiah was overwhelmed with the splendour of his lordship; nothing about a battle or fight is mentioned. He continues to say that Hezekiah sent after him a tribute to Nineveh. This is what makes the case of Jerusalem unique. Nothing tells us that the war ended in a compromise. When Sennacherib relates that the tribute was sent after him to Nineveh, it means that the war did not end with Sennacherib going to Nineveh. That is, although the Assyrian king went back to Jerusalem, Hezekiah felt threatened. What does that mean? Some think that the success was partial or incomplete.[282] Then we have to ask, what does it mean to have a partial success? Did the two kings agree that if Hezekiah paid the tribute, then Sennacherib would not enter the city? Why did Sennacherib accept then that the tribute should be paid in Nineveh? That was not a sign of showing submission as it was known in the Assyrian custom. Also, paying the tribute after the danger was over does not make any sense.

In the light of the notes assembled about the blockade of Jerusalem, a possible solution can be presented in this stage of the study. If Sennacherib chose to enclose Hezekiah in his city, it means he could not enter Jerusalem easily. Hezekiah's Jerusalem was an important city both economically and politically; it would thus be no surprise if a city were fortified and prepared for a predicted attack. It is therefore possible that Sennacherib could not enter the city because Jerusalem was well fortified. The archaeological evidence can support this assumption. Therefore, it is useful to pause briefly on this point.

By and large Jerusalem is the most excavated city in Palestine and Israel,[283] as much effort has been made to reconcile the biblical Jerusalem with the archaeological Jerusalem. Some of the results of these excavations shed light on the events of 701. Therefore, consulting the results concerned with the fortification of Jerusalem and its significance as a fortress city could answer the question of why Sennacherib did not enter the city and also why Hezekiah chose to stay in it.

During the last three decades, efforts have been made to study Jerusalem in its archaeological context. However, a comprehensive work that focuses on the

---

281 Ponchia, S., "Analogie, metafore e similitudini nelle iscrizioni reali assire: semantica e ideolgia", *OA* 26. 3 – 4 (1987), 26, 226.

282 Gallagher, *Sennacherib's Campaign*, 141.

283 Killebrew, A.E. and Vaughn, A.G., "Jerusalem in Bible and Archaeology: Dialogues and Discussions", in Vaughn, A.G. and Killebrew, A.E. (eds.), *Jerusalem in Bible and Archaeology. The First Temple Period* (SBL 18; Atlanta, 2003), 3.

historicity of the biblical accounts of Jerusalem from the tenth century through to sixth century is that by A.G. Vaughn and A.E. Killebrew.[284] From the articles contained in this book, I cite two quotations that are significantly related to our topic; one is about the importance of Jerusalem and the other about the fortification of Jerusalem at the end of eighth century. Concerning Jerusalem, Killebrew maintains that:

"Archaeological discoveries of the last decades have transformed our understanding of Jerusalem and clearly supported maximalist views regarding its size and significance during the eighth-early sixth centuries B.C.E. The undeniable physical remains provide proof that Jerusalem served as a large administrative, political, and residential center with a well-developed environs. Further, it may well have been the most important and impressive center in Judah."[285]

On the other hand, concerning the fortification of Jerusalem, H. Geva maintains that:

"The three sections of fortifications found in the Jewish Quarter belong to the north wall of Jerusalem in First Temple times. They were in two separate but successive stages. First the Broad Wall was built by Hezekiah king of Judah at the end of the eighth century BCE. as part of fortifying Jerusalem against the coming Assyrian invasion. The biblical account relates the story of the fortification of the city together with the king's construction of a water-supply system (2 Chr 32:1–8). "Hezekiah's Tunnel" led the water of the Gihon Spring in the Kidron Valley to the east and outside of the City of David to the Siloam Pool at the southern, lower end of the Central Valley, to the west and outside of the City of David. The wall that encircled the south-western hill descended eastward on the southern slope of Mount Zion above the Hinnom Valley and joined the wall of the city of David at its south end, south of the Siloam Pool. The pool was thus enclosed by the city wall, proving its inhabitants with water even in times of siege. Hezekiah's two important construction projects—the building of a wall around the southwestern hill and the digging of the tunnel—are closely connected. Together they created a complex and effective defensive array whose efficacy was proved when the Assyrian army besieged Jerusalem in 701 B.C.E. and failed to capture the city (2 Chr 32:21–24)."[286]

284 Vaughn, A.G. and Killebrew, A.E. (eds.)., *Jerusalem in Bible and Archaeology. The First Temple Period* (SBL 18; Atlanta, 2003).
285 Killebrew, A.E., "Biblical Jerusalem: An Archaeological Assessment", in A.G. Vaughn and A.E. Killebrew (eds.), *Jerusalem in Bible and Archaeology. The First Temple Period* (SBL 18; Atlanta, 2003), 337–338
286 Geva, H., "Western Jerusalem at the End of the First Temple Period in Light of the Excavations in the Jewish Quarter", in A.G. Vaughn and A.E. Killbrew (eds.), *Jerusalem in Bible and Arcaheology. The First Temple Period* (SBL 18; Atlanta, 2003), 198.

These two statements (about the size and importance of Jerusalem and its forti-fication) certainly came to be supported by other archaeologists. In general, the fact that Jerusalem in Hezekiah's time was prosperous is convincingly asserted by a large number of scholars. They might differ about the time when Jerusalem became significant,[287] but that does not affect the fact that Jerusalem at the time of the attack (701) was certainly a large city.

Therefore, one can conclude that archaeology can answer the question why Sennacherib did not enter Jerusalem.[288] The city was well fortified and that is why Sennacherib chose to blockade the city and use the policy of starving the people inside till Hezekiah gave up. The other point worth mentioning here is the fact that Hezekiah's preparation for war is not indicated only in archaeology, but the biblical text also relates that Hezekiah made some constructions before 701. Although some scholars consider the account of 2 Chr 32 about Hezekiah's building projects to be unhistorical and thus dismiss it,[289] the archaeological evi-dence discussed above could suggest a need to reconsider the account in 2 Chr 32.[290]

But if we accept that the wall saved Jerusalem, why then did Hezekiah pay the tribute? Before we answer this question, we have to remember that the tribute was paid in Nineveh. This means that although Sennacherib went back to Nine-veh, the risk was still there, which made Hezekiah send his tribute. If we consid-er some of the cases in which the blockade was not successful, we realise that the Assyrian king left some troops around the blockaded city and sometimes came back to it as in the cases of Damascus in 733 and Sapiya in 731. One can assume that Hezekiah feared a prolonged blockade that would have isolated him for a long time. In other words, Hezekiah paid tribute because he was afraid of a future attack; that is why he sent him tribute, given the fact that he was left alone in the region as the other kingdoms had showed their submission in ad-vance.

In this case we have to make it clear that Sennacherib did not go to Nineveh because of the heavy tribute he received, as that happened later after he returned

---

287 Na'aman, N., "When and How Did Jerusalem Become a Great City? The Rise of Jerusalem as Judah's Premier City in the Eighth-Seventh Centuries B.C.E", in *BASOR* 247 (2007), 21–56.
288 Mazar, "Monarchy", 173.
289 Gonçalves, *L'expedition*, 488–527; Gallagher, *Sennacherib's Campaign*, 16.
290 2 Chr 32 has details that 2 Kgs and Isa 36–37 do not have. Some scholars assume that these details were from the Chronicler's imagination. A.G. Auld, however, has a different opin-ion. He assumes that the Chronicler had a source other than the book of Kings, and the details that are only in the book of Chronicles, some of them, could be attributed to that source. Auld, A.G., *Kings without Privilege. David and Moses in the Story of the Bible's Kings* (Edinburgh, 1994).

to Nineveh. But the two events, going to Nineveh and paying tribute, were combined in the Assyrian annals to cover the failure.

9. Conclusion to chapter four

Studying the blockade strategy enabled us to understand the military strategy that Sennacherib applied in his attack against Jerusalem and Hezekiah. Having read and discussed the terminology that Sennacherib used to describe his technique in Judah, and having presented similar cases of blockaded cities mentioned in the Assyrian royal inscriptions, we realised that there was a certain pattern in describing a successful blockade. The features of a successful blockade do not apply to the blockade of Jerusalem. The technique was to isolate a city from the rest of the region and prevent the food supply from reaching the city, thus weakening the city from inside and expediting its submission. Sennacherib used the same technique with Jerusalem; however, he left the blockade at a certain point and went to Nineveh. Hezekiah took that as an opportunity to send his tribute and show his submissive behaviour to Sennacherib, because he felt threatened even after Sennacherib had left for Nineveh. Studying other cases, one can assume that Sennacherib probably left troops around Jerusalem to weaken the city. Bearing in mind what happened to Damascus a decade earlier, Hezekiah hastened to send his tribute.

This leads us to conclude that Sennacherib did not return to Nineveh because of the large tribute he obtained from Hezekiah. The assumption that Sennacherib defeated Hezekiah by receiving that tribute is not appealing anymore. But the question that arises from this conclusion is: why did Sennacherib return to Nineveh before he finished his business with Hezekiah? We shall deal with this question later.

Conclusion to part one

The study in this part sets out to explore Sennacherib's conduct in his third campaign against Judah and Jerusalem in 701, and whether his campaign was successful, as the annals claim, or not. The investigation led us to conclude that Sennacherib's strategy with Jerusalem was not completely successful, contrary to what some scholars have argued.

The methodology that has been adopted in this part is new. Unlike previous research, this study investigated what happened in the third campaign by placing the third campaign in its wider context. In other words, the third campaign has been investigated in the context of all of Sennacherib's campaigns, and also in the context of other cases when cities were attacked and suffered an assault very similar to what happened to Jerusalem. Doing so enabled us to know what is significant in the third campaign and accordingly to decide whether or not the campaign was successful.

Structurally, the investigation was divided into three main chapters. In the first chapter, a literary reading of Sennacherib's campaign enabled us to establish the main motives that were focused on in the inscriptions. The military strategy and the economic exaction comprised a large part of the investigation because, expectedly, they were the topoi stressed in the representations of all the campaigns. The discussion led us to conclude that Sennacherib did not use aggressive language in explaining the military actions in representing the third campaign; also, examining the economic exploitation led us to conclude that the largest amount of tribute that Sennacherib received in all of his campaigns was the one he received in his third campaign. This made it tempting to conclude that Sennacherib's campaign against the west was mainly to acquire tribute and to ensure that all the kings and rulers were showing submissive behaviour. This might lead us to conclude that his campaign was successful and that he went back to Nineveh without entering Jerusalem because he did not want to, not because he could not.

Studying the reliefs of the city of Lachish provided us with data supporting the view that the main objective of the reliefs was to show the Assyrian power in assaulting and conquering a very well-fortified city like Lachish. Against those who argued that the reliefs show Sennacherib's non-aggressive treatment of Lachish, I argued that the aim of the main topos in the reliefs was not to convey what happened to the city, but rather how successful the strategy was. Archaeological evidence was used to support this argument. Lachish was destroyed during the attack. This led me to conclude that the text and what is depicted in the reliefs does not necessarily relate what really happened in 701. And it is not wise to depend only on the written text and reliefs to decide whether or not Senna-cherib lost his war with Hezekiah.

To proceed in this study and strengthen my argument, nine cases of block-aded cities were presented and examined to see the way the Assyrian inscrip-tions, in different generations, represented the blockade strategy. The investiga-tion led us to conclude that there was a pattern in presenting the events. The most important topoi to be mentioned are: the fate of the enemy king; the fate of the enemy city; and the tribute. In four cases, either the Assyrian king entered the enemy city or the enemy king himself came out of the city to show submis-sive behaviour. And the Assyrian king went back to his city after solving the problem and receiving tribute. In five cases, however, the Assyrian king had to abandon the blockade because something prevented him from entering the city. In these cases the enemy king stayed safe inside his city, his city remained intact, and no tribute was paid.

In the light of the data provided by our discussion, the case of Jerusalem came to be discussed. Sennacherib went back home without entering Jerusalem or solving his problem with Hezekiah, the rebel. Yet he received a large tribute, albeit in Nineveh. These data tell us something about the campaign. Blockading Jerusalem while conquering other cities means that Sennacherib had a different strategy with Jerusalem. The blockade was meant to weaken the city from inside. This means that Sennacherib could not enter the city because something had prevented him: the walls of Jerusalem. Therefore, the blockade was meant to be set for a longer period. Leaving the blockade and turning to Nineveh without finishing his work with Hezekiah means that his strategy was not quite success-ful and he had to abandon the blockade. But this does not mean that the war ended. The fact that Hezekiah sent his tribute to Nineveh means that a threat still loomed over Jerusalem and Hezekiah took it as an opportunity to appease Sennacherib. In other words, the tribute did not make Sennacherib return to Nineveh, but rather it helped end the war. If we think of Damascus and Sapiya in Tiglath-pileser III's time, the two cities were blockaded, but Tiglath-pileser III had to abandon the blockade for a while. Then he returned to the two cities and finished his work in relation to the two enemy kings. Bearing this in mind, He-zekiah hastened to send his tribute to prevent Sennacherib from coming back to Jerusalem. The question is: what was the urgent matter that obliged Sennacherib to return to Nineveh before finishing the war? There is no answer to this question in the annals; however, other sources might be helpful in dealing with this mat-ter.

Part Two:
Reasons for Sennacherib's Withdrawal from Jerusalem within the Biblical Narratives

Preliminary remarks

Our investigation in the first part of this research led us to conclude that Senna-cherib's return to Nineveh was not the expected result from a king who claims victory: he did not enter Jerusalem, nor did he dethrone Hezekiah the rebel. The oddity in his conduct could be attributed to the fact that there was some-thing that obliged him to return to his city, Nineveh. The Assyrian sources, how-ever, are not of very much help when the matter comes to the question why he lost and what made him return. Scholars, therefore, turn to the biblical accounts to find explanations for the rescue of Jerusalem. Accordingly, in this part of the research the study focuses on the question: why did Sennacherib return? What caused him to go back to Nineveh and receive Hezekiah's tribute there?

Needless to say scholars have put much effort into rationalising Sennacher-ib's unexpected return. Different approaches have been used and some explan-ations have been provided to solve the problem. The most prominent explana-tions have been based on the biblical notes related in 2 Kgs 18–19//Isa 36–37, mainly 2 Kgs 18:13–16, which tells us that Hezekiah surrendered and paid a large tribute; 2 Kgs 19:7//Isa 36:7, which relates that Sennacherib shall hear a ru-mour; 2 Kgs 19:9//Isa 37:9, which tells about the advance of Tirhakah, the Nubian king; and finally, 2 Kgs 19:35//Isa 37:36, which narrates the story of the Angel of the Lord who appeared in the night and smote a large number of Sennacherib's warriors. Attempts have been made to back up one of these explanations and dismiss the others.

One must acknowledge that providing the real reason is far from straightfor-ward. There is more than one piece of evidence that suggests the story has under-gone editorial activity and has been purposely reshaped through generations to agree with their ideology. That, however, does not mean that it is impossible to find reasonable historical explanations. Furthermore, beside the textual prob-lem, there is another problematic point concerning this issue; so many opinions have been given about the matter that it is not simple to differentiate between what the Bible relates and what scholars say. Some opinions have become the-ories and, in turn, these theories have been accepted as facts without discussion. At this stage of dealing with the events in 701 cautious research is needed to go through the plethora of opinions and distinguish between the scholarly conclusions and the biblical data.

To make the task simpler and clearer, one fact should be apparent: the biblical text is the main departure point for this study. However, the way the story and the notes about Sennacherib's return are narrated is rather confusing. On the one hand, three of the notes about Sennacherib's return mentioned above have the word "return" (שוב) in them (2 Kgs 18:14; 19:7, 9), and in the fourth one the word is not mentioned, but the verse after the note (2 Kgs 19:36) relates that Sennacherib actually went back to Nineveh. That caused the possibility that each one might be the reason for Sennacherib's return. On the other hand, no note relates Sennacherib's withdrawal explicitly. That makes it possible to argue against any of the given reasons being the correct explanation of Sennacherib's withdrawal. The argument could easily become circular, and it would be difficult to find a way out. But, one may ask: why is this so? Did the editor of the narrative *mean* to relate it ambiguously, or did he perhaps not have a clear idea of what exactly had happened? Regardless of what the answer might be, we are sure of one fact: the biblical text in the form we now have is the only source available to us regarding the explanation for Sennacherib's return.

Therefore, methodologically, the four biblical notes associated with Sennacherib's return will be discussed one by one. The work in this part is divided into two chapters: in the first chapter the paying of tribute in 2 Kgs 18:13–16 will be discussed at length. In the second chapter, the other three explanations about Sennacherib's return will be considered. The reason why these three notices will be discussed in one chapter is because they are found within the prophetic narrative whose genre is different from that of the account of paying tribute. We shall then consider our conclusion.

Chapter Five: The Paying of Tribute to Sennacherib in 2 Kgs 18:13–16

1. Introduction

Hezekiah's oral message to Sennacherib, "Withdraw from me and whatever you impose on me, I shall bear", provides one of the explanations for Sennacherib's return to Nineveh without entering Jerusalem or punishing Hezekiah. Some scholars assume that Sennacherib did not enter Jerusalem because he accepted Hezekiah's offer to pay a large tribute. Although the assumption looks reasonable up to a point, problems arise when other issues in the narrative are raised in parallel. In this chapter I shall investigate this hypothesis to see if the text really indicates that Sennacherib returned to Nineveh because Hezekiah paid him to do so. The reason for undertaking further investigation—bearing in mind that the text in 2 Kgs 18:13–16 has been discussed many times—is that scholars do not treat equally all the aspects of the problem. Hezekiah's admission that he had done wrong and his offer to pay are not the only things we need to look at in this many-sided matter; other literary and historical analyses are necessary before we accept the view that Sennacherib returned as a result of his receiving a tribute. More specifically, this study identifies three such issues:

1) *The message of the text.* The unity of the text in 2 Kgs 18:13–16 will be discussed. Is the text composed or it is excerpted from a particular document in which similar reports were documented? Literary analysis will be applied to the text to understand the rhetoric and, more importantly, to recognise the message of the text. Does it really relate that Sennacherib went back to Nineveh because of the tribute? On the one hand, the paying of the tribute seems to be connected with Sennacherib's withdrawal; in 2 Kgs 18:14 Hezekiah shows a willingness to pay whatever Sennacherib wants if the latter withdraws, which causes many scholars to take for granted that 2 Kgs 18:13–16 is about the paying of the tribute that results in Sennacherib's return. On the other hand, however, the episode of tribute paying has some ambiguities if the text is read within its wider context.

2) *The ending of the tribute episode.* It is obvious that the text in 2 Kgs 18:13–16 has an ending, but this does not solve the problem. The text does not actually say that Sennacherib went back to Nineveh. In other words, the wider story does not finish with the end that the episode of the tribute has here.

3) *Implications in regard to the historicity of the tribute episode.* How historically reliable is the text? Needless to say, Hezekiah did pay Sennacherib tribute. But the kind of tribute and the circumstances of that tribute still need to

be examined. In this respect, Sennacherib's annals will be of good help when the biblical and Assyrian accounts are compared in order to shed light on the kind of tribute Hezekiah paid.

Careful investigation of these three aspects will assist us in understanding the possible historical situation of 2 Kgs 18:13–16 and, accordingly, help us to draw conclusions concerning the significance of this episode for the whole story. One can tentatively say that the episode is not actually intended to tell us why Sennacherib returned and Jerusalem was saved. Rather, the hypothesis I shall formulate in this study is that, historically speaking, the paying of the tribute was not the main reason for Sennacherib's return. Moreover, I contend that this is reflected in the rhetoric of the text on the paying of the tribute.

Methodologically, this study will proceed as follows. First, the text will be studied using literary and historical approaches in an interrelated way. I will start by discussing the text from an exegetical point of view; a literary analysis is given in this part and an explanation in terms of the compositional process of the episode will be provided. The aim of this approach is to test the unity of the text and to explore whether or not it underwent some processes of development to meet the needs of a different audience. In other words, I will discuss if the text has one or more strata. Additionally, because our passage resembles other passages in the book of Kings that report an attack on Jerusalem or Samaria (as is the case in our text), considering 2 Kgs 18:13–16 in the light of these other texts will be useful. The aim will be to compare our episode with other similar ones and thus to identify what makes 2 Kgs 18:13–16 distinct. Afterwards, I will move on to deal with other issues, including the ending of the episode and the historicity and type of tribute Hezekiah paid to Sennacherib.

It is worth mentioning that I shall not employ the standard notations A (2 Kgs 18:14–16), B1 (2 Kgs 18:13, 17–19:9a//Isa 36:1–37:9a) and B2 (2 Kgs 19:9b–37//Isa 37:9b–37), which were first suggested by B. Stade[291] for the narrative of Sennacherib's invasion. Instead, I simply refer to the events using the verses in which they are described. This is because there is no agreement on what A is, with some confusion over whether it is 2 Kgs 18:13–16, 18:14–16, or 18:14–16 together with 19:36–37. Although the expression "the tribute episode" and similar terms will thus be used repeatedly, I think this is a clearer approach than the disputed division into A and B.

---

291 Stade, B., "Miscellen: Anmerkungen zu 2 Ko. 15–21", *ZAW* 6 (1886), 156–89.

2. Literary analysis of the tribute episode

Under the aegis of literary criticism, many issues have been discussed by scholars with regard to 2 Kgs 18:13–16, including the parameters of the text, its unity, its genre, its composition, its layers and its original context. This has been accompanied in some studies by a consideration of other sources, such as the annals of Sennacherib or other biblical texts similar to the episode in question. The studies undertaken so far clearly show that certain issues have proved to be more interesting to scholars than others. The most prominent issues are whether or not the episode is to be separated from 18:17 ff.; 2 Kgs 18:13 belongs with 18:14–16 or 18:17 ff.; the text is a verbatim excerpt from an archival document or has been edited by the Deuteronomist; and if the episode draws to a recognisable end. In what follows, I shall start by considering the unity of 2 Kgs 18:13–16, proceeding gradually to the other issues involved.

2.1. The relationship between 2 Kgs 18:13–16 and 2 Kgs 18:17–19:37

Although the majority of scholars follow Stade with regard to the division of Sennacherib's story into A (2 Kgs 18:14–16) and B (2 Kgs 18:13, 17–19:37),[292] there are a few who do not accept the division, and have consequently tried to prove that the episode of the tribute payment to Sennacherib is integral to the narrative. In P.R. House's view,[293] for example, the tribute episode is the first stage of the story. He maintains that, although Hezekiah did indeed pay the tribute, this in itself was not enough for Sennacherib, who wanted further assurances of allegiance. The most recent monograph to advance this view is that by Evans,[294] who condemns the source critical method as inadequate and rejects the way in which it separates the tribute paying episode from the rest of the account. He argues that the whole story is coherent, asserting that, at first, Hezekiah promised to pay tribute but when he failed to pay the whole amount Sennacherib responded by sending his military officers to oblige Hezekiah to surrender.

---

292 Six monographs dedicated to the study of this subject support Stade's conclusions. These are: Honor, *Palestine*. Childs, *Crisis*; Clements, *Deliverance*; Gonçalves, *L'expedition*; Camp, L., *Hiskija und Hiskijabild: Analyse und Interpretation von 2 Kön 18–20* (MTA 9; Altenberge, 1990); and Gallagher, *Sennacherib's Campaign*. However, it is worth mentioning that even these studies differ with Stade concerning some of the details concerning the precise starting and finishing points of A and B; for example, Childs and others include 18:13 with vv. 14–16.
293 House, P.R., *1, 2 Kings. The New American Commentary*. Vol. 8 (Nashville, 1995), 362.
294 Evan, *Invasion*.

If we accept the episode of tribute payment as it appears in the text as we now have it, the opinions presented above could be justifiable. This is because the reasons given for arguing that 2 Kgs 18:13–16 is an integral part of the whole narrative are concerned with the meaning of the whole text as it is now, and do not endorse any theory that postulates different sources. However, it is obvious that, if we take seriously the hypotheses of different sources, the episode's integrity in terms of the rest of the narrative can be doubted. In other words, if other issues are discussed such as its genre, the orthography of the name Hezekiah, his portrayal, and the theme (Sennacherib's return being connected with the paying of the tribute), one can find reasons for separating this episode from the rest of the narrative. More details on this will be provided as this study progresses. For now, it is enough to state that we shall conclude that the episode of the tribute is to be separated from the prophetic narrative.

2.2. The rhetoric of vv. 13–16

Whether the episode of the paying of tribute is part of the whole story or not, there is a clear consensus that this part of the narrative is the most historically reliable. It seems indisputable to many that Sennacherib attacked Judah and that Hezekiah paid him tribute to convince him to withdraw. The main support for this assertion is that the episode shares points in common with Sennacherib's inscriptions narrating the same event. This has resulted in some scholars taking the matter for granted and thus focusing on rejecting the historicity of the prophetic narrative in 2 Kgs 18:17–19:37. Indeed, some scholars go further and (in the spirit of Clements)[295] argue that this episode is the only historical part in the story and the rest is legend. Supporters of this view consider the text in 2 Kgs 18:13–16 to be an excerpt from an annalistic document. That said, other scholars doubt the absolute historicity of the tribute episode and question the view that it represents an excerpt from archival materials. It is therefore worth analysing the rhetoric of the text at this stage, so that we may gain a deeper understanding of its nature. In so doing I will draw extensively on C.R. Seitz's argument, as he provides significant insights concerning the rhetorical nature of the episode in question.

---

295 See Clements, *Deliverance*, 14.

2.2.1. Seitz and the status of 2 Kgs 18:13 – 16

In his discussion of the formation of the book of Isaiah as a whole, Seitz[296] fo-cuses on Isa 36 – 39 and the role of these chapters in the Isaian traditions. Pre-dictably, in his discussion he deals with the status of the episode of the paying of tribute in 2 Kgs 18:13 – 16. Although his main concern is the prophetic narrative, Seitz's treatment of 2 Kgs 18:13 – 16 is very significant and has broad implications for our understanding of the episode.

Formulating and critically analysing previous arguments, Seitz moves smoothly from one point to another while presenting his own view on 2 Kgs 18:13 – 16. In his discussion, he presents arguments that have been propounded as far back as the beginning of the nineteenth century. Obviously, he has his own theories that cannot be taken for granted, but that should not obscure the fact that his analysis is a watershed in interpreting 2 Kgs 18:13 – 16, as he presents fur-ther evidence which casts doubt on the historicity of the episode concerned with the paying of tribute.

The first step in his study is to attempt to prove that 2 Kgs 18:13 does not be-long with 18:14 – 16. Accordingly, 18:14 – 16 is an insertion.[297] Among those who argue that 18:13 belongs with 14 – 16, Seitz presents the opinion of H. Wildberger,[298] and then turns rather quickly to discuss—with a kind of agree-ment—the opinions of those who argue that 18:13 does not belong with 18:14 – 16. He commences with Gesenius[299] and Stade[300], whose opinions were wel-comed by a large number of scholars who relied on the evidence that literary and textual criticism provided to support their argument. This evidence was prin-cipally the absence of 18:14 – 16 in Isaiah, the orthography of the name of Hezekiah,[301] the annalistic nature of 18:14 – 16 and the date presented in 18:13. Moreover, attention is drawn to the fact that the plot of the story runs smoothly from 18:13 to 18:17 ff. Seitz thus agrees that for these reasons 18:14 – 16 is separate from 18:13, 17 ff.

---

296 Seitz, C.R., *Zion's Final Destiny. The Development of the Book of Isaiah. A Reassessment of Isaiah 36 – 39* (Minneapolis, 1991).

297 Seitz, *Zion's*, 52.

298 Wildberger, H., *Jesaja 28 – 39*, (BKAT 3; Neukirchen-Vluyn, 1965), 1385.

299 Gesenius, F.H.W., *Philologisch-kritischer und historischer Commentar über den Jesaia* (Leip-zig, 1821).

300 Stade, "Miscellen", 156 – 192.

301 The orthography of "Hezekiah" in 18:14 – 16 where the name is spelt as חזקיה is different from 18:17 – 19:37 where the name is spelt as חזקיהו. Evans argues against this and considers the different spelling of Hezekiah's name in the narrative as inappropriate evidence of different sources. He states: "the issue of the spelling of names may be more indicative of scribal practice than of diverged literary sources." Evans, *Invasion*, 84.

Of course, Seitz is aware that demonstrating 18:14–16 is an insertion was not the sole concern of previous research. Ascertaining the unity of vv. 14–16 and their historical validity were significant points that previous studies took very seriously and firmly endeavoured to prove. Seitz, however, focuses on the intrusive nature of vv. 14–16 that these studies identify. Furthermore, he supports this conclusion using two more arguments when he deals with the matter from a form-critical point of view. First of all, he explores how the title used for Hezekiah in vv. 14–16 is מלך יהודה, while outside vv. 14–16 the title used is חזקיה המלך. Additionally, he notes that the expression מלך יהודה is used in the verses where the kings of Judah and Israel are introduced in the book of Kings (2 Kgs 3:1; 8:16; 13:1; 14:1). This comparison leads him to conclude that the writer of 18:14–16 was also responsible for 18:1–2 and that, accordingly, we should distinguish vv. 14–16 from 18:13, 17 ff. Secondly, by comparing the account of the paying of tribute (18:14–16) with the account of Ahaz (16:5–9), Seitz states that they both share a similar form and theme—the capitulation of the Judean king to the king of Assyria. Therefore, he suggests that the episode in question was constructed to demonstrate continuity between Ahaz and his son, Hezekiah.

Seitz's effort to prove that 18:14–16 is an addition should be seen in tandem with his attempt to show that the historicity of 18:14–16 is not as great as had been previously affirmed. In order to explain the striking similarity of vv. 14–16 with the text of Ahaz's capitulation episode, he states "one hypothesis is that a later editor (post-B) noted a similarity of theme (foreign hostility) in both accounts (2 Kgs 16:5–20 and 18:13, 17–19:37), and especially in the introductory verses (16:5 and 18:13)."[302] This means that, in Seitz's opinion, the episode of the paying of tribute is neither an excerpt from the Judean archives, as some claim, and nor was it composed before 18:13, 17 ff. Nevertheless, Seitz does accept that the episode was not invented entirely by the Deuteronomist. In this regard, he welcomes Childs' argument that the editor of the episode in question depended, in a way, on an archival source, since the text is concerned with the paying of tribute and its amount.[303] However, in Seitz's view this alone does not support the traditio-historical prioritising of 18:14–16 over 18:13, 17 ff. In this lies Seitz's innovation, which should be considered seriously. If vv. 14–16 were edited in the light of the prophetic narrative, then one has to ask Seitz more questions about the trace of 18:13, 17 ff. in the episode in question. Also, if they were built up by editorial action, that would mean that the passage contains more than one layer and that one should be able to find evidence of this

---

302 Seitz, *Zion's*, 59.
303 Seitz, *Zion's*, 54–60.

redactional work within the text of 2 Kgs 18:14–16. Seitz, however, does not discuss these points, which might strengthen his argument.

In order to strengthen his hypothesis, Seitz argues—albeit somewhat weakly —that there is no great similarity between 18:14–16 and the annals of Sennacherib. His argument rests on the statements of Childs and J.B. Geyer, who shed light on the divergences between the two sources. The main points which Seitz draws from the two scholars are the absence of Lachish in the annals of Sennacherib, the non-chronological description of the release of Padî and the inordinately high number of captives reported in the annals,[304] the different theme of each source, and the absence of Hezekiah's attempt to sue for terms with Sennacherib in the annals.[305] To the above points, Seitz adds that there is no mention of Hezekiah's capitulation in the annals. However, Seitz admits that both sources agree that Hezekiah paid tribute, which means he is happy to consider the note about Hezekiah paying the tribute as historically reliable. Eventually, albeit without advancing a truly convincing argument, Seitz agrees with Gonçalves in regarding 18:14–16 as "an official contemporary document", but he then argues that it was *secondarily* inserted into the fuller account (18:13, 17ff.). However, Seitz also quickly asserts that he can see the "hand of a later redactor, who may well have been working with information that had a basis in fact (i.e., Hezekiah paid tribute to the king of Assyria)."[306]

To sum up, Seitz's main concern is to prove that the episode of the paying of the tribute is an insertion, added at a later point to the prophetic narrative by the Deuteronomist. Furthermore, the episode in question, although based on an older source, was composed after the prophetic narrative. The episode was composed for two reasons: to explain continuity between the father, Ahaz, and his son Hezekiah and to clarify the vassal status of Judah in Manasseh's time. In other words, in Seitz's view the real motivation behind the writing of the tribute episode was not to show how the war started and ended, but rather to depict Hezekiah as being similar to his father, Ahaz. Therefore, Seitz does not completely argue against the historicity of the content of the episode, but rather against the view that it was composed before the prophetic narrative. Despite the fact that his contribution to the discussion is significant, especially regarding the intrusive nature of vv. 14–16, there are still weak points in his argument. He does not explain how the Deuteronomist dealt with his source, failing to engage with the question whether the Deuteronomist was faithful to his source or added it to

---

304 See Childs, *Crisis*, 72.
305 Geyer, J.B., "2 Kings XVIII 14–16 and the Annals of Sennacherib", *VT* 21 (1971), 604–606.
306 Seitz, *Zion's*, 66.

the text. Also, if, as he argues, the story of the tribute paying was composed in the light of the story of Ahaz and the prophetic narrative, it would have been helpful if Seitz had revealed the traces of 2 Kgs 18:13,17 ff. in 2 Kgs 18:14–16, something which he makes no attempt to do.

Nevertheless, the way in which the three points—where v. 13 belongs, the historicity and intrusive nature of vv. 14–16, and their relation to Sennacherib's annals—are presented in Seitz's discussion and the conclusion he derives from them establishes a clear need to look anew at the tribute episode. The next step, therefore, will be to explore the episode and simultaneously analyse Seitz's argument.

2.2.2. The status of v. 13

Before we start discussing other opinions, we need to look at v. 13: [307]

ובארבע עשרה שנה למלך חזקיה עלה סנחריב מלך אשור על כל ערי יהודה הבצרות ויתפשם:

And in the fourteenth year of King Hezekiah, Sennacherib, king of Assyria attacked all the fortified cities of Judah and seized them.

The verse as it stands has some notable problems, which have been a subject of research for a long time. The note about the date of the campaign with which the account opens causes discomfort from the start, with the assertion that the attack took place in the fourteenth year of Hezekiah's reign being questionable to say the least. According to 2 Kgs 18:1, 9, 10 Hezekiah was already king of Judah when Samaria fell to the Assyrians in 722, but this cannot be reconciled with 2 Kgs 18:13a which has Hezekiah's reign beginning in 715. The solutions that have been proposed fall mainly into two groups: those which accept the text as it is and accordingly assume that there was another campaign against Judah in 715[308] and those which doubt the text and consider the possibility that a mistake might have made by the author/editor.[309]

---

307 In terms of textual criticism, the Septuagint and the Masoretic text are very similar and not many problems are found in this text.

308 Becking, B., "Chronology: A Skeleton without Flesh? Sennacherib's Campaign as a Case-Study", in L.L. Grabbe, (ed.), *'Like a Bird in a Cage': The Invasion of Sennacherib in 701 BCE* (JSOTSup 363; London, 2003), 46–72. See also, Jenkins, A.K, "Hezekiah's Fourteenth Year. A New Interpretation of 2 Kings xviii 13:-xix 37", in *VT* 26 (1976), 284–289.

309 Rowley, H.H., *Men of God Studies in the Old Testament History and Prophecy* (London, 1963), 113; Wildberger, *Jesaja*, 371. In addition to these two groups, there is another opinion that accepts the text and assumes that 715 was the year when Hezekiah became the sole

Objectivity on such a matter seems to be impossible, and speculating about another campaign in 715 certainly raises more questions than answers. It is agreed that the 701 event is the harshest episode in Jerusalem's history before it fell to Nebuchadnezzar II. Even if we accept that the campaign was peaceful, as Becking suggests,[310] one would have to ask why such an irrelevant event was then mingled with that much more seismic episode. Moreover, it seems hazardous to infer a date of 715 for a first campaign on the basis of 18:13a alone, given that no details about the campaign are reported in either the Assyrian or the biblical records. Thus, solving the chronological problem of v. 13a by speculating about an earlier campaign in 715 is not appealing. The second solution, then, seems more likely, and a mistake may indeed have been made during the writing or editing of the account. This has serious implications for the following discussion. If we agree with M. Cogan that v. 13a is secondary,[311] then this part of the verse does not necessarily have an important effect in deciding where v. 13 belongs in the narrative (i. e. to vv. 14 – 16 or vv. 17 ff?). In other words, considering v. 13a as secondary in the text weakens the assumption that v. 13 has an annalistic genre and should thus belong with vv. 14 – 16 rather than vv. 17 ff.

The second issue concerns the rendering of Hezekiah's name in this verse. While 2 Kings 18:13 has the short reading חזקיה, Isa 36:1 has the long reading חזקיהו. Scholars have used this issue to debate where v. 13 belongs. A. Catastini, following S. Norin,[312] argues that the long reading is the original one based on the Kennicott manuscript of the Hebrew text, and accordingly argues that v. 13 belongs with v. 17 ff.[313] Gonçalves, however, argues for the short reading, based on the Leningrad and Aleppo Codices, and accordingly argues that v. 13 belongs with v. 14.[314] This study takes the view that arguing on this issue pulls one into a never-ending circle. On the one hand, v. 13 could have belonged with v. 14, but the editor of Isaiah took only v. 13 and modified it to agree with v. 17 ff. On the other hand, it is possible that v. 13 was taken from the beginning of the introduction to the prophetic narrative, but the editor of 2 Kings, after inserting vv. 14 – 16, modified v. 13 with v. 14 and thus changed the long reading for the short one.

---

king, while before that he was co-regent. See Gray, J., *I and II Kings. A Commentary* (OTL; London 1977), 75; Sweeney, M.A., *1 and 2 Kings: A Commentary* (OTL; Louisville, 2007), 414.

310 Becking, "Chronology", 57. The author assumes that the campaign was only to secure the paying of the tribute.

311 Cogan, M. and Tadmor, H., *II Kings: A New Translation with Introduction and Commentary.* Includes index (New Haven, 2008), 228.

312 Norin, S., "An Important Kennicott Reading in 2 Kings XVIII, 13", *VT* 32 (1982), 337 – 338.

313 Catastini, A., *Isaia ed Ezechia. Studio di Storia della Tradizione di II Re 18 – 20//Is. 36 – 39* (Rome, 1989), 41.

314 Gonçalves, *L'expediton*, 355.

Both cases are possible. In my opinion, discussion on this matter cannot really help us decide where v. 13 belongs, and I therefore put aside such matters in order to move on.

As for the rest of v. 13b, the text outlines which cities were affected by Sennacherib's action, stressing that it was mainly the fortified cities and not all the cities of Judah. The Hebrew verb תפש indicates that these cities were taken, as the verb means, "to seize possession of a town".[315] The passage tells us of Judah's reduced state; there is no mention of the Judean defence. Obviously, Sennacherib targeted the cities that Hezekiah had fortified to support the kingdom in the military and economic senses. It is clear that the note in the verse seems to be an introduction to a specific account,[316] but that does not mean the verse cannot stand on its own. Whether it introduces a reported invasion (2 Kgs 18:14 – 16) or a narrative (2 Kgs 18:17 – 19:37) is not straightforwardly discerned.

One of the reasons for Seitz's acceptance that 2 Kgs 18:13 belongs with 18:17 ff. is the fact that the story runs smoothly from v. 13 to vv. 17 ff. [317] This statement, however, is not in itself concrete evidence for v. 13 belonging with v. 17 ff. Indeed, other scholars have used the same argument to prove the opposite. B. Long describes the evidence for separating v. 13 from v. 14 as "weak and ambiguous" and considers vv. 13 – 16 to be one unit. He bases his argument on the structure, which progresses smoothly from v. 13 to v. 16.[318] Similarly, Cogan sees v. 13b as belonging with v. 14, arguing that vv. 13b–15 and v. 16 may be excerpts from a Judahite chronicle. His argument—like that of Seitz—is based on the orthography of Hezekiah's name and the titles given to him in the tribute episode and the prophetic narrative.[319] T.R. Hobbs, too, considers vv. 13 – 16 to be a unit very similar to 18:9, and states that it was omitted from Isaiah because of haplography.[320] More recently, Evans concludes that v. 13 belongs to v. 14 on syntactical grounds.[321]

---

315 *HALOT*, תפש 1779.

316 See Gonçalves, *L'expiditon*, 364.

317 See discussion in section 2.2.1.

318 Long, B., *2 Kings: The Forms of Old Testament Literature* (FOTL 10; Grand Rapids, 1991), 205. On this point, Long agrees with Montgomery, who attaches v. 13 to v. 14 because the latter logically needs the former. See Montgomery, J.A., *A Critical and Exegetical Commentary on the Books of Kings* (New York, 1951), 483. Montgomery considers paying the tribute to be an unsuccessful attempt by Hezekiah to buy his freedom.

319 Cogan, *II Kings*, 228.

320 Hobbs, T.R., *2 Kings* (WBC; Dallas, 2002), 247. Hobbs's argument about the haplography is weak and unlikely. The author does not pay any regard to Hezekiah's name in this account. It is improbable that the author/editor of Isa 36 mistakenly omitted vv. 14 – 16 and corrected the short reading of Hezekiah's name into the long reading to bring it into alignment with the pro-

Nevertheless, if we accept the argument of these scholars, and assume that 18:13 belongs to 18:14–16, then the prophetic narrative that begins at 18:17 ff. would need an introduction. The arrival of Sennacherib's officers at Jerusalem would not make any sense without the notice of Sennacherib attacking Judah and conquering the fortified cities, as mentioned in v. 13. Hence, one could argue that if v. 17 needs v. 13, the same also applies to v. 14; the passage in vv. 14–16 needs an introduction to show why Hezekiah paid the tribute. Put plainly, from a structural point of view, both accounts—the paying of the tribute and Sennacherib sending his officers to Jerusalem—need v. 13. It is, therefore, not enough to rely on the structure of the account to decide whether v. 13 belongs with v. 14 or v. 17 ff.; in truth, neither of them can stand without this beginning. Additionally, to do as Seitz does and make a decision on the intrusive nature of vv. 14–16 based on one's reading of whether v. 13 belongs with vv. 14–16 (or not) is not convincing either: v. 13 could belong to vv. 14–16 and, yet, the whole unit vv. 13–16 could be added to v. 17 ff., whose introduction was omitted after the tribute episode was added. Moreover, one cannot draw conclusions based on the style of v. 13, since no sudden change can be identified if it is read with v. 14 or v. 17.

However, one more question does need to be asked in this vein: if vv. 14–16 need v. 13, does v. 13 necessarily need vv. 14–16? The paying of tribute, even if it was successful, seems to be odd in this context. One could wonder if the introduction really suits what follows it. In this respect, it is helpful to compare our text with the other six instances in which a report of an invasion of Judah is given in the book of Kings.[322] In these reports, the introduction of the report usually has a note about Jerusalem, with the capital always being mentioned as the target of the attacker. In 2 Kgs 18:13, however, Jerusalem is not mentioned. In my opinion, v. 14 thus needs an introduction that informs the reader that Jerusalem was attacked, and that is why Hezekiah's offering of tribute is mentioned. Moreover, the conclusion reached at the end of the discussion above—i. e. that v. 13a represents a secondary addition to the text—might be of use to support this argument. This means that v. 13 did not really have the annalistic feature that the note about Hezekiah's date (in the fourteenth year...) would give to the verse. In other

---

phetic narrative. In other words, if the editor was aware of the difference in the name, he must have been aware of the omitted passage as well.

321 Evans, *Invasion*, 92.

322 1 Kgs 14:25–28; 2 Kgs 12:18–19; 2 Kgs 16:5–9; 2 Kgs 24:10–17; 2 Kgs 25:1–15. In 1 Kgs 15:17–22 the text does not mention Jerusalem, but does relate that the king and the people were blockaded.

words, the annalistic feature of v. 13a does not mean necessarily that v. 13 belongs with vv. 14 – 16.

Our investigation has led us to conclude that v. 13 as it stands might well not have originally belonged with v. 14. It is also important to declare that v. 13 might well not have originally belonged with v. 17 ff. either. It is obvious that v. 13 is an "advance notice" of the campaign, i.e. a summary of the whole campaign, while v. 14 and v. 17 both commence stories of what happened to Jerusalem (and to other cities) within the overall story of the conquering of all the fortified cities that is summarised in v. 13. Vv. 17 ff. are the start of a story about Jerusalem, and one can understand that what it narrates took place while the conquest of the cities was still in progress, as is obvious in the case of Libnah. This study proposes, therefore, that v. 13 did not originally belong with v. 14 (against Gonçalves) *and* that it did not originally belong with v. 17 either (against Seitz). It seems to us more likely that at a certain point in the late history of the text, an editor wanted to combine the two stories (i.e. vv. 14 – 16 and vv. 17 ff.) and supplied v. 13 as a single introduction to both. This would explain why the "retrospective overview" of v. 13 is uniquely different from the invasion reports narrated in other biblical texts. It would also help explain the oddities that exist in this verse in relation to the name of Hezekiah and the dating of the campaign. The editor might have felt it important to retain the information he had concerning Hezekiah's paying of the tribute (vv. 14 – 16), but wanted to get that information out of the way before starting on the story of the salvation of Jerusalem, which was more important to him.[323]

2.2.3. Questioning the archival origins of vv. 14 – 16

Despite the enormous body of secondary literature that deals with the story of Sennacherib's invasion, comparatively little has been written about vv. 14 – 16. This is because the majority of scholars take for granted the assertion that the text is a unit and that it is historically authentic because it has archival origins. However, questions arise in this vein that need answers. These include: What does it mean to state that the text of vv. 14 – 16 has an archival origin? What is it in the text that gives it archival features? Is it the information in it, or the style in which the data are edited? How is one to decide that the data are archival? In what follows, I will look closely at these verses in light of such issues.

---

323 For further discussion of why the tribute episode is placed before the narrative story, see Gallagher, *Sennacherib's Campaign,* 148.

2.2.3.1. Connecting vv. 14–15 to v. 13 and v. 16

The first step towards answering these questions is to read the verses and decide on its structural unity:

וישלח חזקיה מלך יהודה אל מלך אשור לכישה לאמר חטאתי שוב מעלי את אשר תתן עלי אשא

וישם מלך אשור על חזקיה מלך יהודה שלש מאות ככר כסף ושלשים ככר זהב

V.14 – *And then, Hezekiah, King of Judah, sent to the King of Assyria at Lachish saying: "I have done wrong. Withdraw from me. Whatever you impose on me, I shall bear." And then the king of Assyria imposed on Hezekiah, King of Judah, 300 talents of silver and 30 talents of gold.*

ויתן חזקיה את כל הכסף הנמצא בית יהוה ובאצרות בית המלך

V.15 – *and then Hezekiah gave all the silver found in the house of the Lord and in the treasuries of the palace.*

בעת ההיא קצץ חזקיה את דלתות היכל יהוה ואת האמנות אשר צפה חזקיה מלך יהודה ויתנם למלך אשור

V.16 – *At that time, Hezekiah cut off[324] the doors of the temple of the Lord and the doorposts that Hezekiah, King of Judah had overlaid (with metal), and gave them to the King of Assyria.*

---

324 A careful reading of this verse demonstrates that it is not straightforward, as the meaning of the verb קצץ and the word האמנות does not seem to be clear in this context. First of all, *HALOT* defines the word קצץ as "to cut off, chop off something". In the present context it defines the verb either as "cut off", or "trim... to steal the gold of decoration". *HALOT* does not give the meaning "to strip", which is usually used to translate the word קצץ in English translations of the Bible. This is not surprising, however, because the verb קצץ occurs fourteen times in the Bible but never has the meaning "to strip". Nevertheless, if we accept the meaning of the word as "cut off", we have to think of the rest of the verse. There are two objects for the verb "cut off": את דלתות and ואת האמנות; what was cut off were the doors and doorposts that Hezekiah plated with metal—not only the metal that was on the doors and doorposts. It is possible that Hezekiah cut off the doors and the doorposts all together and sent them to Sennacherib. Thus, the author meant to show that the tribute was so large that it included not only the metal but the doors as well.

The word "trim" does not seem to be any more appropriate, given that it means cutting the edge off something to make it tidier. However, if the word אמנה is taken to refer to the golden mounting of the door, as *HALOT* defines it, then the word "trim" could have a similar meaning to "strip": Hezekiah stripped the golden mounting of the door and sent it to Sennacherib. Yet the word האמנות does not seem to have that meaning. Although the word is a *hapax legomenon*, one can infer its meaning. The word apparently comes from the verb אמן, which means "to be reliable, to be faithful, to endure". Accordingly, the word האמנות could possibly indicate an object used to support or to secure something else. In this sense, the meaning "doorpost" could be the correct meaning. Eliezer Ben Yehuda defines the word האמנות as columns that hold up the building. See Ben Iehuda, E., *Thesaurus Totius Hebraitatis et veteris et Recentioris*. Vol. 1 (Berlin, 1953), 285. However, to assume that Hezekiah sent the pillars on which the temple was standing is unlikely.

As is obvious, v. 14 turns the reader's attention toward Hezekiah in order to narrate his attitude and his response to Sennacherib's action. Semantically, the event moves smoothly from v. 13 to v. 14. The use of the *waw*-consecutive at the beginning of the verse gives the impression that this verse reports what happened after Sennacherib seized the fortified cities. Within the narrative there is a quotation wherein the message of Hezekiah is related in the first person. With another *waw*-consecutive, the narrator continues the story to relate how much Sennacherib charged Hezekiah. However, if one looks closely at what is narrated in this verse, one might get the impression that the direct speech causes an interruption in the text. The facts narrated in this verse are:

1. Hezekiah takes the initiative to negotiate with Sennacherib;
2. He declares his submission through messengers he sent;
3. The King of Assyria is in Lachish;
4. Hezekiah's message is that he
   a. has done wrong;
   b. asks Sennacherib to withdraw from him; and
   c. will pay whatever Sennacherib demands; and
5. Sennacherib demands that Hezekiah pay what he wants, which is silver and gold.

The facts that the text does not mention are:

1. Where Hezekiah paid the tribute;
2. That Sennacherib returned to Nineveh after taking the tribute; and
3. That there was a siege around Jerusalem.[325]

---

325 The Hebrew word used for besiege is usually צוּר with the preposition עַל. The expression is used several times in the Bible to mean, "encircle" or "lay siege to a city or a person". The use of the word in the book of Kings refers to a military activity with the intent of attacking or of conquering the city by attrition or assault (1 Kgs 15:27; 16:17; 20:1; 2 Kgs 6:24; 17:5; 18:9; 24:11). What is important to note is the fact that the word is not mentioned in the story of Sennacherib's campaign as it is related in the biblical accounts. While 2 Kgs 18:9 clearly mentions the siege of Samaria and its fall to the Assyrian king, 2 Kgs 18:13 – 19:37 does not mention the word צוּר at all; there is no explicit notice of a siege of Jerusalem, although the language of assault is clear in the narrative. In 2 Kgs 18:13 the author relates that Sennacherib went up against all the cities of Judah. The Hebrew word עלה in combination with the preposition עַל does not exactly mean "to go up" but, rather, is a technical term for a military attack. Again, the text does not explicitly refer to an immediate assault against Jerusalem. V. 13 states that Sennacherib went up against all the fortified cities of Judah. Even if we consider the speech of the Rabshakeh in 18:25 as historically reliable, we should note that he does not mention the name of Jerusalem but instead uses the expression "this place".

Despite v. 13 being bound with v. 14 via the *waw*-consecutive, the structure of the event means that it is hard to accept assertions of its supposed unity. First of all, if v. 13 says that all the fortified cities are seized, one would not expect Sennacherib to be at Lachish, given the fact that Lachish was not the last city to be conquered and was probably under siege at that time. We are informed that, at some point, Sennacherib moved from Lachish to Libnah in 2 Kgs 19:8. So, v. 14 assumes that the attacks on the cities were still in progress rather than completed. This means that v. 13 does not match v. 14. It is thus likely that the editor who inserted v. 14 simply tried to bind the verses using the *waw*-consecutive. If this assumption is valid, the logical inconsistency gives us another reason to see v. 14 as an insertion and not bound to the verse preceding it.

In v. 15, however, the reader is informed of Hezekiah's sources for the tribute: the House of the Lord and Hezekiah's own house. The author is interested in telling the reader that Hezekiah actually paid the tribute and does so by relaying where he found the material to do so. Indeed, Hezekiah's action is repeated in v. 16, where it is expressed with the same Hebrew verb נתן. The extra information given in this verse is how Hezekiah got the tribute: by cutting off the doors and the doorposts from the Temple of the Lord and from his house. Concerning this last verse, I align myself with those who consider it to be an addition to vv. 14–15 because of the repetition and the time indicator (thus following Cogan). To sum up, the text of vv. 13–16 does not seem to have unity from a structural point of view. V. 13 does not match the following verse as it is a summary of the whole campaign; vv. 14–15 relate Hezekiah's negotiation and the amount of tribute he paid; v. 16 repeats what is given in v. 15.

2.2.3.2. Redactional features in vv. 14–15

Whether the unit consists of vv. 13–16, vv. 14–16 or vv. 14–15, the archival nature of vv. 14–15 is agreed among almost all scholars. This, however, does not mean that the verses were excerpted verbatim from the archive. In this respect, it is appropriate to start with a quotation from Childs, who says about 2 Kgs 18:13–16 that:

> The style of the account is that of the Deuteronomistic historian (Dtr.) who has obviously used older sources, but who has expressed himself in his own style. Note, for example, the parallel with I Kings 14:25 ff.; II Kings 18:9 ff. In other words, these verses are narrative prose, typical of the author, and not just a copy from an entry in a state archive.[326]

---

326 Childs, *Crisis*, 69–70

Similarly, J. Gray comments on 18:13 – 16, saying:

> In II K. 18:13 – 16, the substantial correspondence with the annals of Sennacherib indicates close reliance on an annalistic source, though the narrative style and summary of details indicates adaptation by the Deuteronomistic compiler. [327]

These statements relay some significant facts. First, the text is not entirely an invention of the Deuteronomist. Secondly, the text is not an exact excerpt either—it is not supposed to be taken as it is and granted complete authenticity as being copied from an archival document. Also, Childs considers the style of the account—narrative prose—as specific to the author.[328] Neither Childs nor Gray sets out what is archival and what is Deuteronomistic in this text.[329] However, one can conclude two points from their statements: first, if we consider Childs' interesting point about the different style used in other texts, specifically 1 Kgs 14:25 ff. and 2 Kgs 18:9 ff., one can understand that the two scholars are concerned with the citation in v. 14 that makes the report more sophisticated. Secondly, they both agree that there was another text/report (whose style was different) behind the text we have now. Is there any way to know why the original text was changed into what we have now? A comparison with other invasion reports might help us ascertain what is an addition and what is original in our text.

Around two decades after Childs's study, T. Vuk elaborates on the idea of the similarity of vv. 13 – 16 to other invasion reports in Kings. This comprehensive study, in which the author presents all the units similar to 2 Kgs 18:13 – 16 that deal with an invasion of Judah or Israel by foreign kings, seeks to detect if there is a special literary genre for such events in biblical texts as well as to determine the text's contents and formal constitutive elements. Vuk's investigation leads him to conclude that there is a typical literary form, which comes from corresponding sources that the Deuteronomist is using, i. e. the annals of the King-

---

327 Gray, *II Kings*, 660.

328 In this respect, one can see how Parker's argument fits in this context. Parker states that the Deuteronomist has his own traditional concepts and formulaic, theological language to express some concepts in his composition (concerning accounts of military campaigns). Parker, S., "Did the Books of Kings make Use of Royal Inscriptions?", *VT* 50 (2000), 366 – 68.

329 Na'aman discusses the possible sources the author of the book of Kings had access to. First of all, he dismisses the idea of archival documents used by the author of the book of Kings and suggests access to other sources, such as temple library materials such as a king list and "the Book of the Chronicles of the Kings of Judah." Na'aman, N., "The Temple Library of Jerusalem and the Composition of the Book of Kings", in A. Lemaire (ed.), *Congress Volume Leiden 2004* (VTSup 109; Leiden, 2006), 129 – 152.

doms of Judah and Israel.[330] Some of his conclusions can be summarised as follows:

1. Vuk notes that there are some texts (among the invasion reports) that are presented without details or description of the event, e.g. 1 Kgs 14:25–28, and that there are other texts that are more sophisticated and contain redactional expansion through the insertion of direct speech and explanations about the events (1 Kgs 15:17–22).[331] In the first case, Vuk suggests that the author wanted to be close to his sources, and the result was what he calls "invasion notes". In other cases, however, where the text is more developed, Vuk suspects that redactional work on the notes that the author got from his sources can be identified—the result is an "invasion narrative". Our text, vv. 13–16, is one of these developed texts. Vuk argues that the influence of that redactional work is tied primarily to the quotation in v. 14. [332] In his opinion, the structure of the speech as well as the use of dialogue is to be evaluated as evidence of non-annalistic writing.[333]

2. The citations that are found in four texts[334] do not affect the basic theme of the invasion and the alignment to the termination. In the case of vv. 13–16, the liberation is reached through the paying of the tribute. In 14:8–14, the focus is on expressing the statement that Joash took the spoils to Samaria. But Vuk is aware that there is a political movement in the other two texts about Asa and Ahaz.

3. The aim of the report is not to explain the victory–defeat theme but to set out the tension between the invasion and its end. Special value is given to the tribute, its amount and its source. So, one should not mix the tribute report with the report of the defeat.

---

330 Vuk, T., *Wiedererkaufte Freiheit. Der Feldzug Sanheribs gegen Juda nach dem Invasionsbericht 2 Kön 18:13–16* (FHTB 1; Jerusalem, 1984). The texts examined in his book are: 1 Kgs 14:25 – 28; 15:17–22; 2 Kgs 12:18–19; 14:8–14; 15:19–20; 15:29–30; 16:5–9; 17:3–6; 23:29–35; 24:10–17; 25:1–15.

331 As for the citation, Evans draws attention to the presence of direct speech in v. 14, which is supposed to be part of an annalistic excerpt. He states: "it seems unlikely... that an archival document would contain the first person speech of the king." However, one must say that Evans does not consider the presence of this citation as a sign of the presence of another source. In his opinion, having archival elements, with or without citations, does not affect the unity of the passage and the whole narrative. See Evans, *Invasion*, 42.

332 Vuk, *Wiedererkaufte*, 33.

333 Vuk, *Wiedererkaufte*, 35.

334 1 Kgs 15:17–22; 2 Kgs 14:8–14; 16:5–9; 2 Kgs 18:13–16.

As for the redactional nature of v. 14, Vuk's conclusions are interesting in the context of this research. His conclusions emphasise the argument of Childs and Gray, i.e. that the style of the invasion reports reflects annalistic material, even though these reports show that the Deuteronomist had his own way of dealing with his material. However, Vuk is more precise in his argument. In his view, the direct speech in v. 14 shows some signs of redactional work and 2 Kgs 18:14b and 18:7 belong to the same redactional level. Vuk is not alone in discussing the redactional nature of the tribute episode (see below). Gonçalves explores Vuk's idea about the redactional nature of v. 14 and the fact that it emerges from the two verbs mentioned in the verse, חטא and שוב. Vuk thinks that v. 14 in this respect reflects v. 7b and 19:7, 28, 33, 36,[335] while Gonçalves argues that one cannot invoke the sense of the verbs חטא and שוב from v. 7b and 19:7, 28, 33, 36. [336] Indeed, Gonçalves goes further and states that there is no reason why v. 14 should have redactional features.

This disagreement between Vuk and Gonçalves on the redactional nature of v. 14 calls our attention to the long discussion on this matter. The discussion about v. 14 being an excerpt or not has been undertaken by two opposing parties who have presented equally strong arguments. The idea that v. 14 has undergone redactional work goes back to the beginning of the last century when A. Šanda argued that the verb חטא unlikely appeared in an annalistic document.[337] The confusion that the verb חטא causes in the verse made Würthwein doubt its originality, and he held that the phrasing emerges from a memory—a common explanation of a vassal vis-à-vis his overlord.[338] In his 1986 article R. Liwak[339] contributes to this discussion when he deals with the style of v. 14. He thinks that the supposed fact that there was a contemporary document from which v. 14 was excerpted is exaggerated. Liwak argues that the condition that Hezekiah sets for paying the tribute is not of a bureaucratic nature; in his opinion, the verse shows Hezekiah negotiating on equal terms with Sennacherib. Furthermore,

---

335 Not in respect to words because v. 7 does not have these words, but rather in respect to content. The wrong that Hezekiah committed is his rebellion against Assyria.

336 Gonçalves, *L'expedition*, 362–65. In his opinion, from a synchronic point of view there is in v. 14 a reference to v. 7b, but not from a diachronic point of view. From a diachronic point of view, v. 14 belongs to an ancient source and v. 7b is a redactional introduction to the narrative of Hezekiah's reign.

337 Šanda, A., *Die Bücher der Könige übersetzt und erklärt: Zweiter Halbband: Das Zweite Buch der Könige* (EHAT 9; Münster, 1912), 249.

338 Würthweint, E., *Die Bücher der Könige: 1. Kön. 17–2. Kön. 25 übersetzt und erklärt* (ATD 11; Göttingen, 1984), 409.

339 Liwak, R., "Die Rettung Jerusalems im Jahr 701 v.Chr.: Zum Verhältnis und Verstandnis historischer und theologischer Aussagungen", *ZThK* 83 (1986),149.

he believes that the use of the two verbs חטא and שוב is meant to indicate a theological view. In Liwak's opinion, although the two verbs have different subjects, according to the Deuteronomistic understanding, rescuing Jerusalem requires admissions of guilt and repentance. In other words, Liwak understands the verbs חטא and שוב as explaining a political action, although their theological dimension is unmistakable.

On the other side, some scholars (in the spirit of Montgomery[340]) have argued for the authenticity of v. 14 as an excerpt from an annalistic document. In the climate of form criticism, Long states: "the speech attributed to Hezekiah is analogous to the confessional statements in legal proceedings in which the guilty party admits wrongdoing."[341] Long's contemporary L. Camp carried out an extensive analysis of 2 Kgs 18–20, rejecting the arguments of scholars who deny the originality of v. 14. In his view, vv. 13b–16 are a reliable report of the events of 701 and seem to be taken from the "*Tagebücher* of the kings of Judah/Israel". His argument is based on an assertion that what this episode relays can be confirmed in Assyrian documents, at least in part.[342] Similarly, L. Berndes[343] argues that there is not much redactional work in v. 14, and he explains the presence of the verb חטא as emulating the Assyrian royal inscriptions in which the cognate Akkadian *ḫaṭû*[344] is commonplace, especially in the Assyrian treaties and the annals where the word echoes Assyrian rhetoric about rebellious foreign kings.

Obviously, the questions concerning the original source of v. 14 are not straightforward. The two camps mentioned above are divided into those who think that v. 14 has undergone redactional activity (especially those that doubt the original text had the word חטא in it) and those who see it as an excerpt from reliable materials. But no one doubts the authenticity of the paying of tribute. However, there is no agreement on how precisely the text is historical. In this respect, one might think that Dion has a point when he states: "in the absence of appropriate indigenous epigraphic documentation, it is difficult to imagine what

---

340 Montgomery, *Kings*, 334.

341 Long, *Kings*, 206.

342 Camp, *Hiskijabild*, 95–105. In his literary analysis of the story of Hezekiah in 2 Kgs 18–20, he isolates vv. 13b–16 along with other verses (2 Kgs 18:1, 2, 4*, 7,8*; 20:21) as stemming from the "Annals of the kings of Judah". But in his literary-historical discussion of the episode of the tribute, he doubts the fact that the negotiation was over the terms of surrender. Ibid, 289–292.

343 Berndes, L., "The Sennacherib Episode: Exegetical Issues," p 5. A short paper presented at OTSEM Conference in Skalholt, September 2010.

344 *CAD*, Ḫ, *ḫaṭû*, 156–157.

kind of official record may have preserved the memory of military defeats and other humiliation suffered by the Hebrew kingdoms."[345] However, that does not preclude the fact that the arguments of the two opposing camps bear some discussion.

To narrow down the discussion about v. 14, one can say that the direct speech is the main problematic issue in this verse—it is either fabricated or it is original. Those who think it is fabricated base their opinion on the fact that the citation is meant to convey a theological theme (in the spirit of Liwak). However, those who think the citation is original rely on the fact that the citation was common in the Assyrian correspondence and there is no reason why we should not consider the citation in v. 14 as being taken from correspondence between Sennacherib and Hezekiah. At this point, one can say that there is merit to both camps' claims. However, one might find it more difficult to rationalise why the citation was fabricated and Hezekiah was portrayed in such a pejorative way. Clearly, the only one who is satisfied with this confession is Sennacherib, who thinks of Hezekiah's rebellion as "wrong doing," otherwise, the author/editor of the text (whether it is the Deuteronomist or not) would not have the same thought about Hezekiah's rebellion even if v. 14 belongs to an early stage of the text. Thus, it is easier to accept the fact that there was correspondence between Sennacherib and Hezekiah and the direct speech in v. 14 was taken from that correspondence.

In addition to the discussion above, I suggest another way of dealing with Hezekiah's confession in v. 14 in order to confirm its originality. Refocusing the discussion and looking at the text from a different angle would be helpful in getting new insights. Whether the citation is an excerpt or the result of redactional activity, its presence in the text in a citation as it is now in the episode, in the first person, could indicate a particular fact. Hezekiah's words in the quotation convey his own view about the war (internal focalisation).[346] It seems that the author lets the reader hear the words of Hezekiah in his confession. This means that the author leads the reader to understand an important aspect of the war—the reason it happened—from Hezekiah's point of view. In the chapter prior to that of Sennacherib's narrative (2 Kgs 17), Israel's downfall is narrated; the author more than once emphasises that the disaster happened because the people of Israel did what was evil in the sight of the Lord (2 Kgs 17:7–18). In chapter 18, however, nothing is mentioned about the people; the attack does

---

345 Dion, P.E., "Sennacherib's Expedition to Palestine", *BCSBS* 48 (1988), 10.
346 Ska, J.L., *Our Fathers Have Told Us. Introduction to the Analysis of Hebrew Narratives* (SubBib 13; Rome 1990), 66.

not seem to be a punishment from God exacted because Judah did not keep his commandments. Nevertheless, we do hear Hezekiah admit that he has done wrong against Sennacherib, which gives the impression that the campaign was not arbitrary but rather a punishment.[347] If so, one can conclude that one of the aims of v. 14 is to reveal the reason for the attack. Paying the tribute then is an offer made to compensate for the wrong that Hezekiah committed, i.e. his rebellion against the Assyrian empire.

Noteworthy in this regard is the fact that Hezekiah is never mentioned in explicitly pejorative language in the Bible. In the book of Isaiah, when the prophet criticises the acts of Judean rulers, Hezekiah's name is never mentioned, even when it is rather clear that the prophet is speaking about Hezekiah (Isa 30). Indeed, when 2 Kings introduces Hezekiah, the author uses highly positive language (2 Kgs 18:1–8). The author probably wanted to maintain that positive depiction of Hezekiah and to put the confession in the first person form to convey Hezekiah's necessary political expediency, and thus the author places himself at a distance from Hezekiah's confession. There is no clear evidence that the author intended to portray Hezekiah in a negative light and there is no theological dimension to the episode of the paying of the tribute (against Liwak).[348] The attitude of Hezekiah is apparently political. From his perspective, the rebellion against Assyria became an offence when he found himself imprisoned in his city (2 Kgs 18:14), while in the Deuteronomist's view Hezekiah's rebellion had a theological value (2 Kgs 18:7). In other words, Hezekiah's confession is confined to certain circumstances, while the Deuteronomist's praise of Hezekiah is presented in a wider context.

To sum up this rather long discussion of the redactional nature of 2 Kgs 18:14–15 then, we could say that the direct speech in v. 14 reflects a kind of diplomatic language. There is no solid ground to assume that the Deuteronomist has fabricated Hezekiah's confession. The quotation seems to be taken from correspondence between Hezekiah and Sennacherib, but we cannot with any certainty ascertain the circumstances of that communication. As for the reason and meaning that this episode has, one can conclude that, by using the citation, the author/editor not only wanted to be close to his sources but also wanted to convey the theme of why Sennacherib attacked Judah: it was not because the people were sinful like the Israelites, or because the king did evil in the sight of the Lord like the Israelite kings, but rather because Hezekiah's rebellion

---

347 Gonçalves, *L'expedition*, 365.
348 See also Irvine, S.A., *Isaiah, Ahaz, and the Syro-Ephraimitic Crisis* (SBLDS 123; Atlanta, 1990), 83–90. The author argues that the confession of Ahaz has theological value and was meant to depict Ahaz negatively.

against Assyria was considered an offence by Sennacherib. Additionally, despite the fact that Hezekiah's name is never mentioned in a pejorative context, v. 14 does not hide that picture of Hezekiah being humiliated. One can thus infer the non-theological aspect of this verse because of Hezekiah's negative presentation. Also, 2 Kgs 18:15 (and indeed v. 16) seems to have an annalistic nature, if we compare 2 Kgs 14 – 15 with other invasion reports in Kings.

However, this does not mean that vv. 14 – 15 are excerpts from an annalistic document. In this respect, I agree with Vuk that there was a kind of unsophisticated invasion report without the direct speech. The quotation (specifically, Hezekiah's confession) could have been added later to the invasion report, which included information about the negotiation between the two parties and relayed how the tribute was an essential means through which to remove a threat against Jerusalem.

2.3. Conclusion of the rhetorical analysis of vv. 13 – 16

We consider that it would be premature to judge that vv. (13)14 – 16 are an excerpt from annalistic documents. This conclusion of ours is based on the discussion above and our inferences about v. 13 not belonging to either v. 14 or vv. 17 ff., on the intrusive nature of vv. 14 – 16, on the way v. 14 reads as a summary of correspondence between the two kings, and on the possibility that v. 16 was added to vv. 14 – 15. The text has clearly undergone different stages and displays some history of editing and redaction. Hence, there is no way to arrive at a consensus of what the original text contained.It is important to clarify, however, that this study does not take the view that vv. 14 – 16 are completely an invention of the Deuteronomist, but rather shares the view that there is more than one sign of redactional activity within the text. If the invasion report in question is compared with other invasion reports, one can notice clearly that there is no one pattern for all the reports and there is no way to decide that any report is an excerpt from the older sources. This, however, should not lead us to dismiss the historicity of the text. Given the fact that the citation is rather reliable, with v. 15 and v. 16 reflecting annalistic documents, one can say that there are some concrete facts: Hezekiah started the negotiation with Sennacherib, he paid him a large tribute, and that tribute was made in order to remove a threat that Jerusalem faced in 701. However, we cannot go further; it is simply not possible to decide conclusively that vv. (13)14 – 16 demonstrate that Hezekiah paid the tribute to make Sennacherib withdraw and that it was only then that Sennacherib returned to Nineveh, although that is what vv. (13)14 – 16 seems to say. To sum up, the discussion about the unity and nature of the episode of the tribute showed that the text is composed and is not an excerpt from the annalistic document. This in a way challenges the assumption that the tribute episode is historically the most reliable section of the invasion narrative. This conclusion will be supported when what is narrated in 2 Kgs 18:14–15 is examined in its wider context and placed in parallel with the Assyrian account of the same event.

3. The ending of the tribute episode

The invasion reports in the books of Kings regularly end with a note stating that the attacker went back after accomplishing his mission. Our text 2 Kgs. 18:13–16, however, ends rather inconclusively with the notice of Hezekiah cutting up the doors and the doorposts of the temple to pay the tribute, which leaves a sense of the story being incomplete. There is no way we can know with certainty if, from the beginning of its history, the text did end there. If in fact the original text told a more complete story, it must have undergone redactional work, so that, as one possibility, the final words were removed from their original place and are now to be found at 2 Kgs. 19:36. If we consider the views of some scholars who think that the text does not need an end, then we could perhaps accept that there is no oddity in the text. Long[349] and Evans[350] argue that we should not be reading this text as Hezekiah's capitulation but rather see the offering of the tribute as the first step—a step which did not work. Other scholars, however, look at the matter differently and argue that the end of this text is in 19:36 f., where Sennacherib returns to Nineveh. At the beginning of the last century this idea was suggested by J. Lewy, who argued that 19:36 was the end of the episode of the paying of the tribute.[351] In agreement with Lewy, S. Parker concentrates on the character of the narrative and notes that the correlation with Assyrian records and the mention of the name of Sennacherib in 2 Kgs 18:13–16 and 2 Kgs 19:36–37 could give good reasons why vv. 36–37 were originally the conclusion of 2 Kgs 18:13–16.[352]

This opinion might be considered strong in some aspects, especially if we consider that it would solve the problem of the lack of an end to the episode of the paying of the tribute. However, the reason it is difficult to accept is that vv. 36–37 narrate the return of Sennacherib as well as his murder by his sons.

---

349 Long, *Kings*, 206.
350 Evans, *Invasion*, 87–137.
351 See Lewy, J., "Sanherib und Hizkia", *OLZ* (1928), 156–7.
352 Parker, S., *Stories in the Scriptures and Inscriptions. Comparative Studies on Narratives in Northwest Semitic Inscriptions and the Hebrew Bible* (New York, 1997), 168, n.34.

This means that the note was written after the death of Sennacherib (681), and thus it would shift the date of the story of the tribute to a later period, at least if we assume that these two verses *are* the end of the episode. Among the scholars who strongly argue that vv. 36–37 belong to 2 Kgs 18:13–16, Berndes tackles this issue and presents an explanation. He agrees with C. Hardmeier that there is a conflation of two distinct stages of history in vv. 36–37, namely Sennacherib's return and his murder. What brings these two events together is the use of "and he dwelt in Nineveh" in v. 36. When looking at other biblical texts this phrase indicates a lapse of time between two events, in our case the return of Sennacherib and his murder by his sons.[353]

Once again, before we accept this hypothesis we have to answer certain questions. When did this combination of events happen? Was it before the combining of the tribute account and the prophetic narrative or after their combination? Why would the note about Sennacherib's death be combined with the delivery of the tribute? It is generally agreed that the death of Sennacherib has a theological meaning, as the attacker who wanted to destroy Judah was destroyed in his own land.[354] So, what is the theological intention of adding v. 37 to the tribute episode? Furthermore, if vv. 13–16 were written under Assyrian supervision, as Berndes suggests,[355] it is unlikely that a Judean scribe would add this notice about the death of the Emperor of Assyria. Also, no notice of any of the kings' deaths is mentioned in the other invasion reports; to end the episode with Sennacherib's death thus serves to cause confusion in the text.

Moreover, the fact that vv. 36–37 is the only place that narrates the end of the attack is pertinent. Both the first episode of the account and the prophetic narrative need this end, just as they both need the beginning in v. 13. Also, if it is indeed an original part or the end of the tribute episode, why does Isaiah have it despite not having the first part of the same account? It is quite improbable that Isaiah omitted part of the episode and kept the end of it.

All of these unanswered questions mean that it is hardly possible to accept the view that vv. 36–37 were originally the end of vv. 13–16. If so, the episode in question lacks an ending, or maybe it was deliberately left like that to indicate that paying the tribute did not mean Sennacherib had returned to Nineveh. If we accept the fact that Sennacherib received the tribute in Nineveh, then the lack of

---

353 Berndes, "Issues", 12–14.

354 Dubovsky, P., "Assyrian Downfall through Isaiah's Eyes (2 Kings 15–23): The Historiography of Representation", in *Biblica*, 89 (2008), 14.

355 Berndes, L., "Dialogic Exegesis of the Sennacherib Episode: The Need for a method that is both Literary and Historical." A Short paper presented at OTSEM conference in Granavolden/ Oslo, in December 2008, 7.

an ending—unlike the other texts—would be understandable. Seitz's theory that the tribute episode was inserted after both the prophetic narrative and the episode of Ahaz showing submission to the Assyrian king once again becomes worthy of further consideration.

4. Implications for the historicity of the tribute episode

The discussion above demonstrated that the hypothesis according to which the account of the paying of tribute to Sennacherib is excerpted from the annals is not strong enough and requires more evidence to prove its trustworthiness. The text in 2 Kgs 18:13–16 is not a unit and it is not an excerpt from an annalistic document. In what follows, this argument will be supported by further discussion; however, the purpose of this current discussion is not to prove that the episode is entirely invented by the Deuteronomist but rather to decide what can be considered as historical within this passage.

First of all, it must be mentioned that this study does not exclude the notion that vv. 13–16 reflect historical events, as mentioned above. However, to insist that it was the only way to make Sennacherib return to Nineveh seems unlikely. At this point in this study of the tribute episode, it is important to place the text in a wider context and read it in parallel with the Assyrian accounts that relate the same event. The aim is to be able to determine whether or not the historical information reported in 2 Kgs 18:13–16 is in line with the information provided by Sennacherib's annals.[356]

When scholars compare the two accounts, they tend to focus on the similarities between them. For example, van der Kooij (although he is aware that the biblical account is scanty and does not relate all the information related in the Assyrian account) considers 2 Kgs 18:13–16 to be historically reliable because of the three common points in the two accounts: the besieging and capturing of Judean fortress cities (v. 13 // Rassam 49–51); the submission of Hezekiah (v. 14a // Rassam 55); and the paying of the tribute (vv. 14b–15 // Rassam 58).[357] In general, van der Kooij presents the widely agreed argument about the authenticity of the tribute episode in the Bible. However, there is another point that needs attention in this respect. It is obvious that the biblical and Assyrian accounts not only show similarities but also differences. Needless to say, scholars are aware of this

---

356 Kofoed, *History*, 51.
357 van der Kooij, A., "Das assyrische Heer vor den Mauern Jerusalems im Jahr 701 v. Ch.", *ZDPV* 102 (1986), 100.

significant fact.[358] Nevertheless, not enough discussion has been devoted to how these differences could direct the debate about the historicity of 2 Kgs 18:13–16.

The most striking note that attracts attention is the location of the paying of the tribute. In the Assyrian account, Sennacherib boasts about the tribute that Hezekiah sent to Nineveh. In the biblical account, however, although the text does not mention it explicitly, the impression is given that the tribute was paid in Lachish. Some scholars assume that the negotiation was in Lachish and the actual payment was in Nineveh, an argument that is mainly based on the note given in 2 Kgs 19:8, which indicates that Sennacherib moved from Lachish to Libnah. In such a view, the negotiation was not initially successful, but eventually worked at a later time.[359] I believe that this solution raises more questions than answers, and another way to approach the matter is necessary.

In the first part of this research in which Sennacherib's campaign against Judah is discussed in the context of the Assyrian royal inscriptions, the discussion of economic exploitation led us to conclude that the tribute that Sennacherib received in his campaigns can be categorised as spot tributes and annual tributes. A spot tribute is what Sennacherib received after he invaded a land, either by entering the capital city of the enemy king or by receiving his tribute from the enemy king who comes out of his city to meet Sennacherib—this was a submission tribute. It was also noted that Hezekiah's tribute does not fit under either of the two categories at hand.[360] It is therefore helpful if the pattern of the tributes seen in the texts that relate the invasion reports in the book of Kings is discussed.

In this respect, Vuk's study of the kinds of tribute that we see in the book of Kings is significant. Having examined the occasions of paying tribute in the invasion reports, Vuk concluded that there are three kinds of tribute: punishment tributes ("*Straftribut*"),[361] favour tributes ("*Gunsttribut*")[362] and submission tributes ("*Unterwerfungstribut*").[363] Vuk counts Hezekiah's tribute among the cases of

---

358 See subsection 2.2.1 above

359 Gallagher, *Sennacherib's Campaign*.

360 See section 4.3.4.1

361 This is a tribute taken when the enemy king enters the city and takes materials from the palace and the temple, e.g. 1 Kgs 14:25–28. In this case this could be considered as booty taken after war.

362 This is the tribute that the (Israelite or Judean) kings send to the enemy king so that the latter may return, e.g. 2 Kgs 12:18–19.

363 This is the tribute that the (Israelite or Judean) kings send to a third party to obtain protection from the enemy king, e.g. 1 Kgs 15:17–22; 2 Kgs 16:5.7–9.

a submission tribute. [364] Before we agree with Vuk about the categorisation of Hezekiah's tribute, however, let us first discuss some other issues.

It appears that what Vuk calls a punishment tribute in the biblical context is what is called booty in the Assyrian context. In both cases, the Assyrian king enters the city and plunders the palace and takes what he finds. A favour tribute, as we might expect, does not have an equivalent in the Assyrian annals. It seems that it was a kind of tribute that an inferior country would pay to a superior one so as to seek protection from a third party. In the case of a submission tribute, although it is found in both the biblical and Assyrian contexts, the mechanism for receiving or paying it is different. Having discussed this kind of tribute in the Assyrian context, the study now turns to the biblical illustration of such a tribute.

According to Vuk, there are four occasions where a submission tribute is paid in the second book of Kings: 2 Kgs 12:18–19; 15:19–20; 17:3; and 18:13–16. In all these cases, apart from Hezekiah's case, the report of the invasion is devoid of citation or direct speech. The main focus is to report the advance of the invader and the paying of the tribute by the Judean or Israelite king. Only in Hezekiah's case do we hear of a negotiation between the invader and the inferior king. Additionally, only in Hezekiah's case are we told anything about the place of negotiation: Lachish. The other significant thing to note is that all the kings of the invaded lands stay put in their cities and do not leave to present their tribute personally to the invader. However, evidence shows that the biblical texts are not historically reliable in this regard. From the annals of Tiglath-pileser III we know that Menahem presented his tribute in Arpad when Tiglath-pileser III invaded the west in 738.[365] Thus, we can conclude that the biblical records do not focus on the manner or the place in which the tribute is paid. Whether the Israelite or Judean kings leave their cities to pay tribute is not of much interest in the biblical accounts. After all, it is a submission tribute. However, the case is not the same in the Assyrian records. As was noted in the discussion above, leaving the city and coming to show submissive behaviour to the Assyrian king was important. Therefore, the characteristics of a submission tribute in the biblical perspective are not the same as in the Assyrian perspective. Bearing this in mind then, there is a need to discuss further the tribute of Hezekiah.

Neither the Assyrian text nor the biblical text relates that Hezekiah left his city to present his tribute. It is therefore certain that he sent his tribute without him being involved in the humiliating action of presenting himself to Sennacher-

---

364 Vuk, *Wiedererkaufte*, 47–8.
365 Tadmor, *Tiglath-pileser III*, 275.

ib. 2 Kgs 18:14a says that he negotiated with Sennacherib in Lachish, while the Assyrian text says nothing about this. Whether or not to accept that there was negotiation, or to assume that Sennacherib received tribute in Lachish, is not based on solid ground. The other invasion reports do not show any interest in mentioning the place of the paying of the tribute. One can safely conclude then that Hezekiah's tribute does not convey the same impression of being a submission tribute as the others do; to call it a submission tribute without qualifying this in some way is not correct.

What is worth noting in Vuk's discussion is that he considers Hezekiah's tribute to be a tribute of submission. He assumes that every instance of tribute has to fit one mould or another and misses the fact that many kings exercise political expediency. On the one hand, Vuk's argument could be understandable given the fact that the biblical texts are scarce and do not give much information about the circumstances of the paying of the submission tribute. On the other hand, reading the text in 2 Kgs 18:14 – 15 in isolation is not helpful. If Hezekiah's tribute is a submission tribute according to the biblical norms, it is not the same in the Assyrian norms. What is it then? Obviously it is not a punishment tribute because Sennacherib did not enter Jerusalem. Nor is it a favour tribute, because there is no third party involved. Is it therefore to be called a submission tribute, given the fact that it was imposed on Hezekiah and he was obliged to pay it? This could hardly be the case because, as mentioned above, a submission tribute does not allow for the terms to be demanded. Perhaps it was simply the ordinary annual tribute a vassal should pay? This is implausible—it was much larger than that. Before saying the last word on this matter, a further point needs to be made.

If we consider the note about Sennacherib moving from Lachish to Libnah as it is narrated in 2 Kgs 19:8, new light can be shed on Hezekiah's tribute. The historical reliability of the prophetic narrative in 2 Kgs 18:17– 19:37 is not to be considered in this stage of the work. In fact, whether it is reliable or not, there is no reason to doubt the note about Libnah, given the fact that Sennacherib conquered a remarkable number of Judean cities and settlements.[366] This means that the correspondence between Sennacherib and Hezekiah in Lachish (if it really happened) did not affect Sennacherib's decision to invade the land and cause the destruction. This supports my conclusion drawn above that

---

366 See Rainey, A.F., "The Fate of Lachish during the Campaigns of Sennacherib and Nebuchadnezzar", in Y. Aharoni (ed.), *Investigations at Lachish: The Sanctuary and* Residency (Lachish V) (Tel Aviv, 1975), 53.

there was in fact no tribute paid in Lachish. The reference to Lachish in 2 Kgs 18:14 then is not intended to convey that a tribute was paid in Lachish.

Thus, accepting the assumption that Sennacherib received Hezekiah's tribute in Nineveh seems the more reasonable option. This is in harmony with the discussion in the first part of the research about Hezekiah's tribute, according to which I concluded that Hezekiah paid his tribute after Sennacherib returned to Nineveh.[367] In this case, Hezekiah's tribute cannot be described as just a submission tribute paid to Sennacherib to return from Judah; instead, it is a tribute paid to appease Sennacherib who found himself in a situation wherein he was obliged to accept the tribute and not to go back to Judah.

5. Conclusion to chapter five

The study in this chapter was motivated by some scholars' assumption (which is mainly based on 2 Kgs 18:13–16) that Sennacherib returned to Nineveh because he accepted the large tribute that Hezekiah offered. The main thing this study sets out to prove is that the text does not necessarily indicate that Hezekiah paid tribute and then Sennacherib returned, and accordingly concludes that—historically speaking—the tribute was not the reason why Sennacherib returned to Nineveh. The literary analysis first leads us to conclude that v. 13 expresses in general what happened during the campaign. It could equally serve to introduce the episode of the paying of the tribute (2 Kgs 18:14–16) and the prophetic narrative (2 Kgs 18:17–19:37). Both accounts need it. This might indicate that v. 13 is a late addition to the whole narrative inserted as a frame by an editor, who combined the tribute episode and the prophetic narrative. Second, literary analysis of v. 14 leads us to conclude that although it is difficult to comment decisively on the verse, it is somewhat easier to agree with scholarly conclusions that the quotation within the verse is likely to be taken from a correspondence between Sennacherib and Hezekiah. In this vein, I particularly seek to draw attention to the literary devices used in v. 14, especially the internal focalisation. Through this, one can identify another theme in the text other than the connection between Sennacherib's return and the paying of the tribute. Thus, vv. 15 and 16 have an annalistic nature and they could reflect an annalistic document.

Although the main point in 2 Kgs 18:(13)14–16 is the tribute, the context within which this theme is expressed tells us that the text has not been excerpted from an annalistic document as one unit. This study, therefore, takes the view

---

367 See section 4.3.4.3

that there was another report behind the present text. Whether or not that text says that Hezekiah paid the tribute and then Sennacherib withdrew is something we cannot know. What is clear is that the assumption that the text in 2 Kgs 18:13 – 16 says that Sennacherib returned because of the large tribute from Hezekiah is not valid.

Moreover, my conclusion is not only based on studying the rhetoric of the story but also on other significant issues. The fact that the text does not end with a regular note about Sennacherib's return causes some doubts about whether the tribute was really the reason Sennacherib returned.

Thus, the forgoing literary analysis helps us to see more than one layer in 2 Kgs 18:13 – 16. Although vv. 14 – 15 and v. 16 seem to belong to an earlier hand,[368] it is possible that they were not taken as a unit. In other words, this literary analysis reveals something about the historical setting of the text. The text as it is shows the attack was because Hezekiah was perceived to have done wrong to Sennacherib. Also, the text lacks any theological comment on the event. From this, one can conclude that the best environment for the text is within the official records. As for its dating, the rather dry portrait of Hezekiah suggests it existed before the prophetic narrative. Also, it is important to mention that the historical reliability of the text should be considered with caution. If the quotation in v. 14 is taken from correspondence between the two fighting kings, and vv. 15 – 16 have certain annalistic features, that does not mean that they are excerpts from annalistic documents. In other words, the note about Hezekiah's confession could be historically reliable, and the note about paying the tribute could also be authentic. However, even if this is the case, that does not mean that the text in 2 Kgs 18:13 – 16 relates the fact that Sennacherib returned to his city because Hezekiah paid him tribute.

---

368 At least according to the material available to the editor in the temple library. See Na'aman, "Temple", 134.

Chapter Six: Three Different Reasons for Sennacherib's Return in the Prophetic Narrative in 2 Kgs 18:17 – 19:37

1. Introduction

Our investigation so far has led us to conclude that Hezekiah did pay a heavy tribute, although the circumstances surrounding the paying of that tribute are not very clear. I concluded that the paying of the tribute was not the reason why Sennacherib returned to Nineveh. 2 Kgs 18:17 ff. continues to narrate some details of what happened when Sennacherib attacked Judah and turned his attention to Jerusalem. Within this account, some essential elements of the event are unfolded and the note about Sennacherib's return is mentioned repeatedly in 19:7, 28, 33, and 36. Nevertheless, there is no way to associate Sennacherib's return with any particular reason with any certainty. When the prophet Isaiah relays the oracle of salvation (19:7), in which he declares that Sennacherib shall return due to his hearing a rumour, the reader expects that this is the end of the war. However, after that oracle, the reader is informed that Sennacherib progresses in his aggressive campaign to go on to conquer another Judean city. Moreover, after hearing about the advance of the Egyptian-Kushite army (19:9a), the reader might think that this is the reason that Sennacherib's invasion of the land comes to a halt and causes him to return. However, the reader is then informed that Sennacherib sends an intimidating letter to Hezekiah (19:9b–13). Only at the end, rather abruptly, is the reader informed that the Angel of the Lord appeared and smote the Assyrian army and that this is what caused Sennacherib to return to his city (19:35).

Thus, the salient question is: what made Sennacherib return to Nineveh? If his return is attributed to the act of the Angel of the Lord (or rather the plague that this denotes), how are we to understand the other two notes about the rumour and the Egyptian-Kushite aid? Are these notes redundant? Do they have any historical reliability? How come they are preserved in the story then? If, on the other hand, Sennacherib's return is not attributed to the act of the Angel of the Lord, which one of the other two reasons is more probable in relation to Sennacherib's return? In this part of the research these questions will be discussed at length. However, before this investigation, some points need to be discussed and clarified.

First of all, we have to admit that the text in the prophetic narrative (2 Kgs 18:17–19:37) is drenched in theology. Therefore, elements in the story that are related to our discussion should be interpreted before they are employed in a historical reconstruction. After all, the notes about Sennacherib's return are given within a particular literary form, which should be considered when dealing with the historicity of these notes.

I agree with Seitz, who asserts that "There is no question that Isa 36 – 37, as it presently stands, is a composite work derived from a traditional process whose precise character is a matter for reasoned speculation. It is not a work authored in a single sitting, or by an eyewitness concerned with reporting "what really happened" in some objective sense."[369] In this statement, Seitz aptly summarises many of the prevalent opinions about the compositional nature of the narrative, starting from Stade right through to the most recent studies made on the text of 2 Kgs 18 – 19.[370] Nevertheless, the work in this research is not concerned with the compositional or redactional nature of the whole prophetic narrative (2 Kgs 18:17– 19:37), as was indeed mentioned in the introduction. Whether or not the text is one unit is not going to be discussed at length in this work. Much effort has been expended on this classic problem, and there is no reason for me to replicate these processes.[371] However, the arguments that such effort yielded are going to be of great help in this investigation. Moreover, I agree with the general consensus that the prophetic narrative evidently consists of distinct parts.[372] Nevertheless, I prefer to be cautious and not to support any of the theories that decide about the beginning and end of each part. In other words, it is not easy to decide the parameters of each part in the complex. For example, it is not possible to decide without speculation where the first confrontation between Sennacherib's officials and Hezekiah's officials ends. Does it end with 2 Kgs 19:8[373] or 19:9a[374] or perhaps with 19:36 – 37? Moreover, it is obvious that the story —despite the fact that it is composed of more than one part—has only one end. Only in 19:36 – 37 is the reader told that Sennacherib actually returned and was killed in his city. But the text does not say explicitly if that happened because of the rumour, the advance of the Egyptian army or because of the annihilation of the Assyrian army by the Angel.

---

369 Seitz, *Zion's*, 94.

370 See Young, R.A., *Hezekiah in History and Tradition* (VTSup 155; Leiden, 2012).

371 See Song-Mi, *Development*.

372 de Jong, M.J., *Isaiah among the Ancient Near Eastern Prophets. A Comparative Study of the Earliest Stages of the Isaiah Tradition and the New-Assyrian Prophecies* (VTSup 117; Leiden, 2007), 361.

373 As is the claim in Laato, A., *Who Is Immanuel? The Rise and the Foundering of Isaiah's Messianic Expectations* (Åbo, 1988), 283 – 288.

374 Childs, *Crisis*, 73 – 94; and Gonçalves, *L'expedition*, 373 – 444.

As for the date of the text (as we have it now) and where it was written, this too is not a topic that is going to be elaborated upon here. In any case, there are some literary features that preclude dating the text too closely to 701.[375] So, in line with the general consensus, I agree that the text was written at some distance from 701. However, that does not mean I see the story as purely an invention of the Deuteronomist or as a legend. On the contrary, I argue that the events narrated in 2 Kgs 18:17–19:37 have their roots firmly in what happened in 701. However, an author/composer made use of these events to convey a theme that he found ideal for the audience of his time. The events of 701 were therefore apparently used to portray Hezekiah as the ideal pious king.

Having said that, it is time to return to the three notes about Sennacherib's return to his city, which are recorded in the report of what happened in 701. The immediate context in which the notes are given will be examined. The study focuses on the historicity of the texts and conclusions will be drawn accordingly. As a result, although we will not obtain an objective history, we will nevertheless be able to make some tentative proposals in that vein.

Methodologically, since the three notes are in the context of the prophetic narrative, they will be dealt with in three separate sections. In the first section, the note about the rumour will be studied. The oracle of salvation in 2 Kgs 19:6–7 in which Isaiah prophesises about the rumour will be scrutinised. The aim of this section is to understand the nature of the rumour and the circumstances in which it is narrated. Therefore, literary analysis will be applied to the text in order to be able to decide about the meaning of the oracle and whether there is a possibility that the rumour is the reason for Sennacherib's return. The second section will be about the Egyptian-Kushite aid that is narrated in 2 Kgs 19:9, and the role of the Kushite army in 701 will be examined. The aim is to decide whether or not their role was significant in that year. Next, the third section will be about the story of the Angel of the Lord in 2 Kgs 19:35. Of course, the story is theology more than history but that does not preclude the idea that this story might have a historical kernel. So, investigations into this matter will be worthwhile. In its methodological approach, the study in chapter six will be similar to chapter five. Literary analysis will help us understand the texts. The discussion, I should say, will be directed toward examining the historicity of these texts in order to know what the reason was behind Sennacherib's odd behaviour. After investigating the nature of the rumour, the role of the Kushites in 701, and the meaning of the story of the Angel of the Lord, we will thus be able to weigh the evidence and discern what is the most reasonable explanation for Sennacherib's return.

---

375 Seitz, *Zion's*, 96.

2. Section One: The Note about the Rumour in 2 Kgs 19:6–7

2.1. Introduction

2 Kgs 19:7 relates that Isaiah prophesies that the Lord will put a spirit in Senna-cherib to cause him to hear a rumour and return to his land, and there the Lord will have him killed. Not a small number of scholars, who think that the prophet-ic narrative is not a legend and has some historical reliability, have suggested that the rumour was the reason why Sennacherib did not conquer Jerusalem and went back to Nineveh without entering Jerusalem and dethroning Hezekiah, the rebel. However, opinions have varied about what the rumour was, because of the complexity surrounding the issue on both literary and historical levels. Re-gardless of what the rumour was about, arguments in favour of the originality of the note about the rumour have come under attack because of the assumption that the whole oracle in 2 Kgs 19:6–7 cannot be historically reliable, in view of it contradicting the picture of Isaiah in Isa 1–35, especially Isa 1:4–8 and Isa 22. Therefore, in my opinion, what causes the note about the rumour to be so par-ticularly difficult to deal with is the fact that it is given within the context of an oracle of salvation announced by the prophet Isaiah. Accordingly, when scholars studied the note about the rumour they focused more on the oracle of salvation, which contains the note about the rumour. This created a larger field to be studied and complicated the issues to be examined. In other words, the authenticity of the rumour came to be studied within the ambit of the au-thenticity of the oracle of salvation. The main question thus became whether Isaiah produced the oracle or not. If he did, how do we reconcile it with other oracles in Isa 1–35 where the prophet Isaiah is seen to take a different view about Hezekiah's policy? Therefore, scholars put a great deal of effort into prov-ing that Isaiah was not always against Hezekiah and his attitude was not always negative in regard to Jerusalem's deliverance (following Seitz).[376] On the other hand, some scholars have argued that the two pictures of Isaiah cannot be rec-onciled and thus the oracle of salvation in 2 Kgs 19:6–7 has come to be dis-missed as an insertion added later for the sake of propagandistic theology (in agreement with Clements).[377]

Before proceeding with the study, a word about Isaiah's attitude toward He-zekiah and Jerusalem is in order. Did Isaiah prophesy the rescue of Jerusalem or not? To start with a concrete fact, it is safe to say that Hezekiah's name is never

---

376 Seitz, *Zion's*, 75–80.
377 Clements, *Deliverance*, 50.

mentioned in the poetic oracles in Isa 1– 35. This means there is no way to know for certain that Hezekiah is the one who is condemned in these poetic oracles, although quite a few scholars have argued that this is the most plausible interpretation. Moreover, there are some texts in Isa 1– 35 which one cannot know for sure whether they are linked to 701 or not. Additionally, there are some texts where the reader finds Isaiah conmending the rulers of Judah, and some texts where Isaiah is found to be against the Assyrians and predicts their failure in attacking Judah. This has allowed some scholars to use some texts to prove Isaiah's pessimistc attitude toward the Judeans and Hezekiah (Isa 1:4 – 8; 22; 30; 31), while other scholars have used other texts to prove Isaiah's optimistic attitude toward the people of Judah (Isa 10:16; 29:1 – 8; 30:27 – 33; 31:1 – 9), and argued that Isaiah could have envisaged that God would deliver Zion, in keeping with the Zion tradition found in Ps 46, 48, and 76.[378] Other scholars, however, stand in the middle and assume that Isaiah's response to Hezekiah in 2 Kgs 19:6 – 7 should be read in light of Hezekiah's prayer and proverb in 2 Kgs 19:3 – 4. Thus, it is possible that Isaiah changed his approach and prophesied the rescue of Jerusalem after seeing Hezekiah's changed attitude.[379]

The problem is more complicated than appears at first sight. To decide which text can be related to 701 is a task that demands going through the book of Isaiah to sift out the secondary from the primary materials and discern which parts of First Isaiah can be dated to the Assyrian period and particularly to the 701 event. Being selective and studying only some texts in order to decide about Isaiah's attitude during the period when Jerusalem was blockaded is not to build on solid ground. Therefore, in order to do the biblical texts justice more thorough study should be undertaken bearing in mind the different themes in Isaiah's prophecies: the Davidic dynasty, the Judeans, and Jerusalem.

In other words, we cannot say a *priori* (a) that certain texts are definitely the words of Isaiah of Jerusalem, (b) that his authentic words demonstrate a consistently negative attitude on his part towards Hezekiah, (c) that a negative attitude towards Hezekiah precludes a negative attitude towards the Assyrians, and (d) that texts which manifest a negative attitude towards the Assyrians must therefore be inauthentic. Nor do we know in detail the complete set of events that took place during the whole ministry of Isaiah of Jerusalem, so as to be able to relate a particular text with certainty to the events of 701 and no other year. The judg-

---

378 Day, J., *God's Conflict with the Dragon and the Sea. Echoes of a Canaanite Myth in the Old Testament* (Cambridge, 1985), 88 – 139.

379 Darr K.P., "No Strength to Deliver: A Contextual Analysis of Hezekiah's Proverb in Isaiah 37:3b", in R.F. Melugin and M.A Sweeney (eds.), *New Visions of Isaiah* (JSOTSup 214; Sheffield 1996), 232 – 245.

ment as to which texts are the authentic words of Isaiah of Jerusalem, and which are added later, must be made in a complex interaction with other judgments about the sequence of events and the attitudes of the people involved. It is not necessary—in fact it is not possible —to reach absolute certainty about the correct attribution of words presented as Isaiah's in Isaiah and in 2 Kings, before investigating the historical events of 701. Therefore I may proceed with evaluating the historicity of the explanations that have been offered for Sennacherib's return from blockading Jerusalem. I shall of course consult some texts about which there is a widespread consensus, such as Isa 1:4–8. But I shall not focus on Isaiah's attitude towards Hezekiah and Jerusalem. Rather, I hope the fruits of my investigation might contribute to more detailed studies of his attitude, of whether it changed in the course of his ministry, and of how it related to his attitude towards Assyria which, despite being "the rod of God's anger", could still be condemned for arrogance and cruelty.

Since what is said about the rumour is very much connected with the oracle of salvation, in the present study I suggest another way of approaching this oracle and thus drawing a conclusion about the authenticity of the rumour. First of all, I shall investigate what the text in 2 Kgs 19:6–7 is telling us, its meaning, its context and its function within the narrative. A careful critical reading of the text will eventually help us tease out a conclusion about the historicity of the text in general and the rumour in particular. The main question the investigation should lead us to answer is: does the oracle in 2 Kgs 19:6–7 provide an explanation for Sennacherib's unexpected behaviour? The question of what the rumour was about should, in my view, thus be deferred to a later stage in this study during the investigation of the role of the Kushite army in 701 and the story of the angel of the Lord.

Methodologically, this section proceeds as follows. The function of the oracle will be treated first. Next, a thorough literary analysis will be carried out on the oracle, wherein the literary features of the text, its form, syntax, and meaning, will be scrutinised. The aim of this investigation is to decide about the date and the compositional nature of the text in 2 Kgs 19:6–7. This will then eventually enable us to draw our conclusions regarding the historicity of the note about the rumour. It is important to mention briefly that the sign that Isaiah gives to Hezekiah in 2 Kgs 19:29–31 is connected with the oracle and will thus be investigated as well.

2.2 The function of the oracle within the narrative

Structurally, the note about the rumour is placed in the middle of the narrative; between the first (oral) message of Sennacherib and his second (written) message. After Rabshakeh's intimidation of Hezekiah and the Jerusalemites who were standing at the wall of the city in 2 Kgs 18:19 – 25; 18:27 – 35, the text directs attention to the attitude of the people and Hezekiah's officials in 18:36 – 37. Regarding Jerusalem, the text relates the attitude of Hezekiah in 19:1 – 5; being agitated by the news, he sends messengers to the prophet Isaiah asking him to raise his petition to the Lord for the sake of the remnant. In 19:6 – 7, Isaiah utters an oracle of salvation in which the note about the rumour is related. After that, in 19:8 the scene changes to take the reader again outside the walls to narrate the return of the Rabshakeh to Sennacherib in Lachish. The note about Tirhakah is given in 19:9a; and then in 19:9b-13 the text relates the second message of Sennacherib. Immediately, in 19:14 – 9 the reader hears the prayer of Hezekiah. Without any notice about sending messengers to Isaiah, in 19:20 – 34 the prophet utters three oracles in answer to Hezekiah's prayer. After the oracles, in 19:35 the note about the Angel of the Lord is given, and in 19:36 – 37 the note about Sennacherib's return and his murder by his sons are narrated.

It is obvious that what is narrated in 2 Kgs 19:6 – 7 is fulfilled at the very end of the narrative in 2 Kgs 19:36 – 37. Whether the retardation of fulfilling the oracle is attributed to narrative technique (K.A.D. Smelik)[380] or to the assumption that different sources have been compiled into one is something that has been debated for a long time. It is not the task of this study to consider this matter further. For now it is sufficient to declare that, regardless of whether the prophetic narrative is one unit or more, the function of the information given in 2 Kgs 19:6 – 7 is not necessarily affected. It is clear that the story does not end with the rumour note but develops further, with the tension inherent in the event rising and creating suspense for the reader. The question arising from this is what, given the fact that the war did not finish after Isaiah's oracle, the function of the oracle in the narrative actually is. From the content of the oracle one can safely conclude that it declares the end of the war and the way Sennacherib is going to leave Jerusalem and go back to his city. More than that, information about his death (by sword) is also provided. However, the oracle does not say exactly when that would happen. Therefore, whether the narrative is one unit or more

---

380 Smelik, K.A.D., "Distortion of Old Testament Prophecy. The Purpose of Isaiah xxxvi and xxxvii", in A.S. van der Woude (ed.), *Crisis and Perspective. Studies in Ancient Near Eastern Polytheism, Biblical Theology, Palestinian Archaeology and Intertestamental Literature* (OS 24; Leiden, 1985), 74 – 84.

does not affect the function of the oracle. In any case, it foretells the way the war will finish and the fate of Sennacherib. Accordingly, we cannot assume that the place of the oracle within the narrative is confusing; neither can we assume that the rumour is not the reason why Sennacherib withdrew because the events (i. e. sending the written message to Hezekiah) continue in the narrative.

2.3. The literary analysis of 2 Kgs 19:6 – 7

Applying literary analysis to Isaiah's response to Hezekiah helps us read the text closely and carefully, so that we may be able to discern its meaning and the compositional nature of this brief message. Therefore, in order to do justice to the text it is better to start by analysing the different expressions used in vv. 6 – 7. The insights offered by scholars are indispensible in this task; presenting their arguments and carefully discussing them will affect the way this study approaches the meaning and compositional process of the note about the rumour.

The text says:

ויאמר להם ישעיהו כה תאמרון אל אדניכם כה אמר יהוה אל תירא מפני הדברים אשר

שמעת אשר גדפו נערי מלך אשור אותי

הנני נתן בו רוח ושמע שמועה ושב לארצו והפלתיו בחרב בארצו

> And Isaiah said to them, "Thus you shall say to your lord, "Thus says the Lord: do not fear the
> words that you heard by which the servants of king of Assyria have rebuked me. Behold I am
> setting in him a spirit and he shall hear a rumour and he shall return to his land and shall be
> killed with sword."

As the discussion about the literary analysis of the text has more than one aspect, I divide this sub-section into categories in order to make the work more systematic.

2.3.1. The form of the oracle in 2 Kgs 19:6 – 7

As for the *form* of the message, because of the messenger formula ("Thus says the Lord") and the reassurance formula ("Do not fear"), followed by the announcement of salvation, scholars rightly agree that the genre of this prophecy is an oracle of salvation. Compare Ex 14:13 – 14; Josh 8:1 – 2; Isa 7:1 – 9; 2 Chr 20:1 –

17.[381] It announces an act of deliverance performed by God (putting His spirit in Sennacherib) and the retreat of the enemy, as well as the reason for that retreat—hearing a rumour. In other words, it displays how the end of the attack against Judah will transpire. When discussing the form of the oracle, scholars have not gone any further than deciding it is an oracle of salvation. After agreeing on its form, they immediately discuss the content of the oracle and find themselves obliged to face the difficulty of discussing Isaiah's different attitude in this oracle compared to other texts in Isa 1– 35. I hold that the discussion about form must go further. In this regard, Westermann can be of great help. He categorises this oracle as an oracle in a narrative context. These oracles are found in reports of a situation, and have specific features.[382] In Isa 1– 39, he distinguishes between "those found in the context of narrative and those which are transmitted in collections of the prophetic words."[383] For those that are in a narrative context, Westermann groups three stories in which Isaiah gives oracles of salvation: Isa 7; 37; 38. In all cases, the oracle is given in a threatening situation; it proclaims an act of deliverance by God accompanied by a sign.[384] This discussion reveals two significant points: first, if the oracle in 2 Kgs 19:6 – 7 belongs to a particular set of oracles which have a certain pattern, one may ask whether it is thus appropriate to compare it with other oracles in Isa 1– 35 to decide about its meaning and Isaiah's attitude. Secondly, if we accept that there is a pattern for such oracles, then it is obvious that the sign given by Isaiah in 2 Kgs 19:29 – 31 is connected to the oracle, and should therefore be considered a continuation of the oracle. As for the first point, it is likely that there was a tradition responsible for the three oracles of salvation (Isa 7; 37; 38). This tradition portrays Isaiah as having a positive attitude towards the deliverance of Jerusalem and the Davidic dynasty. As for the second point about the sign, I think it is important to include what is happening in 2 Kgs 19:29 – 31 in the discussion about the oracle. However, I defer this discussion until after I have discussed the nature of the oracle.

2.3.2. Syntax of the oracle

It is obvious that the oracle is presented as direct speech. God's message starts with an order given to Hezekiah not to fear the words that he had heard. Then,

---

381 Long, *Kings*, 220. Thus also Wildberger, *Jesaja*, 382; Sweeney, M.A., *Isaiah 1 – 39: With an Introduction to Prophetic Literature* (FOTL 16; Grand Rapids 1996), 468.
382 Westermann, C., *Prophetic Oracles of Salvation in the Old Testament* (London, 1991), 15.
383 Westermann, *Oracles*, 67.
384 Westermann, *Oracles*, 70.

with a second relative pronoun אשר, the text relates what kind of words Hezekiah is urged not to fear: the words with which the servants of the Assyrian king slandered God. However, some scholars assume that the second relative pronoun does not fit the sentence because it is unusual in Hebrew syntax.

In v. 7 there are four verbs connected with *waw*-consecutives. Two verbs express God's activities and the other two denote Sennacherib's activity. It is obvious that the issue is between God and Sennacherib. The activities of Sennacherib are reactions to God's initiatives. The non-verbal clause הנני נתן בו רוח is followed by a verb with a *waw*-consecutive. This means that the action is sequential and the translation of the verbs that follow should be '*I shall set in him a spirit and then he shall hear...he shall return...and I shall have him killed.*' The spirit then causes Sennacherib to hear about something, regardless of the authenticity of what Sennacherib hears. In any case, the phrase "*and he shall return*" is to be closely connected with what precedes, so that we are to understand the returning to Nineveh as a consequence of what Sennacherib hears.[385] To conclude, one can say that syntactically v. 7 is well formed and it gives the message that the meaning of the oracle is meant to be theological more than historical: the return and death of Sennacherib is attributed to God's action.

2.3.3. The date and compositional nature of 2 Kgs 19:6 – 7

As for the *meaning* of the text and its *unity*, scholars do not agree. Different arguments have been proposed for the unity of the text, its originality, historicity, and date. However, all these arguments focus on distinguishing what is theology from what is history in this text. In what follows, I present the different arguments offered by scholars who have interpreted this oracle while discussing in detail the structure and meaning of the oracle.

The efforts of German-speaking scholars stand out when it comes to the meaning of the oracle and its originality. There is common agreement that even if it is not the entire oracle, part of it belongs to the original stage of the narrative. Wildberger explains and supports this theory best, although he was not the first to hold such a position. First, he agrees with B. Duhm that the phrase in 2 Kgs 19:6b ("with which the rogues of the Assyrian king slandered me") is a later addition, because if the Rabshakeh was slandering God, then Hezekiah would have the opportunity to hope, not to fear.[386] Then, Wildberger argues that using the plural form נערי to refer to the speaker does not fit the con-

---

385 Young, E., *The Book of Isaiah: Volume 2, Chapters 19 – 39* (Grand Rapids, 1969), 476.
386 Duhm, B., *Das Buch Jesaia* (HKAT III/1; Göttingen, 1914), 239.

text; it was only the Rabshakeh who was speaking. The other point is the use of the word גדף instead of חרף. After consulting other biblical texts where the word occurs, Wildberger concludes that the word גדף is relatively late. Therefore, according to Wildberger and others, the concluding part of 2 Kgs 19:6b is taken to be a late addition. 2 Kgs 19:7, however, belongs to the original stage of the text.[387] To defend its originality, again Wildberger offers an explanation that embraces the common opinions about the meaning and originality of this verse. He strengthens his argument by comparing what is happening in v. 7 with other biblical texts. His discussion can be summarised as follows:

- First of all, he draws attention to other occasions in the Old Testament where a spirit causes delusion and confusion, mainly 1 Kgs 22:20 ff. Also, Wildberger recalls other texts where a spirit (from God) causes unrest and unexpected behaviour in the person it enters (1 Sam 16:14; Judg 9:23; Num 5:14; Isa 29:10; 19:14.
- As for the rumour, Wildberger considers it an act of the spirit, and it is not surprising that the rumour causes terror when a person is forced to receive the spirit, especially when comparing v. 7 with Isa 28:19. So, the rumour, which was caused by the spirit, caused terror in Sennacherib and made him act in a strange manner.
- As for the last part of v. 7, which contains the note about Sennacherib's death in his own land, Wildberger begins in a tentative way but then confirms his conclusion. He is aware of the fact that prophesying about Sennacherib's assassination could mean the phrase is an insertion. However, he argues that the fact that the note about Sennacherib's death does not say that he would be killed by his sons indicates its authenticity, as it does not precisely describe the exact way in which Sennacherib was going to be murdered.[388] In this, he also consults other biblical texts like 1 Kgs 14:10 – 14; 16:4; 21:24; Amos 7:11 and Jer 22:12 f.

One can safely say that, in Wildberger's reading, the similarity that v. 7 shares with other biblical texts supports its originality. Wildberger's discussion was welcomed by Camp, who concludes in his study that v. 7 belongs to the original part of the narrative.[389]

On the other hand, Würthwein has a different opinion about the oracle and considers it to be a late addition to the story. However, he does not support his

---

387 Wildbereger, *Jesaja*, 1410. See also Kaiser, O., *Isaiah 13 – 39. A Commentary* (OTL; London, 1974), 383.
388 Wildberger, *Jesaja*, 1411.
389 Camp, *Hiskijabild*, 157.

argument with a thorough critical analysis of the text, briefly arguing that the unexpected liberation of Jerusalem and Sennacherib's assassination in his city inspired the Deuteronomist to edit the prophet's announcement. Thus, the unexpected return of Sennacherib was interpreted as an act of the Lord.[390]

It is obvious that the scholars whose opinions are presented above thought that the text in 2 Kgs 19:6–7 grew in stages and some of it was added at a later stage of this growth. However, there is agreement that v. 7 is authentic and reflects historical reality: Isaiah announces the withdrawal of Sennacherib because of a rumour and his death in his own land. However, this assumption needs further scrutiny. In what follows, I again read the text in vv. 6–7 and provide an argument different from those which have been suggested so far. In my discussion I use the same methodology Wildberger used to come to a different conclusion about the originality of vv. 6–7.

First of all, I agree with the scholarly consensus that the second part of v. 6 (the note about slandering God) is later. However, I use Dubovsky's argument about the verb גדף to prove that this part of the oracle is connected with the end of it (end of v. 7). Dubovsky argues that using the verb גדף radically changes the interpretation of Assyrian behaviour. According to Num 15:30–31, the verb גדף indicates a crime that must be punished by death.[391] So, Sennacherib blasphemed and that is why he deserves to die. One may conclude that the note about slandering God is thus well connected with the note about Sennacherib's death.

As for the meaning of the word רוח, it is understandable that Wildberger refers to other texts; there are several references in the Old Testament to particular types of spirit. As mentioned in the discussion above, there is an evil spirit that disturbs and torments a person (1 Sam 16:14,16,23; 18:10; 19:9), and a lying spirit who entices a person (1 Kgs 22:22; 2 Chr 18:21). Moreover, there is also a spirit of deep sleep that seals the eyes of the prophets so they cannot see (Isa 29:10) and a spirit of dizziness that makes the person stagger.[392] In all these texts the way the spirit acts within a person is explained; the reader knows what kind of spirit it is and what its characteristics are. To shed further light on this, let us again look at the example most often used by scholars, i.e. 1 Kgs 22:20ff. The text, as one reads it simply, relates a story about God and the angels in heaven. The Lord asks who can entice Ahab; and a spirit responds that he is able to entice Ahab by making Ahab's prophets prophesy lies. So, the text is clear on the role of the spirit: it

---

390 Würthwein, *Bücher*, 424–425.
391 Dubovsky, "Assyrian downfall", 10.
392 Wildgerger, *Jesaja*, 1411.

makes a person give false prophecy and, eventually, Ahab believes it. Whether this is original or not is not the task of this study to conclude. But it is clear that explaining what is happening in 2 Kgs 19:7 by comparing it to 1 Kgs 22:20 ff is not helpful. The spirit that the Lord puts in Sennacherib in v. 7 is not identified. It is not clear whether it is a lying or enticing or agitating spirit. It says that the spirit will make Sennacherib hear a rumour. Such a note is not common in the Bible. The text does not say that a spirit will make others declare a rumour, which Sennacherib will then hear and go home. The act of the sprit, according to the text, is within Sennacherib himself. Therefore, I see difficulty in connecting the role of the spirit within Sennacherib to the hearing of the rumour. Some scholars have tried to solve the problem by explaining the note about the spirit as indicating the emotional turmoil inside Sennacherib. Montgomery refers to Ezek. 2:2; 3:12, 14 to suggest that the spirit in 2 Kgs 19:7 is "the uncanny pre-sentiment of evil, hardly personified."[393] Other scholars assume that v. 7 indicates a sort of unrest in the psyche of Sennacherib that would cause him to return to his city.[394] This interpretation, I think, complicates the matter unnecessarily. If we accept that the note about the spirit refers to some unrest inside Sennacherib, then one would need to ask how that could be connected with the rumour. Before moving on, a further word about the rumour is due.

The word שמועה is no less ambiguous. It is not said in the text what Sennacherib would hear. The word שמועה, despite the several occurrences in the Bible, does not refer to a lie or unrealistic fact; it simply means a 'report' or 'news'.[395] However, as Wildberger argues, it could cause terror when it is unexpected, and the hearer could behave oddly. This could lead us to conclude that the text relates that Sennacherib was agitated by the rumour, more than by the spirit. To conclude this discussion about the spirit and the rumour, I argue that there is some clumsiness in the text that makes it difficult to connect the spirit with the rumour.

As the reader continues with the text in v. 7, a note about Sennacherib's death is given. With this piece of information the reader knows that the aim of the oracle is not limited to relating only the end of the attack, but also the death of Sennacherib himself. It is obvious that with the note about Sennacherib's death the oracle goes beyond answering Hezekiah's request about saving Jerusalem. Since Sennacherib died 20 years later, one can thus conclude that the whole of v. 7 is a later addition.[396]

---

393 Montgomery, *Commentary*, 491.
394 Oswalt, J.N., *The Book of Isaiah. Chapters 1 – 39* (NICOT; Grand Rapids, 1986), 647.
395 *HALOT*, שמועה, 1555 – 1556.
396 Kaiser, *Isaiah*, 391.

To sum up my discussion about the unity and originality of 2 Kgs 19:6–7, I argue that it is far from certain that the text is a unit that goes back to the historical Isaiah. As has been demonstrated above, the note about slandering God and Sennacherib's death are connected to each other. I conclude, then, that both belong to the same hand. And since the note about Sennacherib's assassination is later—at least 20 years after the attack—this means that Sennacherib's attack was considered a blasphemy that required death according to the law. Whether these two notes stem from the same hand responsible for the note about the spirit and Sennacherib's return is not clear; it is possible that they were added later.

Anyway, the difficulty in connecting the act of the spirit with hearing the rumour on the one hand, and connecting Sennacherib's death with his return on the other, does not support the assumption that the oracle was original and composed at an early stage of the narrative. More likely, the note about the rumour and the return belong to an earlier stage of the original story, while the note about slandering God and Sennacherib's death were added later.

2.4. Historical reliability of 2 Kgs 19:6–7

Having decided that the text in 2 Kgs 19:6–7 is not original and has undergone a compositional process, one must concede nonetheless that this does not mean that the oracle does not reflect any historical reality. It is quite possible that a later compiler should have drawn on historical material when making his interpolations. There is good reason to think that the mention of a rumour in the oracle is an instance of such a historically accurate interpolation. The oracle consists of three elements: the putting of a spirit into Sennacherib, his hearing of a rumour, and his death in Nineveh. The first element can be explained without implying historical accuracy; the compiler introduces the spirit in order to attribute Sennacherib's unexpected return and death to divine intervention—this is a typical *theologoumenon*, a theological interpretation of a historical event. Of the other two elements the latter, Sennacherib's death in his land, we know to be historical. It is therefore reasonable to suppose that the compiler's reason for including it is to offer an acceptable interpretation of historical events. The remaining element, the rumour Sennacherib is supposed to hear, still requires explanation. There are two motivations which we can, with confidence, attribute to the compiler on the grounds of the other two elements of the oracle: introducing a theological explanation for Sennacherib's return and death, and giving a historical account of those events. Of these only the latter can reasonably be supposed to explain the comment concerning the rumour. This is because the claim that Sennacherib will hear a rumour is both (a) difficult to understand as a act of divine intervention related to the spirit mentioned, and (b) redundant for the purposes of giving a theological explanation, since the claim concerning the spirit achieves this already. Therefore the most parsimonious account of the intentions of the compiler must attribute the mention of the rumour to the motivation of giving a historical account. The only other option would be to postulate a third independent reason for the mention of the rumour; as said above, such a postulation is redundant. Therefore I suggest that the rumour belongs to what historically happened in 701. There was a rumour and Sennacherib's performance in the land of Judah was affected by this rumour. The author of the story wanted to connect this rumour to God, and hence introduced the note about the spirit. Then, the story took another shape. Sennacherib returns because of a rumour that was caused by God. The end of the attack, then, is attributed to God; not to the rumour. In this regard, the interpretation of the note about the spirit as indicating God's intervention is reasonable.[397]

If it is true, as I argue, that the rumour is the historical reason for Sennacherib's return, the content of that rumour will be of significant historical interest. However, seeking to know the content of the rumour will require further investigation. Much effort has been employed in attempting to explain the rumour. Some scholars assume that the rumour is about the advance of the Egyptian-Kushite army.[398] This is because of the note recorded in 2 Kgs 19:8 – 9 about Tirhakah. Other scholars, however, think that the rumour has something to do with political unrest in Assyria or Babylonia.[399] Wildberger, however, asserts that the content of the rumour cannot be known.[400] In my opinion, the matter needs more work to give a possible solution. I defer that for later.

2.5. The sign given by Isaiah in 2 Kgs 19: 29 – 31

As mentioned above, giving a sign is a way of confirming the content of an oracle.[401] Therefore, in this part of the study the sign that Isaiah gave to Heze-

---

397 Cogan, however, refers to 1 Kgs 22:20 – 23 to conclude that the spirit indicates a divine intervention that would make Sennacherib behave unexpectedly. See Cogan and Tadmor, *II Kings*, 234. Blenkinsopp reads v. 7 in the light of 1 Sam 16:14 – 16,23; 18:10; 19:9 – 10 and suggests that God will put an evil spirit in Sennacherib as He did with Saul to bring about his end. See Blenkinsopp, *Isaiah*, 475.
398 Watts, J.D.W., *Isaiah 34 – 66* (WBC 25; Dallas, 2002), 35.
399 Kaiser, *Isaiah*, 378.
400 Wildberger, *Jesaja*, 1410.
401 See above 2.3.1.

kiah is examined to see how much it further contributes to our exploration of what happened in 701. Before going deeper into the critical analysis, a word about how this sign is connected to the oracle of salvation in 2 Kgs 19:6–7 is in order. One can see that structurally and thematically the sign is at some distance from the oracle, but this problem can be explained.

As it is made clear, 2 Kgs 19:29–31 describes a sign given by the prophet Isaiah to Hezekiah. The sign is located almost at the end of the narrative about Sennacherib, where the role of Isaiah is very prominent in scenes leading up to the end of the narrative. After Sennacherib sends two messages to Hezekiah (2 Kgs 18:18–35; 19:10–13), the latter prays (2 Kgs 19:14–19). The prophet Isaiah afterwards sends an answer to Hezekiah's prayer, which consists of a series of three oracular responses: a taunt poem (2 Kgs 19:21–28), a sign (2 Kgs 19:29–31) and a prophecy (2 Kgs 19:32–34). After Isaiah's answer, the narrative concludes with the Angel of the Lord smiting the Assyrian army (2 Kgs 19:35) and Sennacherib's withdrawal to Nineveh (2 Kgs 19:36–37).

Structurally, 2 Kgs 19:29–31 seems distinct from the poem that precedes it because of its different literary genre and linguistic character. Whereas the poem has a threatening flavour towards Assyria, the sign is more comforting to Israel.[402] Furthermore, vv. 29–31 appear to be distinct from the prophecy that follows because of the change in the theme, with vv. 29–31 describing a sign of the survival of a remnant from the house of Judah and vv. 32–34 relating an oracle that predicts the immediate deliverance of Jerusalem and Sennacherib's return to his city. One can conclude that the sign in 2 Kgs 19:29–31 does not connect structurally with its immediate context. It is therefore possible to assume that the sign was removed from its original place within the narrative in the process of composition.

As for the thematic point, what the sign contains does not seem to be connected with the oracle. While the oracle speaks about a rumour, the sign (as was mentioned above) speaks about eating and planting. Comparing this sign with the other two signs that Isaiah gives in chapters 7 and 38, one can realise that the sign does not necessarily reflect the content of the oracle. The giving birth of the young woman in Isa 7:14 does not seem to be connected with what the oracle announces about the kings of Aram and Israel in Isa 7:7–8. In the same way, the sign about the shadow in Isa 38:8 does not seem to be connected with what the oracle relates about Hezekiah's healing in 38:4–6.

Thus, one can conclude that any assumptions about the disconnection between the oracle in 2 Kgs 19:6–7 and the sign in 2 Kgs 19:29–31 on structural

---

402 Young, *Isaiah*, 497.

and thematic grounds are not valid. On this basis then, the study proceeds to investigate whether or not vv. 29–31 are inserted and how much they reflect the events of 701. I will start with a literary analysis focusing on the meaning of the verses regardless of their date, before exploring how they relate to the context.

2.5.1. Literary analysis of 2 Kings 19:29–31
My analysis begins with a close reading of v. 29, which describes the sign.

2.5.1.1. Analysis of v. 29
וזה לך האות אכול השנה ספיח ובשנה השנית סחיש ובשנה השלישית זרעו וקצרו ונטעו כרמים

ואכלו פרים

And this is for you the sign, you shall eat this year what grows of itself, and in the second year what springs of the same, and in the third year sow and reap and plant vineyards and eat their fruit.[403]

The sign concerns what people are going to eat for the two years during which there will be no sowing or planting; only in the third year shall people sow, plant vineyards and eat their fruit. The language of the sign is not straightforward and some expressions make understanding this verse difficult. For example, the Hebrew word used for eating (אכול) is in the infinitive absolute and thus does not indicate a certain tense or the person to whom the sign is given; the word could mean 'you (sg. or pl.) shall/may/should eat...' despite the fact that the first pronoun in the verse is in the second person, which indicates Hezekiah, as from the context of the verse we know that Hezekiah and his people are involved in the sign. Moreover, the two words used in the text for what people shall eat do not appear regularly in the Bible. The word סחיש is a *hapax legomenon* and its meaning is derived from the context. *HALOT* defines it as "self-seeded plant 'growing by itself after the harvest of the second year.'"[404] The word ספיח occurs only three times in the Bible outside the context of Sennacherib's campaign against Judah; twice in Leviticus (25:5, 11) and once in Job (14:19). *HALOT* gives different meanings of the word for the two occurrences. In Leviticus (and in

---

403 Concerning textual criticism, the text has some minor problems, especially in relation to the last series of imperative verbs. While 2 Kgs 19:29 has the last verb in imperative form, Isaiah 37:30 has the verb in the infinitive absolute, although this variant does not change the meaning of the text.
404 *HALOT*, סחיש, 749.

2 Kgs 19:29; Is 37:30), ספיח means 'second growth' and is glossed with "what has not been sown in the Sabbath year grows subsequently from seed which has fallen aside." For Job, however, *HALOT* suggests the conjectural reading of סחיפה,[405] perhaps because the first meaning does not fit in the context.[406]

Thus, from the verse one can understand that the Judeans will not undertake their normal agricultural activities for two years; otherwise they would not have eaten what grows by itself, regardless of what kind of plant is meant. It should be noted that the text does not say why people are not undertaking agricultural activities. Is it because they were not able to resume normal work because of Sennacherib's presence in the area or is it for an unrelated reason? The text alone does not allow one to answer this question with confidence.

Most of the scholars who have discussed these verses have focused their attention on dealing with the problem concerning the connection between the immediate deliverance and the predicted length of time the sign will be fulfilled (three years). In other words, the main question is: if Sennacherib withdrew immediately, why could people not sow for two years? A few scholars argue that Sennacherib withdrew and people did not sow seeds because of the destruction the Assyrian army caused in the area. However, people did not starve because divine providence ensured that the after-growth was so abundant that it sufficed for two years.[407] Others have suggested that the duration of time involved could be much shorter than three years, being instead only fourteen to fifteen months if one assumes that the prediction comes at the end of the first year of occupation.[408] Others have argued that the two years of suffering were due to the Assyrian presence in the area.[409] Some scholars, on the other hand, have doubted whether the sign is really in its original context and preferred to consid-

---

405 *HALOT* ספיח, 764. See also Gordis, R., *The Book of Job* (CNTSS; New York, 1978), 151. The meaning of the word סחיפה suggested in this book is "torrent or downpour."

406 It is worth noting Cogan's assertion that a word with the same three radical letters 'sph' appears as a loan in the late Babylonian dialect of Akkadian as *sippīḫu*, which means 'wild growth.' Cogan, M. and Tadmor, H., *II Kings*, 238. The word in Akkadian, however, is attested in only one text and it does not have the exact meaning given by Cogan. *CAD, sippīḫu* has: "The field for cereal cultivation is at PN's disposal for *sippīḫu* and for cultivating the weeds for PN's, he will weed the field and perform the s., [he will pay] the *šibšu* tax for any field he does not leave fallow just like his upper or lower neighbors (pay)." CAD, S, *sippīḫu*, 300.

407 Cogan and Tadmor, *II Kings*, 238. Clarke has a similar opinion; see Clarke, A., *Clarke's Commentary: Second Kings* (electronic edition). Logos Library System; Clarke's Commentaries (2 Ki 19:29) (Albany, 1999).

408 Oswalt, *Isaiah*, 664.

409 Widyapranawa, S.H., *The Lord is Savior: A Commentary on the Book of Isaiah 1–39* (ITC; Grand Rapids, 1990), 247.

er it a later addition.[410] Another view holds that the year of Isaiah's prediction was a sabbatical year followed by a jubilee, meaning people could not sow owing to religious obligations.[411] Scholars who hold this view think that the law for the sabbatical year given in Lev 25 illustrates what Isaiah predicts.[412] The idea that people do not sow for two years and yet will have enough to eat (the word ספיח is used) reflects the idea of a sabbatical year.

We can see then that several interrelated issues are involved, including the presence or absence of the Assyrian army in the area, not sowing because of religious obligation or because of affliction, the immediate deliverance of the city of Jerusalem and the provenance of the text. The links are not easy to identify, but if we look at the sign from a different angle, possible explanations do appear. I will discuss the opinions outlined above and outline a scenario that could bring them together satisfactorily. I start with the notion that the people were not sowing because it was a sabbatical year.

This view is not free from difficulties as there is no historical evidence that a sabbatical year was practised in Judah during the pre-exilic period.[413] Similarly, however, there is no archaeological evidence that the Assyrian presence in the area continued for a long time.[414] Moreover, if the prediction was in the autumn or winter as mentioned above, expecting people to eat wild wheat would make little sense because the harvest time would have already passed and people would already have had their supplement for the whole year.[415] O. Borowski's study of agriculture in Iron Age Israel elucidates this discussion. The study seeks to establish the agricultural calendar of the time by consulting literary and archaeological sources. The key materials are the Israelite festivals, agricultural seasons, and the tenth-century Gezer calendar, which contains an inscription relating to agricultural practices. Borowski shows that the agricultural year starts with autumn (October, November, December) and winter (January, February, March), progressing to spring (April, May, June) and summer (July, August, September). The agricultural season for the ploughing and sowing of the main crops, such as wheat and barley, is in late autumn and early winter, meaning harvest would be in April to June.[416]

---

410 Gonçalves, *L'expedition*, p. 486; Auvray, P., *Isaïe* (Paris, 1957), 156.
411 Clover, R., *The Sabbath and Jubilee Cycle*. Volume 1 (Garden Grove, 1992), 29–132.
412 Montgomery, *Commentary*, 497.
413 See also Young, *Isaiah*, 495.
414 Faust, "Settlement", 184–186.
415 Clover, *Sabbath*, 45.
416 Borowski, O., *Agriculture in Iron Age Israel* (Winona Lake, 1987), 57–91. On the main kinds of crops that Judah grew, see Faust, A. and Weiss, E., "Judah, Philistia and the Mediterra-

If we assume that the sabbatical year was observed, calculating the years from the reference given in 1 Macc 6:53 (which declares that 163/2 was a sabbatical year), year 702/701 would indeed be a candidate for a sabbatical year.[417] However, a weakness in this view is the explanation given about the sabbatical year in Lev 25, which scholars holding this view did not consider. Lev 25:5 says: "you shall not reap what grows of itself in your harvest or gather the grapes of your undressed vine." This means that in the seventh year both sowing and harvesting are prohibited. Moreover, when people wonder how they will have enough to eat if they do not sow, Lev 25:20–22 says: "I will send you such a blessing in the sixth year that the land yield enough for three years." This means that people are not going to starve because they have extra food from the abundant harvest of the sixth year. In other words, the text does not say that people are going to eat ספיח or סחיש. Eating wild growth does not seem to be a blessing or a sign of deliverance; rather, it refers to a time of suffering and need. That is obvious from the contrasting pictures that Isaiah gives for the first two years and the third year. E. Young provides good support for the contrasting picture of sterility of the first and second year and the fertility of the third year. He argues that using the infinitive absolute for eating (אכול) in the two years contrasts with the imperatives in the third year; in the imperatives there is a definiteness that is lacking in the infinitive.[418] One can say (with Young) that the Jerusalemites will suffer for two years and that only in the third year will the situation improve. To sum up, the view of the sabbatical year does not properly answer the question why people could not sow for two years.

Concerning the presence of the Assyrian army in the area, it is impossible to know with certainty how long the army stayed. Furthermore, the withdrawal of Sennacherib does not in itself necessarily indicate that the area was free from Assyrians; it is quite possible that Sennacherib could have left some troops behind until Hezekiah gave up and paid the tribute. Alternatively, some troops could have gone to the area around Jerusalem while Sennacherib was conquering the 46 cities of Judah. In this regard, Oded's discussion supports the argument here. The author asserts that damaging the agriculture of the land being attacked is part of the wartime acts the Assyrians used to perform for more than one reason, like punishment, pressure and depriving the people of food

---

nean World: Reconstructing the Economic System of the Seventh Century B.C.E.", BASOR 338 (2005), 80–83.

417 Wright, C., "Sabbatical Year", *ABD*, 5, O-Sh, 860.

418 One has to say that Young is depending on Isaiah's version of the account where there is a slight textual difference from the 2 Kings version.

sources.[419] Regardless of this, to assume that the Assyrian presence only lasted for days is not reasonable at all; the blockade of the city could have extended from weeks to months, which would have been enough time to cause great damage to agriculture. Indeed, at particular times, such a disruption could have had a grave impact even on the crops of the following year. Thus, the brief presence of the Assyrians in the area could have been enough to cause great damage, which does not contradict the fact that deliverance was relatively immediate, if we do not speak about some hours or a few days.

This leads us to the second point about eating. In order to eat cultivated or wild wheat, people must be able to harvest. Being able to harvest makes it necessary to accept that the Assyrian army left in the same year it arrived. This is because, if the Assyrians were in the area, they would not have allowed the Jerusalemites to harvest whatever the plant was. The sign, therefore, if we are to understand it literally, emphasises the fact that the army was not in the area for a long time (against Gonçalves and Auvray).[420]

Also, as mentioned above, eating wild growth is not a sign of abundance or prosperity but instead suggests a time of hardship and distress that will be over in the third year. Interpreting the sign in this way fits the context. V. 30, which follows the sign, speaks about a surviving remnant after Sennacherib's attack. Both the deprivation in the two years and the reduction of the population to a remnant (a group of people not the whole state) indicate that a misfortune happened to the state. It seems clear then that the people (at least those remaining) suffered after Sennacherib's attack and only in the third year did prosperity return to the land.

2.5.1.2. Analysis of vv. 30 – 31

ויספה פליטת בית יהודה הנשארה שרש למטה ועשה פרי למעלה כי מירושלם תצא שארית

ופליטה מהר ציון קנאת יהוה תעשה זאת

V. 30 And again the surviving remnant of the house of Judah shall take[421] *root down and bear fruit above, (v. 31) because from Jerusalem shall come out a remnant and from Mount Zion a band of survivors. The zeal of the Lord shall do this.*

There are three points worth pausing over in these two verses:

---

419 Oded, B., "Cutting Down Orchards in Assyrian Royal Inscriptions – The Historiographic Aspect", in *JAC* 12 (1997), 93.
420 As for Gonçalves and Auvray, see section 2.5.1.1.
421 There is no Hebrew word for this verb in the sentence, but it is added out of linguistic necessity.

1. Syntactically, v. 30 exhibits a problem. The subject of the sentence is 'the remnant', whose gender, in Hebrew, is feminine. The first verb יֹסֵף agrees with the subject as its form is also feminine. However, the second (definite) verb in the sentence is עשה and it is in the masculine form, which does not agree with the gender of the subject. This could be a spelling mistake.

2. The subject פליטה is in the construct chain, i.e. the remnant of the house of Judah. The genitive here seems to be exegetical, i.e. genitive of definition not partitive genitive. The text does not say a remnant from Judah, but rather the remnant, the house of Judah. On the other hand, v. 31 defines the remnant as coming from Jerusalem and Mount Zion. The movement is thus from the house of Judah to Jerusalem and finally to Mount Zion.[422]

3. The expression בית יהודה is found quite often in the Bible. Zobel suggests that this expression is used in the prophetic books as a term in contrast to "house of Israel."[423] It is unlikely that the term was used to indicate a small group from the state of Judah, but rather to refer to the whole state as a political entity. Moreover, it is not typical for the expression to be used in the context of speaking about the remnant. It is, therefore, striking to see the expression in the present context where the prophet is speaking about a group of people who survived a catastrophe.

Discussion of the second and third points helps us to decide what kind of remnant the author is speaking about in these two verses, unpicking whether the remnant is historical or eschatological. As was established above, Sennacherib's army destroyed many cities and settlements of Judah but Jerusalem was spared. Thus, on the one hand, one expects the remnant to be a group of people, not the whole state. On the other hand, the author uses the expression 'the house of Judah', which indicates the whole state, to refer to the remnant. Accordingly, the remnant in these verses is understood to be Judah the state. However, this does not fit with the context of the event. It is implausible to refer to those who survived the attack as 'the house of Judah' because this is not a historical reality. One can understand that Isaiah is not speaking about a historical remnant, but rather an eschatological one.[424] Indeed, this assumption can be supported by another argument.

---

422 Hausmann argues that the accumulation of names (house of Judah, Jerusalem and Zion) is to remove any doubt about the positive future for Judah. Hausmann, J., *Israels Rest: Studien zum Selbsverständnis der nachexilischen Gemeinde.* (Stuttgart, 1987), 131–134.

423 Zobel, H.-J., "יהודה", *ThDOT*, 5,492–3.

424 This goes against Hasel, who argues that because of the use of 'the house of Judah' the oracle indicates that the prophet is not speaking about the future remnant, but rather a historical

At the beginning of the book of Isaiah, the prophet describes the country as a wasteland (1:5–9). In vv. 7–9 the reality is described: countryside and cities have been devastated and Jerusalem is left alone, isolated. Many scholars agree that these verses refer to the events of 701.[425] What is related to our discussion in Isa 1:5–9 is the fact that the prophet in this text speaks also about a 'remnant' (Isa 1:9). However, the 'remnant' in this context refers to those who survived the military attack. That is clear from the context, with vv. 7–8 relating two of the military activities practised by the enemy: eating the harvest of the land and besieging Jerusalem. The tone of the prophet, however, is not optimistic at all and there is no theological perspective in his description of the remnant (at least in vv. 4–8).[426] It is thus unlikely that Isa 37:31–32 and Isa 1:5–9 come from the same person and the same time because they differ radically in the way they look at Jerusalem after the attack. If Isa 1:5–9 refers to a historical remnant, then Isa 37:31–32 cannot refer to a historical reality. The two verses (Isa 37:31–32) could possibly have been inserted at a later period when an understanding of the 701 event became more theological. Thus, it seems clear to me that the text of Isa 37:31–32//2 Kgs 19:30–31 is not from the historical Isaiah.

2.5.2. Conclusion and dating of 2 Kgs 19:29–31

Two clear conclusions about the text can be drawn from the above analysis. First, there is no contradiction in 2 Kgs 19:29 between the immediate deliverance and the delayed agricultural activities. The sign is used to establish the fact that there will be starvation and distress for two years but this crisis will come to an end in the third year. 2 Kgs 19:30–31, however, speaks about an eschatological remnant that will prosper and flourish in the future. In the light of these conclusions, dating the sign (v. 29) and the oracle about the remnant (vv. 30–31) to the same period seems implausible. The sign seems to describe the condition of a besieged state, and it reflects the reality of what happened in 701. Moreover, it echoes Isaianic ideology.[427] The oracle about the remnant, however, reflects a

remnant. When he comments on the next verse, however, he argues that the prophet does not appear to speak of the military or political inviolability of Zion/Jerusalem. Hasel, G., *The Remnant: The History and Theology of the Remnant Idea from Genesis to Isaiah* (AUM 5; Berrien Springs, 1972), 335.
425 Williamson, *Isaiah*, 63–73.
426 Hasel, *Remnant*, 316: "the context of 1:8–9 shows that these 'survivors' are not the community of faith which would emerge from God's purging judgment as the eschatological remnant." It was thus because of God's grace that these were saved.
427 Seitz, C.R., *Isaiah 1–39* (BCTP; Louisville 1993), 251. Childs, *Crisis*, 276. Both scholars (with others) argue that it has similar features with the sign given to Ahaz in Isa 7.

later development of the theme of the remnant.[428] We should not, therefore, ascribe the oracle to the same time as the sign.

It has been suggested that the sign and the oracle were one unit because of the agricultural metaphor presented in the oracle. [429] The prosperity of the third year in v. 29 is echoed in vv. 30 – 31, where the prophet depicts the prosperity of the remnant that will come to take root and bear fruit. In both cases, God is the active agent. However, this argument has flaws. The sign in v. 29 can stand on its own; it conveys information about agricultural activities that should not necessarily be read in the context of the restoration of the nation. However, when the oracle was added, the sign then came to be understood as indicating the future restoration of the nation. This intimate relationship between the recovery of the land after war and the salvation of the nation is similarly attested in other biblical texts, the prime example being Amos 9:14 – 15, which is considered to be secondary.[430] The theme of the verses is that the Israelites will prosper again and will be planted in their land. Amos 9:14 – 15 also shares similar wording with the Isaianic sign, with both utilising metaphors involving planting vineyards and eating fruit.

To sum up, 2 Kgs 19:29 reflects the situation of Judah after the 701 attack, while 2 Kgs 19:30 – 31 is a later addition.

2.6. Conclusion to section one

The main goal of the investigation undertaken in this section was to examine the oracle in 2 Kgs 19:6 – 7 and the sign in 2 Kgs 19:29 – 31, which was presumed to be connected with the oracle of salvation. The aim was to see if the text provides an explanation for Sennacherib's unexpected behaviour or not. Having analysed the literary features of the oracle, we were able to draw some conclusions. First of all, the function of the oracle seemed to foretell the end of the attack on Jerusalem, regardless of whether or not the narrative is one unit or contains more than one unit. Secondly, the literary analysis revealed the theological nature of the oracle. Its genre and syntax indicate that the oracle has a theological orientation.

---

428 See Clements, R.E., "שאר", ThDOT, 14, 280. See also Housmann, Israels, 131. The author argues that it is better to think that the verse serves an eschatological function.
429 E.g. Young, Isaiah, 497.
430 Andersen, F.I. and Freedman, D.N., Amos (AB, 24 A; New York, 1989), 921 – 926. J.D. Smoak has a different explanation for the text: see Smoak, J.D., "Building Houses and Planting Vineyards: The Early Inner-Biblical Discourse on an Ancient Israelite Wartime Curse", JBL 127 (2008), 19 – 35.

On the other hand, the examination of the compositional nature of the text led us to conclude that the text was composed after the death of Sennacherib, and it is unlikely that the prophet Isaiah could have been the source for this oracle even if he was the source of inspiration for it. However, two important points have to be clarified. First, if the text of the oracle has editorial features, that does not mean it is historically unreliable. From the discussion of the note about Sennacherib's death, we concluded that the text does indeed have a historical kernel. Also, from the way it reveals the circumstances of Sennacherib's return, one can tell that the text communicates the idea that Sennacherib's return was unexpected. Secondly, if the text is late, that does not mean that this study confirms the assumption that Isaiah was completely negative and did not prophesy the deliverance of Jerusalem. It is true that there are some texts in Isa 1–35 where Isaiah is depicted as criticising Hezekiah's policy (Isa 30–31; especially Isa 22), but there is no way to know if he ever uttered any prophecy for Jerusalem concerning Sennacherib's attack. To sum up, 2 Kgs 19:6–7 reflects a historical reality, and the assumption that there was a rumour that surprised Sennacherib is, in my opinion, reasonable.

Similarly, the investigation about the sign led us to conclude that the text explains the reality of what happened after the attack. Isaiah, through this sign, is not prophesyng a delayed salvation of Jerusalem, but rather prophesying the well-being of the Jerusalemites after two years of hardship. Again, whether or not Isaiah himself said these words is difficult to ascertain. Nevertheless, comparing this text with Isa 1:4–8 reveals a very similar attitude on the part of the prophet. In any case, the sign reflects a historical reality that could have taken place after the attack and the military activities of Sennacherib's army in 701.

3. Section Two: The Role of Egyptian-Kushite Army in 701

3.1. Introduction

Despite the fact that the military role of the Egyptian-Kushite forces in the events of 701 against the Assyrians is indisputable, it is unknown how supportive that role was. One must say that the scarcity of Egyptian sources and some anomalies which have been identified in the Assyrian and biblical accounts, which recount the episode concerning the Egyptian-Kushite role, make it extremely difficult to decide with any certainty the exact role of these forces in the campaign. Whether they came to support their allies in the southern Levant or their aim was to counter Assyrian expansion and control territory that could eventually lead to an attempt to reach Egypt and conquer it, one cannot tell.[431] Nevertheless, some attempt in this vein is necessary, since this study is not principally concerned with the relations between Egypt and Assyria but rather with the Egyptian-Kushite role and how far the presence of the Egyptians and the Kushites affected the outcome of the battle in relation to Sennacherib's attack on Judah. The main question discussed in this section is therefore whether the Egyptian-Kushite presence in the southern Levant was so significant as to hinder Sennacherib in his quest to take Jerusalem and to cause him to return to Nineveh before he could accomplish his aim.

3.2. The Egyptian-Kushite presence in the Assyrian and biblical sources

One of the issues that Sennacherib's annals and the biblical accounts in 2 Kgs 18–19//Is 36–37 differ about in depicting the 701 event is their presentation of the Egyptian-Kushite forces in the course of the event. The text in the annals is generous in recording the place where the Egyptian-Kushite forces confronted Sennacherib, the composition of the enemy (kings of Egypt), Sennacherib's bravery, the result of the battle, and the taking of prisoners. The biblical accounts, however, provide a brief passage about Sennacherib receiving a report about the advance of Tirhakah, king of Kush, who had set out to fight Sennacherib (2 Kgs 19:9). Nothing is mentioned about the development or the result of the battle. The difference between the two accounts lies not only in the amount of information but also in the place where the Egyptian-Kushite forces fight the Assyrian army: while the annals relate that the confrontation was in the vicinity of Elteqeh (a site in southern Palestine not far from the city of Ekron [Tel Miqne]), the biblical accounts do not give precise information about the place. Before relating the note about Tirhakah, 2 Kgs 19:8 tells the reader that Sennacherib left Lachish and went to Libnah. It does not say clearly that Sennacherib went to confront Egyptian forces at Libnah. Moreover, in his description of the composition of the enemy, Sennacherib mentions (twice) "kings of Egypt" and cavalry of the king of *Meluḫḫa* (i.e. Nubia); and among the prisoners he mentions "the charioteers and sons of kings of Egypt" and "the charioteers of the king of *Meluḫḫa*". No note about the presence of the king of *Meluḫḫa* is given

---

431 For more discussion on the Assyrian-Egyptian relationship before 701, see Zamazalova, S., "Before the Assyrian Conquest in 761 B.C.E.: Relations between Egypt, Kush and Assyria," in J. Mynářová (ed.), *Egypt and the Near East – the Crossroads: Proceedings of an International Conference on the Relations of Egypt and the Near East in the Bronze Age, September 1–3, 2010.* (Prague, 2011), 297–328.

in the episode. In the biblical account, however, it is Tirhakah, "the king of Kush", who advances to fight Sennacherib (see below).

It is important, therefore, to bear in mind these differences when the role of the Egyptian-Kushite forces in Sennacherib's campaign against Judah is discussed. One might ask if the two accounts speak about one army that fought the Assyrians at Eltekeh and then went to aid Hezekiah, or if there were two armies, one that fought the Assyrian at Eltekeh and the other led by a Kushite commander that fought Sennacherib separately in the region of Judah. Some efforts have been made in discussing these issues in order to create harmony between the Assyrian and biblical presentations of the Egyptian-Kushite forces and accordingly to decide on the supportive role of these forces against the Assyrians. It is worthwhile to present some of these scholarly attempts and discuss them.

3.3. Scholarly opinions

In discussing the identity of the commander of the Egyptian expedition in Eltekeh, N. Na'aman argues, "the phraseology suggests that it was not the same Egyptian expedition mentioned in the Bible led by the Nubian prince Tirhakah (2 Kings xix 9) but an earlier campaign."[432] Similarly, Gallagher rejects the possibility that there was a link between the presence of the Egyptians at Eltekeh and the report about Tirhakah in 2 Kgs 19:9. He considers the Assyrian annals as reliable, while dismissing the biblical note about Tirhakah as not reliable on the basis of literary and archaeological evidence.[433] He supports the idea that there was a rumour about the Egyptian advance, but he considers the presence of Tirhakah's name wrong, and it was added later. The Egyptian army, however, never encountered the Assyrian army as far as it concerns the attack against Judah; and there was no time when the two armies engaged in battle. The Egyptian army was very far, maybe in Egypt, when Sennacherib heard about it while besieging and fighting in the Judean region. On the other hand, Mayer presents a different scenario when he assumes that "Eltekeh and Tamnâ were part of the group of 46 Judean sites Sennacherib conquered."[434] Given the fact that the 46 cites belonged to Hezekiah, as Sennacherib relates in his annals, in this case,

---

432 Na'aman, N., "Sennacherib's Campaign to Judah and the Date of the *lmlk* Stamps", *VT* 29 (1979), 65.
433 Gallagher, *Sennacherib's Campaign*, 123–124.
434 Mayer, "Sennacherib's", 177. The author assumes that the two cities may have been located far south of Ekron.

even if Mayer does not say that explicitly, one can conclude that the two Egyptian-Kushite expeditions mentioned in the annals and the Bible were one force. Knauf, however, reads the events of 701 differently and argues, "when Sennacherib advanced from Bīth-Daganna to Eltekeh, an Egyptian army was nowhere in sight."[435] In his view, the Egyptian forces only approached at the very end of the campaign when these forces stepped in to outflank the Assyrian army, which by now must have been diminished after more than 50 sieges. There was no battle at Eltekeh, because the three parties, Assyrians, Egyptians and Judeans came to terms.[436] One can safely say that Knauf and Mayer agree about the way they see the Egyptian-Kushite expedition: it was only one. Like Mayer, Knauf suggests that Sennacherib heard about the advance of the Egyptians when he besieged Jerusalem. The note about Tirhakah in 2 Kgs 19:9 refers to the Egyptian force that was fighting in Eltekeh. Thus, the two expeditions are one, in Knauf's view.

Similar to Na'aman, Aubin asserts that Sennacherib's uncertain phraseology, when he describes the Egyptian army in the episode of Eltekeh, provides shaky evidence of the existence of two armies. The Kushite-Egyptian armies were divided into two contingents. While the Egyptian-Kushite army fought and was defeated by Sennacherib in Eltekeh, Tirhakah's army, which appeared after Sennacherib conquered Ashdod and Lachish, subsequently won the battle and defeated the Assyrians. And finally, in a recently published article, J. Vidal presents his opinion on the matter when he discusses the outcome of the battle that took place at Eltekeh. In his view, 2 Kgs 19:9 is not reliable because it belongs to a later prophetic narrative. He therefore simply does not discuss the presence of the Egyptian army in the Judean region.[437]

One must say that the uncertain and divergent opinions about the two pictures of the Egyptian-Kushite forces presented in the Assyrian annals and biblical accounts emanate, of course, from the different ways that both sources tell the reader about the Egyptian-Kushite role in the event. Accordingly, scholars not only differ in deciding the number of the armies, but also in regard to the role of the Egyptian-Kushites in the outcome of the campaign. On the one hand, the anachronism in 2 Kgs 19:9a concerning Tirhakah, king of Kush, caused both Vidal and Gallagher to consider the note as late and the work of a Deuteronomistic redactor; the real confrontation then, was only with the Assyrians at Eltekeh. The Egyptian-Kushite presence in the west, therefore, was not significant

---

435 Knauf, "Berezina", 144.
436 Knauf, "Berezina", 141–149.
437 Vidal, J., "Some Remarks on the Battle of Altaqu", in G. del Olmo Lete, *et al.* (eds.), *The Perfumes of Seven Tamarisks. Studies in Honour of Wilfred G.E. Watson* (AOAT 394; Münster, 2012), 77–78.

to Judah, even if Sennacherib was not completely defeated in the battle at Eltekeh.[438] Whether or not Sennacherib won his battle against Hezekiah, that did not have much to do with the confrontation at Eltekeh. On the other hand, Sennacherib's phraseology in the note about his real enemy at Eltekeh caused Na'aman and Aubin to assert that there were two Egyptian-Kushite armies, not just one. In Aubin's view, the presence of the Kushite army in the area was very significant, and moreover, it was the reason why Jerusalem was rescued. Looking at the event from a different angle, the lack of chronology in narrating the event caused Knauf and Mayer to struggle to explain the event and discern how many army divisions there were in the campaign. Both scholars reject the idea that there were two confrontations with the Assyrians; rather, there was only one at Eltekeh, although they differ about the timing of the confrontation. In Knauf's view, the confrontation in a way weakened the Assyrian army and obliged Sennacherib to come to terms. For Mayer, however, the Egyptian-Kushite army did not cause a serious threat to the Assyrians.

3.4. Discussing the scholarly views

At this point, we have to remind ourselves that the above discussion was presented to help us decide about the Egyptian-Kushite role in the campaign and whether or not Sennacherib withdrew after hearing about the approach of the Kushite king, Tirhakah. The discussion about the divisions of the Egyptian-Kushite army was necessary in order to give us a better understanding of the Egyptian-Kushite role in the campaign. This discussion, however, merits some more scrutiny.

There is one fact that all sources (and scholars) agree about, which is the active participation of the Egyptian-Kushite forces in the 701 events, regardless of the outcome of their participation. Of course, it is not a surprise to hear about the Egyptian aid to the Levant, as it is not the first time that the Egyptians confronted the Assyrians in order to support their allies in the southern Levant before the Assyrian king, Esarhaddon, finally conquered Egypt.[439] But, as noticed, the debate is about how significant the role was. Strangely, in the previous discussion, the archaeological inferences have not been seriously consulted. I assume that archaeology can support the discussion, since the evidence provided by excavations can illuminate our knowledge about the outcome of Sennacherib's campaign.

---

438 Gallager, *Sennacherib's Campaign*, 121; Vidal, "Remarks", 78–79.
439 The Egyptian supported Hanunu of Gaza against Sargon II in 711.

Needless to say, archaeological discussions and studies connected with Sennacherib's campaign are numerous. And, they almost all agree that the outcome of the 701 event is attested in many sites and cities all over Judah.[440] Dealing with the settlement and demography of Judah in the seventh century, A. Faust[441] dedicates considerable space to discussing the extent and intensity of Sennacherib's campaign. In this study, he summarises the consensus and presents his own conclusions based on a new examination of the evidence. His conclusions, therefore, are significant to our discussion and deserve to be noted. As far as the Shephelah is concerned, Faust asserts, "the Shephelah was the most densely settled part of Judah, with a large number of sites, and the majority of Judah's towns and cities... The excavated Iron Age sites in this region were practically all destroyed by the Assyrians...".[442] The sites that were affected by Sennacherib are: Lachish, Tell Beit Mirsim, Tel Halif, Tel Batash, Tel Beth-Shemesh, Tel Goded, Maresha, and Tel 'Eton.[443] Traces of destruction were found not only in the Shephelah, but also in the Highlands of Judah, Ramat Rahel, Hebron and Kh. Rabud.[444] E. Bloch-Smith made another study that contributed to the discussion about the sites that were destroyed by Sennacherib.[445] Although Bloch-Smith is cautious about the conclusions concerning the highlands of Judah, she supports Faust's conclusion about the Shephelah. In her opinion Sennacherib's strategy to destroy those sites was not without reason. As she states, "Sennacherib appears to have secured the Judahite sites in the lowlands, the Shephelah foothills, and the northern Negev in order to encircle the highlands and isolate Jerusalem."[446]

From this, one can safely conclude that Sennacherib went through Judah destroying sites that were of militaristic and economic significance. Additionally, the strategy of isolating Jerusalem demonstrates that Sennacherib was aware of the possibility that Judah would get support from its allies, namely the Egyptian-Kushite allegiance. Therefore, hearing about their advance would not have

---

440 See Stern, E., *Archaeology of the Land of the Bible, vol. II: The Assyrian, Babylonian and Persian Period (732 – 332 E)* (ABRL; New York, 2001), 10. Vaughn, *Archaeology*, 44; Blakely, J.A. and Hardin, J.W., "Southwestern Judah in the Late Eighth Century B.C.E.", *BASOR* 326 (2002), 14 – 38.
441 Faust, "Settlement", 168 – 194.
442 Faust, "Settlement", 172
443 Faust, "Settlement", 172 – 173.
444 Faust, "Settlement", 178.
445 Bloch-Smith, E., "Assyrians Abet Israelite Cultic Reform: Sennacherib and the Centralization of the Israelite Cult", in J.D. Schloen (ed.), *Exploring the Longue Durée. Essays in Honor of Lawrence E. Stager* (Winona Lake, 2009), 35 – 44.
446 Bloch-Smith, Centralization", 38.

been a surprise for Sennacherib. If this was so, the argument about the significant role of the Egyptian-Kushite support to Hezekiah begs a question. No matter
where or when the Egyptian forces met Sennacherib's army, at the end of the
campaign or at the beginning, with one army or two armies, it appears from
the archaeological evidence that their presence did not cause a serious threat
to the Assyrians. Sennacherib did reduce and weaken the kingdom of Judah
and quell the revolt in the southern Levant and the Egyptian-Kushite armies
did not hinder him from doing that, even if they confronted him once or
twice. Therefore, to assume that Sennacherib retuned to Nineveh after he
heard about the Tirhakah is unlikely.

The discussion as presented above leads us to another crucial point in the
study, i.e. the connection between the rumour in 2 Kgs 19:7 and the note
about Tirhakah in 2 Kgs 19:9. Is the rumour really about the advance of Tirhakah?

3.5. The connection between 2 Kgs 19:7 and 2 Kgs 19:9a

This part of the study discusses the connection between the rumour and the note
about Tirhakah. Some scholars assume that the two notes are related to each
other and the rumour of which Isaiah speaks in the oracle of salvation is the
note of Tirhakah that surprises Sennacherib and has him go back to his
city.[447] Basically, this suggestion is grounded on the two verses that follow the
note of the rumour, 19:8–9a. In v. 9a the text says that Sennacherib 'heard'
that Tirhakah went out to fight him. So, scholars connected this news (about Tirhakah) with the hearing about the rumour. At this point this suggestion deserves
some attention.

3.5.1. Literary analysis of 2 Kgs 19:9a
Reading the text closely will be helpful:

וישמע אל תרהקה מלך כוש לאמר הנה יצא להלחם אתך

And he heard about Tirhakah, King of Kush, "Behold, he has gone out to fight against you."

---

447 Montgomery, *Commentary*, 491. Hardmeier, C., *Prophetie im Streit vor dem Untergang Judas*
(BZAW 187; Berlin, 1990), 288–290. The author is comparing the event of 588, when Jerusalem
fell to Nebuchadnezzar, with 701 .

The information given about the advance of Tirhakah is placed within a context that does not seem to be well connected with the rest of the narrative. In 2 Kgs 19:8, the text relates that the Rabshakeh left Jerusalem for Lachish to meet Sennacherib, who had left to fight in Libnah. Moreover, after relaying the information about Tirhakah, the text in 2 Kgs 19:9b relates that Sennacherib sent a message to Hezekiah. Despite the attempt to find coherence and consistency between vv. 8–9 and the rest of the narrative,[448] source-critical analysis finds it difficult to view the sections in a similar way.[449] On both sides, one can say, the assumption that the rumour was about Tirhakah finds support. Therefore, arguing about whether vv. 8–9 are part of the text or not does not benefit research about the role of the Egyptian-Kushite army or answers the question of whether or not Tirhakah hindered Sennacherib from taking Jerusalem. Nevertheless, literary analysis helps us to figure out what this brief text says.

First of all, v. 9a seems to be isolated. The main subject in v. 8 is the Rabshakeh, but suddenly in v. 9a the subject switches to Sennacherib. Also, the reference to the name Tirhakah has created a long debate, as Tirhakah was not king of Nubia in 701. Yet, Kitchen argues for the possibility of Tirhakah's participation in 701 as he claims that he was 20 years old then.[450] However, the problem is not only with the reference to the name but also with the title, the King of Kush. According to the annals of Sennacherib, the Kushite king did not participate in the war (whether it was Tirhakah or another one). So, mentioning the name with the title makes one doubt the accuracy of this brief note. However, on the one hand, the way the sentence is composed does not affect the fact that the Egyptian-Kushite force had a role in 701. On the other hand, one cannot tell whether the rumour mentioned in v. 7 is about the advance of Tirhakah. Moreover, one cannot say that Tirhakah hindered Sennacherib in his efforts to take Jerusalem.

3.5.2. The role of the Egyptian-Kushite aid in the wider context

To assume that the rumour was about Tirhakah could be supported from the number of references to Egyptian military aid to Judah and Israel in the Old Testament. 2 Kgs 7:6 relates a story of how Samaria was rescued from an Aramean siege. The text says, *"the Lord had caused the Arameans to hear the sound of chariots and horses and a great army, so that they [the Arameans] said to one another,*

---

448 Evans, *Invasion*, 88–111.
449 Gray views vv. 8–9 as editorial bridges between the two versions of the same delegation. Gray, *II Kings*, 663
450 Kitchen, *Egypt*, 550–559.

"Look, the king of Israel has hired the Hittite and Egyptian kings to attack us! So they got up and fled in the dusk and abandoned their tents and their horses and donkeys. They left the camp as it was and ran for their lives". In his commentary on this verse, Gray assumes that "a rumour had reached them [the army of Aram] of the activity of 'the kings of the Hittites' and of Muṣri, and it is not impossible that this rumour had been fomented by one of the prophets by the authority of Elisha."[451] Similarly, Jer 37:5 tells of the withdrawal of the Chaldeans when they heard that the Egyptian army came out to fight them. The text says, *"Meanwhile, the army of the Pharaoh had advanced from Egypt, and the Chaldeans who had been blockading Jerusalem had, on hearing the report, broken off operations and withdrew."* Here too, the lifting of the siege is attributed to Egyptian military intervention.[452] In both cases, the withdrawal of the enemy, which surrounds the city, is accounted for hearing about the advance of the Egyptian forces.

One can readily conclude that the presence of Egyptian aid to Judah is expected by the reader of the story and, in general, of the Old Testament. To connect the note about the rumour with the advance of Tirhakah might at first seem rather rational. If so, the connection assumed between the rumour and Tirhakah ought to fit in well with the conclusions made up earlier, i.e. the insignificant role of the Egyptians and the strong connection between Sennacherib hearing the rumour and his return to Nineveh. If not, then one should make some revisions in order to hold all the arguments together. This is where the arguments of some scholars, in my opinion, are weak.

3.6. Conclusion to Section Two

Obviously, what causes confusion in the debate about the rumour is the lack of comprehensiveness and inclusiveness that can assemble the variant phases when this matter is tackled. It is not enough to deal with just one aspect to obtain a decisive conclusion. Historical-critical analysis of the text, alone, is not sufficient to gain a clear idea. To argue historically about the role of the Egyptian-Kushite forces, and decide whether that role was significant or not, would not explain the clumsiness in the text, especially 2 Kgs 19:7 and 2 Kgs 19:9. However, to read the text synchronically and oversimplify the discussion by relying on the note of 'hearing' in 2 Kgs 19:7 and 19:9 might lead us to some facts that contradict the historical reality illuminated by both archaeological and lit-

---

451 Gray, *II Kings*, 524.
452 Carroll, R.P., *Jeremiah. A Commentary* (OTL; London, 1986), 673.

erary evidence. Reaching all the angles of the discussion, therefore, is – albeit difficult – important if we want to gain a reasonably clear idea about what happened.

In the work presented above, therefore, I have tried to discuss two points: the role of the Egyptian-Kushite forces in Sennacherib's third campaign and the connection between the rumour and the advance of Tirhakah. The conclusion of my study may be summarised as follows:

1. Because of the devastating action of Sennacherib in the southern Levant and the catastrophic condition he left Judah with, one can safely say that even if the Egyptian-Kushite army came to confront Sennacherib, it did not cause Sennacherib to return.
2. The note about the rumour is connected with Sennacherib's return to Nineveh. If the Kushites did not cause Sennacherib to return, then the rumour could not be about the advance of Tirhakah.
3. The tradition that connects the rumour with the note about Tirhakah emanated from the fact that the Egyptian aid to the Levant has its history in the biblical text.

4. Section Three: The Angel of the Lord in 2 Kgs 19:35

4.1. Introduction

Having discussed the first three explanations given for the deliverance of Jerusalem, it is time to deal with the fourth. This one is based on 2 Kgs 19:35, which relates how the Angel of the Lord visited the camp during the night and annihilated many of the Assyrian soldiers, so that Sennacherib went back to Nineveh unexpectedly. According to this passage, it is not the tribute or the rumour or Tirhakah that made Sennacherib withdraw but rather a divine intervention that ended the attack.

It has to be admitted that discussing this explanation for the rescue of Jerusalem is not a straightforward matter. The main difficulty is that the story has such a theological and religious outlook that makes the task of searching for history in this matter almost impossible. It should not be a surprise that scholars go to opposite extremes when they discuss this text. Interpretative opinions go between considering the text as authentic,[453] to regarding it as a

---

453 Young, *Isaiah*, 505.

legend.[454] Between these two opinions, some scholars sought to see in the story of the Angel of the Lord a text that communicates a message to the reader about God's rescue of Jerusalem.[455]

Some scholars have gone further and associated this story with 2 Sam 24 and interpreted the event as an epidemic spreading amongst the army and killing many of them. This theory has had a wide range of supporters; some have presented considerable arguments and some have simply accepted the conventional opinion (see below). However, this matter warrants closer scrutiny. After discussing these scholarly opinions, I shall investigate further this theory. My main concern is not only what the Angel of the Lord denotes, but also whether the Angel of the Lord (or whatever it might be taken to indicate) was really the reason why Sennacherib returned.

4.2. What does the note mean?

As mentioned above, v. 35 is a dense theological explanation of the reasons behind Sennacherib's withdrawal. However, some scholars argue that the story of the Angel of the Lord has a historical kernel, one that provides a reasonable explanation for Sennacherib's return. These scholars assume that the reference to the angel implies a plague that spread among the Assyrian army and killed an immense number of the warriors. Supporters of this view include those who strengthen their statement with argument and those who just accept the idea without evidence or argumentation.[456] The arguments of the first group are assembled and presented in a relatively recent article by K. Radner, who follows C. Boutflower (and others) in basing her argument on other occasions when the Assyrian army suffered disastrous epidemics. Radner declares: "The fact

---

454 Clemants, *Deliverance*, 26.

455 B.S. Childs, *Isaiah* (OTL; London, 2001), 277.

456 Supporters of the second group include Adams, who argues "the Assyrian army was providentially decimated by an outbreak of plague." He takes the view that there was no military encounter between the Assyrians and the Egyptians. Adams, W.Y., *Nubia: Corridor to Africa* (London, 1977), 264. J.H. Breasted argues that it was not only the plague that made Sennacherib return but also another factor, stating that the "overwhelming catastrophe, together with disquieting news from Babylon, forced him hastily to retire to Nineveh". See Breasted, J.H., *A History of Egypt from the Earliest Times to the Persian Conquest* (London, 1906), 552. See also Bruce, F.F., *Israel and the Nations: From the Exodus to the Fall of the Second Temple* (Grand Rapids, 1963), 72; Wilson, J.K., "And He Shall Hear a Rumour..." (Isaiah 37:7; 2 Kings 19:7), in J.K. Aitken, K.J., Dell *et al* (eds.), *On Stone and Scroll. Essays in Honour of Graham Ivor Davies* (BZAW 420; Berlin, 2011), 371–374.

that also the Assyrian army was ravaged repeatedly by epidemics is clear from the evidence of the Eponym Chronicles which at times supplements the routine mention of the destination of the Assyrian army with the note *mūtānu* "mass death; epidemic": for the year 802, the entry reads "to the sea; epidemic"; for 765, "to Ḥatarikka; epidemic"; and for 759, "revolt in Guzana; epidemic."[457] She goes further in stating "the most famous Assyrian army epidemic is that which forced Sennacherib (704–681) to end his 701 campaign into Palestine."[458] Radner's grounds for her judgement are the story in Herodotus and 2 Kgs 19:35.[459]

This view has been challenged strongly by Aubin, who dealt with the matter from different angles.[460] His argument can be summarised in four points: (1) the biblical text does not speak of a plague. However, there are other examples in the Bible where an epidemic is explained as an angel's instrument, such as Ex. 9:11; 2 Sam 24 so why should the author not use the same language in this story? (2) the Assyrian's multi-pronged offensive would have made it hard for a disease to strike a crippling blow to the army as a whole; (3) the story of Herodotus does not say explicitly that the mice caused the plague (see below); and (4) why did Sennacherib not come back to Hezekiah and attack Jerusalem after his army had recovered?[461]

Although Aubin's argument is stimulating, it is obvious that his objections to the theory are based on questions that can hardly be answered by the biblical text. In his first and fourth points he basically interrogates the way the text is written and why it was not written more explicitly.

---

457 Radner, K., "The Assyrian King and His Scholars: The Syro-Anatolia and the Egyptian Schools", in M. Luukko *et al.* (eds.), *Of God(s), Trees, Kings and Scholars. New Assyrian and Related Studies in Honor of Simon Parpola* (ST 106; Helsinki 2009), 230; Kitchen, K., "Egypt, the Levant and Assyria in 701", in H. Brunner, *Fontes Atque Pontes* (Wiesbaden, 1983), 251. The commentators are even more cautious in dealing with this part of the narrative, seeming to avoid a decisive explanation for v. 35. Wildberger, for example, argues that one should be very cautious about speculating and answering the question why Sennacherib returned unexpectedly like that (Wildberger, *Jesaja*, 1438); and Blenkinsopp also states that the intervention of the Angel of the Lord "illustrates the element of the sudden in the way the divine can irrupt into human lives" (Blenkinsopp, *Isaiah*, 478).
458 Radner, "Assyrian", 230.
459 See also Frahm, *Einleitung*, 11.
460 Aubin is not the first to argue against this theory, e. g. Kaiser states, "The assumption that the instrument of death was a plague is basically an inadmissible rationalization of the miracle" (Kaiser, *Isaiah*, 395). Similarly, Cogan argues that the explanation of "plague or pestilence visited upon the Assyrians represents later theological rationalization of the miraculous deliverance" (Cogan, *II Kings*, 239).
461 Aubin, *Rescue*, 120–22.

Anyway, it is clear that both supporters and opponents of the theory have provided reasonable arguments that mean it is not straightforward to decide which side to support. Moreover, scholars from both camps have used Herodotus to argue for and against the plague theory. At this point of the work, therefore, reading the text of Herodotus will be helpful in comparing the two stories:

> *Next on the throne after Anysis was Sethos, the high priest of Hephaestus. He is said to have neglected the warrior class of the Egyptians and to have treated them with contempt, as if he had been unlikely to need their services. He offended them in various ways, not least by depriving them of the 12 acres of land which each of them had held by special privilege under previous kings.*
>
> *As a result, when Egypt was invaded by Sennacherib, the king of Arabia and Assyria, with a great army, not one of them was willing to fight. The situation was grave; not knowing what else to do, the priest-king entered the shrine and, before the image of the god, complained bitterly of the peril which threatened him. In the midst of his lamentations he fell asleep, and dreamt that the god stood by him and urged him not to lose heart; for if he marched boldly out to meet the Arabian army, he would come to no harm, as the god himself would send him helpers.*
>
> *By this dream the king's confidence was restored; and with such men as were willing to follow him – not a single one of the warrior class, but mixed company of shopkeepers, artisans and market-people – he marched to Pelusium, which guards the approaches to Egypt, and there took up his position.*
>
> *As he lay here facing the Assyrians, thousands of field-mice swarmed over them during the night, and ate their quivers, their bowstrings and the leather handles of their shields, so that on the following day, having no arms to fight with, they abandoned their position and suffered severe losses during their retreat.*
>
> *There is still a stone statue of Sethos in the temple of Hephaestus; the figure is represented with a mouse in its hand, and the inscription: "Look upon me and learn reverence."*[462]

Boutflower directs attention to the common points the story of Herodotus shares with the biblical story: they both speak about a disaster that happens during the night, which is framed as a divine interposition obtained by a king who desperately prays to his god for such help.[463] This supports the idea that the two stories imply a kind of mysterious happening that befell the Assyrian army and forced Sennacherib to withdraw. Boutflower goes further to state that "both accounts point unmistakably to pestilence as the natural agency employed."[464] He backs up his position with reference to 1 Sam 6 where the plague is connected with mice and 2 Sam 24 where the plague is connected with the Angel of the

---

462 Aubin, *Rescue*, 94–95.
463 Boutflower, C., *The Book of Isaiah: Chapters 1–39 in the Light of the Assyrian Monuments* (London, 1930), 286.
464 Boutflower, *Isaiah*, 287.

Lord. Moreover, he argues that the author did not use the expression 'plague'.[465] Gray agrees with Boutflower and asserts "the two are not irreconcilable, as mice are notorious bearers of plague."[466] Laato too holds this view and argues that there is a possibility to see a trace of plague in both stories. Herodotus's story might contain allusion to actual facts, such as the destruction by plague of Sennacherib's army.[467] The picture for other scholars is not as clear as it looks. L.L. Grabbe, for example, thinks it is unfortunate that the story of Herodotus has been interpreted in the light of the biblical story of the angel. He, therefore, argues strongly for what is unique and distinct in Herodotus's story. First of all, he states that the story of mice is independent and should be examined on these grounds. There is nothing in the story that refers to plague or to an epidemic that struck the Assyrian army. In Grabbe's view, Sennacherib was defeated not by the killing of his army but rather by the army becoming unable to fight. He states: "When Herodotus's account is read in its own right, without interpretation in the light of the biblical, it tells us of an Egyptian defeat of Sennacherib. The defeat was not by normal force of arms but entailed some unusual happening."[468] This unusual happening is something that Grabbe attributes to the role of the Egyptian army, thus agreeing with Aubin.[469]

4.4. Discussion and conclusion to section three

The above makes the following issues clear:
i.   V. 35 has attracted the attention of many scholars who consider it as the verse that relates the end of the 701 event.
ii.   Because of its theological nature, scholars have used other biblical texts in tandem to interpret its somewhat opaque meaning.
iii. Other extra-biblical sources, mainly Herodotus, have been seen as corroborating the story because of their common elements.
iv.   Conclusions on v. 35 have been decisive; supporters of the plague theory assert that the plague was devastatingly large and had a remarkable effect on the whole campaign, making Sennacherib return to his city before entering

---

465 Boutflower, *Isaiah*, 287–88.
466 Gray, *II Kings*, 694.
467 Laato, *Immanuel*, 270.
468 Grabbe, L.L., "Of Mice and Dead Men: Herodotus 2. 141 and Sennacherib's Campaign in 701 BCE", in L.L. Grabbe (ed.), *'Like a Bird in a Cage.' The Invasion of Sennacherib in 701 BCE* (JSOTSup 363; London, 2003), 137.
469 Grabbe, "Mice", 137–39.

Jerusalem. Opponents, however, dismiss the whole idea and argue that v. 35 is editorial; this verse was intended to theologise the story.

It is undeniable that scholarly work on v. 35 is notable and that any additional work will have to be built on what has been done so far. One, however, can go further in this discussion, and this will be the contribution of this work to the debate about v. 35 where the arguments of the scholars will be used to fit with new perspectives on the topic.

It is obvious that what is refered to in v. 35 puts an end to the attack but not to the whole story (given the fact that Hezekiah paid tribute after Sennacherib returned to his land). Are we supposed to dismiss the reference to the Angel of the Lord and consider it a fiction in the same sense that a fairy tale is fiction? Or should we instead consider it a theological explanation of an event or fact that actually happened at some point in the attack? The first option seems unlikely; after all, using an angel to explain an extraordinary event in the Bible is not an uncommon device. On the other hand, if we assume that the event related in v. 35 has a historical kernel, we must be careful how to interpret it and apply it in our story. The claim that the Angel of the Lord smites the army without a sword gives the impression that Sennacherib was not defeated in the battle; instead, the number of Sennacherib's men was suddenly reduced. What immediately comes to mind to explain such an event is a plague, quite apart from other biblical texts in which the Angel of the Lord is associated with a plague.

So, let us assume for now that there was a plague. What scholars do not speak about is what happens if we apply this assumption to the story. If we accept that Sennacherib lost an enormous number of his army, then his acceptance of the fact that he lost the war and returns to his city would be understandable. But one faces a challenge when continuing with the story. Our investigation in the first part of this study, which dealt with the Assyrian account of the campaign, and in chapter five, which dealt with the paying of tribute (2 Kgs 18:13 – 16), led us to conclude that Sennacherib was forced to return. Only afterwards, Hezekiah sent his very large tribute. The sending of tribute makes sense if Hezekiah, even after Sennacherib's return, felt threatened; thus, Sennacherib's absence from the Judean region clearly did not completely remove the threat. Our discussion also led us to assume that Sennacherib left some troops around Jerusalem, something not uncommon in Assyrian military history. Bearing in mind what happened to Damascus when Tiglath-pileser III left his troops around Damascus in 733 and came back the following year, and also what happened to Samaria when it was besieged for three years, the same strategy cannot be excluded with regards to the campaign in Jerusalem.

So, if we continue to accept the occurrence of a plague, we need to think how that plague affected the campaign. The narrative as it is related in the Bible informs us that there were at least three military units: one around Jerusalem, one at Lachish and another one at Libnah. In this case, Aubin's point about the Assyrian multi-pronged offensive is worth considering again. He argues that dividing the army into units makes it hard for a disease to strike the whole army. Of course, an epidemic could still affect a significant number of units. But that would not give a reasonable cause for Sennacherib's return. Moreover, suggesting that Sennacherib's army was destroyed by the epidemic would definitely exclude the notion that he left troops around Jerusalem. Returning to Nineveh with excessive losses would mean Hezekiah no longer had a reason to fear Sennacherib and pay him a large tribute to appease his already defeated enemy.

To sum up, v. 35 might have a historical kernel.[470] However, to conclude that the losses resulting from the plague were massive and were the reason Sennacherib retreated is not accurate. In later stages, when the event was re-edited, this fact took on a more prominent place in the story and thus was a suitable way for the editor to relate the divine intervention. This might explain why the return is emphasised more in the story, just as our discussion led us to conclude at the beginning of this study.

5. Conclusion to chapter six

This chapter set out to examine the three notes given in the prophetic narrative (2 Kgs 19:7, 9a, and 35) that some scholars consider could explain the reason for Sennacherib's return to his city without entering Jerusalem or dethroning Hezekiah. The aim of the investigation was to seek to decide which of the notes is more likely to explain Sennacherib's return: did he return because of a rumour, or because of the Egyptian-Kushite aid, or because of the Angel of the Lord (or plague) decimated the Assyrian army? Methodologically each note was examined in a separate section. Literary analysis was employed on the texts to help reach historical conclusions.

As for the rumour in 2 Kgs 19:6 – 7, it seems to function as a telling of Sennacherib's return within a theological framework. The text contains elements showing that it was written after Sennacherib's death, and there is no way to know whether Isaiah could have spoken it. However, this discussion led us to

---

470 Millard, A.R., "Story, History, and Theology", in A.R. Millard, *et al.* (eds.) *Faith, Tradition & History. Old Testament Historiography in Its Near Eastern Context* (Winona Lake, 1994), 63.

conclude that the text relates a historical element: Sennacherib's death. More-over, Sennacherib's return is presented as unexpected. This coheres with the con-clusion that was drawn from the first part of this research where Assyrian in-scriptions were examined.

As for the Egyptian-Kushite aid related in 2 Kgs 19:9a, the main concern of the investigation has been how significant the role of the Egyptian-Kushite army was and if it really scared Sennacherib into returning to his land. The con-clusion reached was based on archaeological evidence. Given the fact that Sen-nacherib caused a lot of damage in the Levant and reduced Hezekiah's kingdom, it is unlikely that the Egyptian-Kushite aid was sufficiently significant to make Sennacherib return. Hence, the rumour that was supposed to make Sennacherib return cannot be about Tirhakah's advance.

As for the story of the Angel of the Lord related in 2 Kgs 19:35, despite the theological outlook of the note, one cannot decide that the whole story is fiction. Again, it tells of something unexpected happening, which coheres with the con-clusion of the Assyrian part of this research. However, whatever the story indi-cates does not seem to be a reasonable solution in the wide context of the story. There might have been a plague or epidemic in Sennacherib's army, but that would not affect Sennacherib's entire army because his army was divided into units. Also, if we accept the assumption that the angel (plague) struck such a great number of Sennacherib's army, and that as a result of this Senna-cherib returned, then we have difficulty explaining why Hezekiah sent a large tribute after the danger was over.

To sum up, the investigation leads us to conclude that among the three ex-planations for Sennacherib's return, the Egyptian-Kushite aid is to be excluded. The story of the Angel of the Lord might refer to something that did happen, with remarkable results, but did not of itself make Sennacherib return. The rumour, however, seems to provide a reasonable explanation for Sennacherib's return. The question that arises from this is what was the rumour about that made Sen-nacherib return? In what follows, I provide an answer that might be hypotheti-cal, but not impossible.

If we recall our discussion about the rumour in section one of this chapter, we understand that the rumour was connected with Sennacherib's return. This means that the theory of Tirhakah's advance is not valid in this context because the Egyptian-Kushite role, as was concluded in section two, was not significant and it did not make Sennacherib return. Likewise, the Angel of the Lord (pla-gue), even if we accept it has a historical kernel, did not make Sennacherib re-turn. Thus the rumour could not have been about a plague or epidemic that struck the Assyrian army.

Two scholars, however, suggested that Sennacherib's return was due to unrest caused by rebels back in Babylon. Von Ranke argues, "Sennacherib was compelled to abandon the siege, principally, it appeared, on account of commotions which had broken out in Babylon."[471] In a similar vein, Young declares, "it would seem more likely that the report was one that came to the king from some other part of his vast empire, such as Nineveh or Babylon."[472] Both of them, however, did not go further to support their argument. In what follows I shall present an argument in favour of their suggestions.

Sennacherib led another military campaign against Babylon in 700. There he accomplished a three-fold task: defeating the leader of the rebellion, Mušēzib-Marduk, in Bit-Dakkuri; marching toward Bīt-Yakīn to force Merodach-Baladan to flee; taking Bēl-ibni back to Assyria, whom Sennacherib had set on the throne of Babylon three years previously, and establishing his (Sennacherib's) son on the throne of Babylon. There is no doubt that this campaign was to quell the revolt against Assyrian hegemony. That is clear from the items of booty that Sennacherib took in the course of his campaign; only prisoners are mentioned in the annals. It is not known if Bēl-ibni revolted or if he was taken because he was incompetent.[473] One can safely say, however, that Bēl-ibni could not control the state. Accordingly, while Sennacherib was in the southern Levant, the condition in the south of the empire was not stable.

Another question might arise from this conclusion: if the case was so urgent, why did Sennacherib not launch a war against the Babylonians in the same year he returned from the west (701)? Why did he wait a year later (700)? It seems that Sennacherib had to postpone going to Babylonia until 700 because he needed time to reassemble his army and prepare himself for another war. Additionally, having studied the annals of Ashurnasirpal, Liverani argues that there was a certain season for launching a war: spring time.[474] So one can conclude that Sennacherib waited for the right time to lead his army to Babylonia.

Thus the suggestion that Sennacherib heard a rumour about the rebellion in Babylon while he was besieging Jerusalem is rational, even if it is speculative.[475]

---

471 von Ranke, L., *Universal History: The Oldest Historical Group of Nations and the Greeks* (London, 1884), 79.

472 Young, *Isaiah*, 476.

473 Brinkman, J.A., *Prelude to Empire: Babylonian Society and Politics 747 – 626 B.C.* (Philadelphia, 1984), 59 – 60.

474 Liverani, *Ashurnasirpal*, 147 – 148.

475 Wildberger, *Jesaja*, 1410. The author argues that nothing is known about such unrest in Babylon.

Chapter Seven: Conclusion

This research has attempted a reconstruction of Sennacherib's campaign against Judah in 701. The purpose of this resconstruction has not been to reach a definitive picture of the events of 701 but rather to come to the best possible hypothesis based upon a wide study of the relevant texts.

The events of the 701 campaign, according to my reconstruction, are as follows. First Sennacherib attacks Judah. He then blockades Jerusalem, meanwhile attacking other cities. At this stage Sennacherib hears a rumor (possibly concerning a revolt in Babylon). As a result of this Sennacherib returns to Nineveh. Hezekiah then sends tribute to Sennacherib in Nineveh, which Sennacherib accepts. I have discussed the hypotheses that before Sennacherib returns to Nineveh (a) a plague breaks out amongst his troops and/or (b) an Egyption army advances on him. I have argued that whether or not these events occurred, they cannot have caused Sennacherib's return and therefore play no role in the causal chain of events. This is because in either case it would not have made sense for Hezekiah to send tribute to Sennacherib in Nineveh after his departure. The fact that Hezekiah does so shows that Sennacherib remained a threat to Jerusalem even after leaving. Had he been driven away by plague or defeated by an Egyption army this would not have been so.

The two points of contention concerning the 701 campaign are whether or not Sennacherib lost the battle, and for what reason he returned to Nineveh. The position defended in this discussion – that Sennacherib *lost the battle*, and left *because of the rumour of 2 Kgs 19:7* – does not constitute a new suggestion. However previous discussions have failed to show the full weight of the argument in favour of this conclusion. In particular they have neglected to examine the campaign of 701 in the light of the wider military activities of Senncherib as well as other Assyrian kings. As a result even those who have argued that Sennacherib's campaign in 701 is not a complete success do so on grounds which might easily have been defeated by broader evidence. By drawing a general criterion for success in battle, from a wide study of Assyrian warfare it has been possible to put forward firm grounds for thinking that such a criterion cannot plausibly be considered to have been met in the 701 campaign. Likewise even those who have argued that Sennacherib returns to Nineveh as a result of the rumour fail to offer convincing explanations of the nature of this rumour. Those who suggest that it corresponds to a plague or an Egyption attack have no explanation for why Hezekiah nonetheless sends tribute to Sennacherib in Nineveh. Those who like myself hold that the rumour is likely to relate to a revolt in Babylon leave this as an unargued hypothesis. I have attempted to show what considerations can be given in favour of this hypothesis. Though these have turned out to be relatively speculative they nonetheless constitute a plausible case.

In order to argue for this reconstruction of the 701 campaign I divided my discussion into two parts. In part one I deal with Assyrian texts, in part two, biblical texts. Part one began by examining the literary conventions and formulae of the texts under examination. The language used about the 701 campaign taken on its own might suggest that Sennacherib did not intend to act with aggression against Jerusalem and Hezekiah. This view has been thought to be corroborated on the one hand by the reliefs of the attack on Lachish, which neither depict the city being destroyed nor burned but only conquered, and on the other hand by the large tribute taken by Sennacherib, which it has been suggested, shows that Sennacherib's aims were ecominic rather than destructive. However, I have argued that this view is undermined by the archeological evidence which shows that Lachish and other cities *were in fact destroyed*. Therefore the lack of aggression on the part of Sennacherib suggested by the inscription and the reliefs cannot be taken as veridical.

In the remainder of part one I developed a criterion for success in military campaigns based on the pattern of the military exploits of Sennacherib and other Assyrian Kings. It was noted that, wherever a battle is concluded successfully, the enemy king is described as showing submission to the Assyrian attacker either by coming out of his city and paying tribute directly or by allowing the Assyrian king into his city and paying tribute within his own palace. In no case other than the 701 campaign of Sennacherib is an Assyrian king described as receiving a tribute without the inclusion of a description of the submission of the enemy king at the location of the battle. It may be inductively inferred from this that had the 701 campaign been successful at the point of Sennacherib's departure, Hezekiah would have been made to pay tribute on the spot, and the inscriptions would include a description of this event. Since no such description appears in the inscriptions relating to the 701 campaign it was concluded that the campaign was not a success at the point of Sennacherib's departure.

Part one established that Sennacherib had not defeated Jerusalem when he departed to Nineveh. This agrees with the biblical version of the story. Part two addressed the question why Sennacherib departed at this time. Since the Assyrian sources provide no explanation for Sennacherib's return, part two dealt with the biblical evidence. The scholarly debate concerning the reason for Sennacherib's return to Nineveh has focussed on four notes given in the Bible in 2 Kgs 18 – 19.

These note are: the paying of tribute in 2 Kgs 18:13 – 16; the hearing a rumour in 2 Kgs 19:7; Egyptian-Kushite aid in 2 Kgs 19:9a; and the appearance of the

Angel of the Lord in 2 Kgs 19:35. All these explanations were examined and discussed at length. Our conclusions were as follows:

- As for the paying of tribute, the investigation led us to conclude that the text in 2 Kgs 18:13–16 is not a unit taken from an annalistic document as has been suggested. Thus the assumption that this text is most historically reliable because of its annalistic origin is not valid. Also, there was reason to think that the text does not necessarily indicate that Hezekiah offered his tribute and that Sennacherib then returned afterwards. The text does not end with an account confirming his return as other biblical invasions reports have. We know that Hezekiah offered his tribute to Sennacherib in order that his forces might withdraw, but the whole circumstance of that offer is not clear. What this study suggests is that Hezekiah paid tribute in Nineveh. If this is correct then it cannot have been the tribute that made Sennacherib return, because he was already in his land when Hezekiah paid it. It might however be possible that Hezekiah offered his tribute while Sennacherib was in Nineveh so that Sennacherib might remove the troops he left after he returned to Nineveh.
- As for the rumour, there is no way to know if Isaiah really reported it or not. However, the investigation of this matter led us to conclude that the note about hearing a rumour is difficult to explain as a divine action, and so there is no obvious theological justification for its inclusion in the text. Though the rumour is mentioned in a theological context—it follows the report of the spirit which God is said to place in Sennacherib—there is no way to know whether this is the context in which it originated. It is difficult to explain its presence in the text without the assumption that it had historical precedent.
- As for the Egyptian-Kushite aid, this study excluded the view that Sennacherib withdrew because he was surprised by the advance of Tirhakah. The decision on this matter was based on the archaeological evidence that showed that Judah suffered from Sennacherib's campaign and many sites were destroyed. In this case, the presence of the Nubian king was not so significant in the field.
- As for the Angel of the Lord, the conclusion reached was not decisive. Some scholars dismiss the whole story because of its theological framework. I argued that this is not necessarily a sufficient reason to dismiss it, and that it might have related to a historical occurrence. However, I also suggested that such an occurrence could not have been the main reason to make Sennacherib withdraw.

To sum up, the conclusions made above oblige us to narrow down the possibilities for the reason for Sennacherib's return. It is not because of the paying of tribute, nor is it the presence of Tirhakah that obliged Sennacherib to return. If the Angel of the Lord (plague) was not the main reason, then the rumour must have had a significant role in Sennacherib's return.

The question of the nature of the rumour was also discussed. Although only a speculative conclusion could be possible I suggested that news about trouble in Babylonia might be the answer. The unsettled condition in Babylonia, and the campaign that Sennacherib launched in 700 would provide some support for this assumption.

Bibliography

Achenbach, A., "Jabâ und Atalja – zwei jüdische Königstöchter am assyrischen Königshof. Zu einer These von Stephanie Dalley", *BN* 113 (2002), 29 – 38.

Adams, W.Y., *Nubia: Corridor to Africa* (London, 1977).

Albenda, P., "Assyrian Wall Reliefs: a Study of Compositional Styles", in H. Waetzoldt and H. Hauptmann (eds.), *Assyrien im Wandel der Zeiten, XXXIXe Rencontre Assyriologique Internationale, Heidlberg 6 – 10 Juli 1992* (Heidelberg, 1992), 223 – 226.

Andersen, F.I. and Freedman, D.N., *Amos* (AB, 24 A; New York, 1989).

Athas, G., *The Tel Dan Inscription: A Reappraisal and a New Introduction* (JSOTSup 12; London, 2003).

Aubin, H.T., *The Rescue of Jerusalem. The Alliance between Hebrews and Africans in 701 BC.* (New York, 2002).

Auvray,P., *Isaïe* (SB; Paris, 1957).

Bär, J., *Der assyrissche Tribut und seine Darstellung: Eine Untersuchung zur imperialen Ideologie im neuassyrischen Reich* (AOAT 243; Neukirchen-Vluyn, 1996).

Barnett, R.D., Bleibtreu E. and Turner G., *Sculptures from the Southwest Palace of Sennacherib at Nineveh* (London, 1998).

Becking, B., "Chronology: A Skeleton without Flesh? Sennacherib's Campaign as a Case-Study", in L.L. Grabbe (ed.), *'Like a Bird in a Cage': The Invasion of Sennacherib in 701 BCE* (JSOTSup 363; London, 2003), 46 – 72.

Ben Iehuda, E., *Thesaurus Totius Hebraitatis et veteris et Recentioris.* Vol. 1 (Berlin, 1953)

Berndes, L., "The Sennacherib Episode: Exegetical Issues," An unpublished short paper presented at OTSEM Conference in Skálholt, September (2010).

Berndes, L., "Dialogic Exegesis of the Sennacherib Episode: The Need for a method that is both Literary and Historical." An unpublished short paper presented at OTSEM conference in Granavolden/Oslo (December 2008).

Blakely, J.A. and Hardin, J.W., "Southwestern Judah in the Late Eighth Century B.C.E.", *BASOR* 326 (2002), 11 – 64.

Blenkinsopp, J., *Isaiah 1 – 39. A New Translation with Introduction and Commentary* (AB 19; New York, 2000).

Bloch-Smith, E., "Assyrians Abet Israelite Cultic Reform: Sennacherib and the Centralization of the Israelite Cult", in J.D. Schloen (ed.), *Exploring the Longue Durée. Essays in Honor of Lawrence E. Stager* (Winona Lake, 2009), 35 – 44.

Boardman, J., *The Cambridge Ancient History, III part 2, The Assyrian and Babylonian Empires and other States of the Near East, from the Eighth to Sixth Century* (Cambridge, 1991).

Borger, R., *Babylonisch-Assyrische Lesestücke* (AO 54; Rome, 1979).

Borger, R., *Beiträge zum Inschriftenwerk Assurbanipals* (Wiesbaden, 1996).

Borowski, O., *Agriculture in Iron Age Israel* (Winona Lake, 1979).

Bostock, D., *A Portryal of Trust: The Theme of Faith in the Hezekiah Narratives* (PBM; Milton Keynes, 2006).

Boutflower, C., *The Book of Isaiah: Chapters 1 – 39 in the Light of the Assyrian Monuments* (London, 1930).

Breasted, J.H., *A History of Egypt from the Earliest Times to the Persian Conquest* (London, 1906).

Brinkman, J.A., *Prelude to Empire: Babylonian Society and Politics 747–626 B.C.* (Philadelphia, 1984)

Bruce, F.F., *Israel and the Nations: From the Exodus to the Fall of the Second Temple* (Grand Rapids, 1963).

Camp, L., *Hiskija und Hiskijabild: Analyse und Interpretation von 2 Kön 18–20* (MThA 9; Alterberge, 1990).

Carroll, R.P., *Jeremiah. A Commentary* (OTL; London, 1986).

Catastini, A., *Isaia ed Ezechia. Studio di Storia della Tradizione di II Re 18–20//Is. 36–39* (Rome, 1989).

Childs, B.S., *Isaiah and the Assyrian Crisis* (SBTh 3; London, 1967).

Childs, B.S., *Isaiah* (OTL; London, 2001)

Clarke, A., *Clarke's Commentary: Second Kings* (Albany, 1999).

Clements, R.E., "שאר", *ThDOT*, Vol. XIV, 272–286.

Clements, R.E., *Isaiah and the Deliverance of Jerusalem. A Study of the Interpretation of Prophecy in the Old Testament* (JSOTSup 13; Sheffield, 1980).

Clements, R.E., *Jerusalem and the Nations. Studies in the Book of Isaiah* (HBM 16; Sheffield, 2011).

Clover, R., *The Sabbath and Jubilee Cycle.* Vol. 1 (Garden Grove, 1992).

Cogan, M., *Imperialism and Religion: Assyria, Judah and Israel in the Eighth and Seventh Centuries B.C.E.* (SBL 19; Missoula, 1974).

Cogan, M. and Tadmor, H., *II Kings: A New Translation with Introduction and Commentary.* Includes index (AB 11; New Haven, 2008).

Crouch, C., *War and Ethics in the Ancient Near East: Military Violence in the Light of Cosmology and History* (BZAW 407; Berlin, 2009).

Dalley, S., "Yabâ, Atalyā and the Foreign Policy of Late Assyrian Kings" *SAAB* 12 (1998), 83–98.

Dalley, S., "Recent Evidence from Assyrian Sources for Judean History from Uzziah to Manasseh", *JSOT* 28 (2004a), 387–401.

Darr, K.P., "No Strength to Deliver: A Contextual Analysis of Hezekiah's Proverb in Isaiah 37:3b", in R.F. Melugin and M.A Sweeney (eds.), *New Visions of Isaiah* (JSOTSup 214; Sheffield 1996), 219–256.

Day, J., *God's Conflict with the Dragon and the Sea. Echoes of a Canaanite Myth in the Old Testament* (Cambridge, 1985).

de Jong, M.J., *Isaiah among the Ancient Near Eastern Prophets. A Comparative Study of the Earliest Stages of the Isaiah Tradition and the New-Assyrian Prophecies* (VTSup 117; Leiden, 2007).

Dion, P.E., "Sennacherib's Expedition to Palestine", *ÉgT 20* (1989) 5–25.

Dorsey D., *The Roads and Highways of Ancient Israel* (Baltimore, 1991).

Dubovsky, P., "Tiglath-pileser III's Campaigns in 734–732 B.C.: Historical Background of Is 7; 2 Kgs 15–16 and 2 Chr 27–28", *Bib* 87 (2006), 153–170.

Dubovsky, P., "Assyrian Downfall through Isaiah's Eyes (2 Kings 15–23): The Historiography of Representation", *Bib* 89 (2008), 1–16.

Duhm, B., *Das Buch Jesaia* (HKAT III/1; Göttingen, 1914).

Elat, M., "The Impact of Tribute and Booty on Countries and People within the Assyrian Empire", in H. Hirsch and H. Hunger (eds.), *Afo Beiheft 19* (=CRRAI 28), Horn, 244–251.

Eph'al, I., *The City Besieged. Siege and Its Manifestations in the Ancient Near East* (CHANE 36; Leiden, 2009).

Evan, P.S., *The Invasion of Sennacherib in the Book of Kings. A Source-Critical and Rhetorical Study of 2 Kings 18–19* (VTSup 125; Leiden, 2009).

Fales, F.M., "Moving around Babylon: On the Aramean and Chaldean Presence in Southern Mesopotamia", in E. Cancik-Kirschbaum et al (eds.), *Babylon: Wissenskultur in Orient und Okzident* (TBSAW1; Berlin, 2011)", 91–111.

Fales, F.M., "Tiglat-Pileser III tra annalistica reale ed epistolografia quotidiana.", in F.P. Daddi & M.C. Guidotto (eds.), *Narrare gli Eventi. Atti del Convengo degli Egittologi e degli Orientalisti Italiani in Margine alla Mostra "La Battaglia di Qadesh"* (SA 3; Rome, 2005), 163–191.

Faust, A. and Weiss, E., "Judah, Philistia and the Mediterranean World: Reconstructing the Economic System of the Seventh Century B.C.E.", *BASOR* 338 (2005), 71–92.

Faust, A., "Settlement and Demography in Seventh-Century Judah and the extent and Intensity of Sennacherib's Campaign" *PEQ* 140, 3 (2008).

Frahm, E., *Einleitung in die Sanherib-Inschriften* (AfO 26; Wien, 1997).

Frahm, E., "Sîn-aḫḫē-erïba", in H. Baker (ed.), *The Prosopography of the Assyrian Empire*. Vol. 3, Part I: P-Ṣ (Helsinki, 2002), 1113–1127.

Frahm, E., "New Sources for Sennacherib's 'First Campaign'", in J.M. Cordoba and P.A. Miglus (eds.), *Assur und sein Umland*, ISIMU VI (2003), 129–146.

Fuchs, A., *Die Inschriften Sargon II aus Khorsabad* (Göttingen, 1994).

Fuchs, A., "Über den Wert von Befestigungsanlagen", *ZAVA* 98 (2008), 45–99.

Galil, G., review of F.M. Fales, *Guerre et Paix en assyrie: Religion et imperialism. Les Conférences de l'école Pratique des Hautes études* (Paris, 2010).

Gallagher, W.R., *Sennacherib's Campaign to Judah. New Studies* (SHCANE 18; Leiden, 1999).

Galter, H.D., "Die Zerstörung Babylons durch Sanherib", *SO* 55 (1984), 161–173.

Geyer, J.B., "2 Kings XVIII 14–16 and the annals of Sennacherib", *VT* 21 (1971), 604–606.

Geva, H., "Western Jerusalem at the End of the First Temple Period in Light of the Excavations in the Jewish Quarter", in A.G. Vaughn and A.E. Killbrew (eds.), *Jerusalem in Bible and Arcaheology. The First Temple Period* (SBL 18; Atlanta, 2003), 183–208.

Gordis, R., *The Book of Job. Commentary New Translation and Special Studies* (MS 2; New York, 1978).

Gonçalves, F., *L'expedition de Sennachérib en Palestine dans la littérature hébraïque ancienne* (Ébib 7; Paris, 1986).

Grabbe, L.L., *Can a "History of Israel" Be Written?* (JSOTSup 245; Shefield, 1996).

Grabbe, L.L., "Of Mice and Dead Men: Herodotus 2. 141 and Sennacherib's Campaign in 701 BCE", in L.L. Grabbe (ed.), *'Like a Bird in a Cage.' The Invasion of Sennacherib in 701 BCE* (JSOTSup 363; London, 2003), 119–140.

Gray, J., *I and II Kings. A Commentary* (OTL; London 1977).

Grayson, A.K., "The Walters Art Gallery Sennacherib Inscription", *AfO* 20 (1963), 88–91.

Grayson, A.K., *Assyrian and Babylonian Chronicles* (TCS 5; Locust Valley, 1975).

Grayson, A.K., "Königslisten und Chroniken B. Akkadisch", *RIA* 6/1 (1980), 86–135.

Grayson, A.K. and Novotny, J., *The Royal Inscriptions of Sennacherib, King of Assyria (704–681 BC), Part1* (RINAP 3/1; Winona Lake, 2012).

Hardmeier, C., *Prophetie im Streit vor dem Untergang Judas* (BZAW 187; Berlin, 1990).

Hasel, G., *The Remnant: The History and Theology of the Remnant Idea from Genesis to Isaiah* (AUM 5; Berrien Springs, 1972).

Hausmann, J., *Israels Rest: Studien zum Selbsvertändnis der nachexilischen Gemeinde* (BWANT 7; Stuttgart, 1987).

Hobbs, T.R., *2 Kings* (WBC 13; Dallas, 2002).

Honor, L.L. *Sennacherib's Invasion of Palestine: A Critical Source Study* (COHP 12; New York, 1926)

House, P.R., *1, 2 Kings* (NAC 8; Nashville, 1995).

Irvine, S.A., *Isaiah, Ahaz, and the Syro-Ephraimitic Crisis* (SBLDS 123; Atlanta, 1990).

Jankowska, N.B., "Some Problems of the Economy of the Assyrian Empire", in I.M. Diakonoff (ed.), *Ancient Mesopotamia. Socio-Economic History* (Moscow, 1969), 253–276.

Jeffers, J., "Fifth-Campaign Reliefs in Sennacherib's Palace 'Palace without Rival' at Nineveh", *Iraq* 73 (2011), 78–116.

Jenkins, A.K, "Hezekiah's Fourteenth Year. A New Interpretation of 2 Kings xviii 13 – xix 37", in *VT* 26 (1976), 284–289.

Kaiser, O., *Isaiah 13–39. A Commentary* (OTL; London, 1974).

Katzenstein, H.J., *The History of Tyre: From the Beginning of the Second Millennium B.C.E. until the Fall of the Neo-Babylonian Empire in 538 B.C.E.* (Jerusalem, 1973).

Killebrew, A.E. and Vaughn, A.G., "Jerusalem in Bible and Archaeology: Dialogues and Discussions", in Vaughn, A.G. and Killebrew, A.E. (eds.), *Jerusalem in Bible and Archaeology. The First Temple Period* (SBL 18; Atlanta, 2003), 1–10.

Killebrew, A.E., "Biblical Jerusalem: An Archaeological Assessment", in A.G. Vaughn and A.E. Killebrew (eds.), *Jerusalem in Bible and Archaeology. The First Temple Period* (SBL 18; Atlanta, 2003), 329–346.

Kitchen, K., "Egypt, the Levant and Assyria in 701 BC", in H. Brunner and M. Görg (eds.), *Fontes Atque Pontes: eine Festgabe für Hellmut Brunner* (ÄAT 5; Wiesbaden, 1983), 243–253.

Kitchen, K.A., *The Third Intermediate Period in Egypt (1100–650BC)* (Warminster, 1986).

Knauf, E.A., "Sennacherib at the Berezina", in Grabbe, L.L. (ed.), *'Like a Bird in a Cage': The Invasion of Sennacherib in 701 BCE* (JSOTSup 363; London, 2003), 141–149.

Kofoed, J.B., *Text and History. Historiography and the Biblical Text* (Winona Lake, 2005).

Kuan, J.K., *Neo-Assyrian Historical Inscriptions and Syria-Palestine* (JDds 1; Hong Kong 1995).

Kuhrt, A., "Sennacherib's Siege of Jerusalem", in A.K. Bowman *et al.* (eds.), *Representations of Empire: Rome and the Mediterranean World, Proceedings of the British Academy 114* (London, 2004), 13–33.

Laato, A., *Who is Immanuel? The Rise and the Foundering of Isaiah's Messianic Expectations* (Åbo, 1988).

Laato, A., "Assyrian Propaganda and the Falsification of History in the Royal Inscriptions of Sennacherib", *VT* 45 (1995), 198–226.

Leichty, E., *The Royal Inscriptions of Esarhaddon, King of Assyria (680–669 BC)* (RINAP 4; Winona Lake, 2011).

Levine, L.D., "The Second Campaign of Sennacherib", *JNES* 32 (1973), 312–317.

Levine, L.D., "Sennacherib's Southern Front: 704–689 B.C.", *JCS* 34 (1982), 28–58.

Levine, L.D., "Preliminary Remarks on the Historical Inscriptions of Sennacherib", in H. Tadmor and M. Weinfeld (eds.), *History, Historiography and Interpretation. Studies in Biblical and Cuneiform Literatures* (Jerusalem, 1983), 58–75.

Lewy, J., "Sanherib und Hizkia", *OLZ* 31 (1928), 150–163.

Lie, A.G., *The Inscriptions of Sargon II, King of Assyria* (Paris, 1929).

Liverani, M., "The Ideology of the Assyrian Empire", in M.T. Larsen (ed.), *Power and Propaganda. A Symposium on Ancient Empire* (Mesopotamia 7; Copenhagen, 1979), 297–317.

Liverani, M., *Studies in the Annals of Ashurnasirpal II, 2: Topographical Analysis* (Rome, 1992).

Liverani, M., "The Age of Sennacherib", in C. Lippolis (ed.), *The Sennacherib Wall Reliefs at Nineveh* (Mesopotamia 15; Firenze, 2011), 7–22.

Liwak, R., "Die Rettung Jerusalems im Jahr 701 v. Chr.: Zum Verhaltnis und Verstandnis historischer und theologischer Aussagungen", *ZThK* 83 (1986), 137–166.

Long, B., *2 Kings: The Forms of Old Testament Literature* (FOTL 10; Grand Rapids, 1991).

Luckenbill, D.D., *The Annals of Sennacherib* (OIP II; Chicago, 1924).

Luckenbill, D.D., *Ancient Records of Assyria and Babylonia, 2. Historical Records of Assyria from Sargon to the End* (Chicago, 1927).

Martin, W.J., *Tribut und Tributleistungen bei den Assyrern* (SO 8/1; Helsingforsiae 1936).

Mayer, W., *Politik und Kriegskunst der Assyrer* (ALASPM 9; Münster 1995).

Mayer, W., 'Sennacherib's Campaign of 701 BCE: The Assyrian View' in Grabbe, L.L. (ed.), *'Like a Bird in a Cage': The Invasion of Sennacherib in 701 BCE* (JSOTSup 363; London, 2003), 168–200.

Mazar, A., "The Divided Monarchy: Comments on Some Archaeological Issues", in I. Finkelstein and A. Mazar (B. B. Schmidt, ed.), *The Quest for the Historical Israel. Debating Archaeology and the History of Early Israel* (SBL 17; Atlanta, 2007), 159–180.

Millard, A.R., "Sennacherib's Attack on Hezekiah", *TB* 36 (1985), 61–77.

Millard, A.R., *The Eponyms of the Assyrian Empire 910–612 BC* (SAAS 2; Helsinki, 1994).

Millard, A.R., "Story, History, and Theology", in A.R. Millard, *et al.* (eds.) *Faith, Tradition & History. Old Testament Historiography in Its Near Eastern Context* (Winona Lake, 1994), 37–64.

Montgomery, J.A., *A Critical and Exegetical Commentary on the Books of Kings* (ICC; New York, 1951).

Na'aman, N., "Sennacherib's 'Letter to God' on his Campaign to Judah", *BASOR* 214 (1974), 25–39.

Na'aman, N., "Sennacherib's Campaign to Judah and the Date of the *lmlk* Stamps", *VT* 29 (1979), 61–86.

Na'aman, N., "Forced Participation in Alliance in the Course of the Assyrian Campaigns to the West", in M. Cogan *et al.* (eds.), *Ah...Assyria. Studies in Assyrian History and Ancient Near Eastern Historiography Presented to Hayim Tadmor* (SH 33; Jerusalem, 1991), 80–98.

Na'aman, N., "The Temple Library of Jerusalem and the Composition of the Book of Kings", in A. Lemaire (ed.), *Congress Volume Leiden 2004* (VTSup 109; Leiden, 2006), 129–152.

Nadali, D., "Sennacherib's Siege, Assault, and Conquest of Alammu", in *SAAB* 14 (2002–2005), 113–128.

Nadali, D., "Sieges and Similes of Sieges in the Royal Annals: The Conquest of Damascus by Tiglath-pileser III", *Kaskal: Rivista di storia, ambienti e culture del Vicino Oriente Antico* 6 (2009), 137–150.

Nadali, D., "Assyrian Open Field Battles. An Attempt at Reconstruction and Analysis", in J. Vidal (ed.), *Studies on War in the Ancient Near East. Collected Essays on Military History* (Münster, 2010), 117–152.

Norin, S., "An Important Kennicott Reading in 2 Kings XVIII, 13", *VT* 32 (1982), 337–338.

Oded, B., *War, Peace and Empire: Justifications for War in the Assyrian Royal Inscriptions* (Wiesbaden, 1992).

Oded, B., "Cutting Down Orchards in Assyrian Royal Inscriptions – The Historiographic Aspect", in *JAC* 12 (1997), 93–98.

Oswalt, J.N., *The Book of Isaiah. Chapters 1–39* (NICOT; Grand Rapids, 1986).

Parker, S., *Stories in the Scriptures and Inscriptions. Comparative Studies on Narratives in Northwest Semitic Inscriptions and the Hebrew Bible* (New York, 1997).

Parker, S., "Did the Books of Kings Make Use of Royal Inscriptions?", *VT* 50 (2000), 357–378.

Parpola, S., *Neo-Assyrian Toponym* (AOAT 6; Kevelaer, 1970).

Piepkorn, A.C., *Historical Prism Inscriptions of Ashurbanipal* (AS 5; Chicago, 1933)

Pitard, W.T., *Ancient Damascus. A Historical Study of the Syrian City-State from Earliest Times until its Fall to the Assyrians in 732 B.C.E.* (Winona Lake, 1987).

Pognon, H., *L'inscription de Bavian: texte, traduction et un glassaire* (Paris, 1879–1880).

Ponchia, S., "Analogie, metafore e similitudini nelle iscrizioni reali assire: semantica e ideolgia", *OA* 26. 3–4 (1987), 232–255.

Postgate, J.N., *Taxation and Conscription in the Assyrian Empire* (StPol 2; Rome, 1974).

Radner, K., "Esarhaddon's Expedition from Palestine to Egypt in 671BCE: A Trek to Negev and Sinai", in D. Bonatz, *et al* (eds.), *Fundstellen Gesammelte Schriften zur Archäologie und Geschichte Altvorderasiens ad Honorem Hartmut Kühne* (Wiebaden, 2008), 305–314.

Radner, K., "The Assyrian King and His Scholars: The Syro-Anatolia and the Egyptian Schools", in M. Luukko *et al.* (eds.), *Of God(s), Trees, Kings and Scholars. New Assyrian and Related Studies in Honor of Simon Parpola* (ST 106; Helsinki 2009), 221–238.

Radner, K., "After Elteqeh: Royal Hostages from Egypt at the Assyrian Court", in H.D. Baker *et al* (eds.), *Stories of Long Ago. Festschrift für Michael D. Roaf* (AOAT 397; Münster, 2012), 471–480.

Rainey, A.F., "The Fate of Lachish during the Campaigns of Sennacherib and Nebuchadnezzar", in Y. Aharoni (ed.), *Investigations at Lachish: The Sanctuary and Residency (Lachish V)* (Tel Aviv, 1975), 47–60.

Rawlinson, G., *Phoenicia* (London, 1889).

Reade, J., "Ideology and Propaganda in Assyrian Art", in M.T. Larsen, *Power and Propaganda: A Symposium on Ancient Empire* (Copenhagen, 1979).

Reade, J., "Ideology and Propaganda in Assyrian Art", in M.T. Larsen (ed.), *Power and Propaganda. Mesopotamia. Copenhagen Studies in Assyriology* (Mesopotamia 7; Copenhagen, 1979), 329–343.

Rowley, H.H., *Men of God: Studies in the Old Testament History and Prophecy* (London, 1963).

Russell J.M., *Sennacherib's "Palace without Rival": A Programmatic Study of Texts and Images in a Late Assyrian Palace* (Pennsylvania, 1990).

Russell, J.M., *The Final Sack of Nineveh. The Discovery, Documentation, and Destruction of King Sennacherib's Throne Room at Nineveh, Iraq* (New Heaven, 1998).

Russell, J.M., *Writing on the Wall. Studies in the Architectural Context of Late Assyrian Palace Inscriptions* (MC 9; Winona Lake, 1999).

Šanda, A., *Die Bücher der Könige übersetzt und erklärt* (EHAT 9; Münster, 1912).

Seitz, C.R., *Zion's Final Destiny. The Development of the Book of Isaiah. A Reassessment of Isaiah 36–39* (Minneapolis, 1991).

Seitz, C.R., *Isaiah 1–39* (BCTP; Louisville 1993).

Ska, J.L., *Our Fathers Have Told Us. Introduction to the Analysis of Hebrew Narratives* (SubBib 13; Rome, 1990).

Smelik, K.A.D., "Distortion of Old Testament Prophecy. The Purpose of Isaiah xxxvi and xxxvii", in A.S. van der Woude (ed.), *Crisis and Perspective. Studies in Ancient Near Eastern Polytheism, Biblical Theology, Palestinian Archaeology and Intertestamental Literature* (OS 24; Leiden, 1985), 70–93.

Smoak, J.D., "Building Houses and Planting Vineyards: The Early Inner-Biblical Discourse on an Ancient Israelite Wartime Curse", *JBL* 127 (2008), 19–35.

Song-Mi, P., *The Development of the Hezekiah Complex: Literature, History and Theology* (Ph.D Dissertation, Harvard University, 2010).

Stade, B., "Miscellen: Anmerkungen zu 2 Ko. 15–21", *ZAW* 6 (1886), 156–89.

Stern, E., *Archaeology of the Land of the Bible, vol. II: The Assyrian, Babylonian and Persian Period (732–332 BCE)* (ABRL; New York, 2001).

Suleiman, A., *Al-kitāba al-mismārīya wal-ḥarf al-'arabī* (Cuneiform Writing and Arabic Alphabet) (Ph.D. Dissertation, Mosul n.d).

Streck, M. (ed.), *Assurbanipal und die letzten assyrischen Könige bis zum Untergange Niniveh's*. (VB 7; Leipzig, 1916).

Sweeney, M.A, *Isaiah 1–39: With an Introduction to Prophetic Literature* (FOTL 16; Grand Rapids 1996)

Sweeney, M.A., *1 and 2 Kings: A Commentary* (OTL; Louisville, 2007).

Tadmor, H., *The Inscriptions of Tiglath-pileser III King of Assyria. Critical Edition, with Introductions, Translations and Commentary* (IASH; Jerusalem, 1994).

Tadmor, H., "Propaganda, Literature, Historiography: Cracking the Code of the Assyrian Royal Inscriptions", in M. Cogan (ed.), *"With My Many Chariots I have Gone up the Heights of the Mountains". Historical and Literary Studies on Ancient Mesopotamia and Israel* (IES; Jerusalem, 2011), 3–24.

Tadmor, H., "History and Ideology in the Assyrian Royal Inscriptions", in M. Cogan (ed.), *"With My Many Chariots I Have Gone Up the Heights of Mountains". Historical and Literary Studies on Ancient Mesopotamia and Israel* (IES; Jerusalem, 2011), 25–46.

Tadmor, H., "Observations on Assyrian Historiography", in M. Cogan (ed.), *"With My Many Chariots I Have Gone Up the Heights of Mountains". Historical and Literary Studies on Ancient Mesopotamia and Israel* (IES; Jerusalem, 2011), 47–56.

Telfer, C.K., "Toward a Historical Reconstruction of Sennacherib's Invasion of Judah in 701 B.C. with Special Attention to the Hezekiah-Narrative of Isaiah 36–39", *MAJTh* 22 (2011), 7–19.

Uehlinger, C., "Clio in a World of Pictures –Another Look at the Lachish Reliefs from Sennacherib's Southwest Palace at Nineveh", in L.L. Grabbe (ed.), *'Like a Bird in a Cage' The Invasion of Sennacherib in 701 BCE.* (JSOTSup 363; London, 2003).

Ussishkin, D., *The Renewed Archaeological Excavations at Lachish (1973–1994)*, Vol. I (MS 22; Tel Aviv, 2004).

Ussishkin, D., The *Conquest of Lachish by Sennacherib* (PIA 6; Tel Aviv, 1982).

Ussishkin, D., "Sennacherib's Campaign to Philistia and Judah: Ekron, Lachish, and Jerusalem" in Y. Amit *et al.* (eds.), *Essays on Ancient Israel in Its Near Eastern Context. A Tribute to Nadav Na'aman* (Winina Lake, 2006), 338–357.

van der Kooij, A., "Das assyrische Heer vor den Mauern Jerusalems im Jahr 701 v. Ch.", *ZDPV* 102 (1986), 93–109.

Vaughn, A.G., *Theology, History, and Archaeology in the Chronicler's Account of Hezekiah* (ABS 4; Atlanta, 1999).

Vaughn, A.G. and Killebrew (eds.), A.E., *Jerusalem in Bible and Archaeology. The First Temple Period* (SBL 18; Atlanta, 2003).

Vidal, J., "Some Remarks on the Battle of Altaqu", in G. del Olmo Lete, *et al.* (eds.), *The Perfumes of Seven Tamarisks. Studies in Honour of Wilfred G.E. Watson* (AOAT 394; Münster, 2012), 75–83.

Vuk, T., *Wiedererkaufte Freiheit. Der Feldzug Sanheribs gegen Juda nach dem Invasionsberich 2 Kön 18:13–16* (FHTB 1; Jerusalem, 1984).

Watts, J.D.W., *Isaiah 34–66* (WBC 25; Dallas, 2002).

Westermann, C., *Prophetic Oracles of Salvation in the Old Testament* (London, 1991).

Widyapranawa, S.H., *The Lord is Savior: A Commentary on the Book of Isaiah 1–39* (ITC; Grand Rapids, 1990).

Wildberger, H., *Jesaja 28–39* (BKAT 3; Neukirchen-Vluyn, 1965).

Williamson, H.G.M., *A Critical and Exegetical Commentary Isaiah 1–27. Vol 1 Commentary on Isaiah 1–5* (ICC; London, 2006).

Wilson, J.K., "And He Shall Hear a Rumour…" (Isaiah 37:7; 2 Kings 19:7), in J.K. Aitken, K.J. Dell, *et al* (eds.), *On Stone and Scroll. Essay in Honour of Graham Ivor Davies* (BZAW 420; Berlin, 2011), 371–374.

Winckler, H., *Die Keilschrifttexte Sargons, nach den Papierabklatschen und Originalen. Band 1* (Leipzig, 1888).

Wright, C., "Sabbatical Year", *ABD*, 5, O-Sh, 857–861.

Würthweint, E., *Die Bücher der Könige: 1. Kön. 17–2. Kön. 25 übersetzt und erklärt* (ATD 11; Göttingen, 1984).

Yamada, S., *The Construction of the Assyrian Empire. A Historical Study of the Inscriptions of Shalmaneser III (859–824 BC) Relating to His Campaigns to the West.* (CHANE 3; Leiden, 2000).

Yurco, F.J., "Sennacherib's Third Campaign and the Coregency of Shabaka and Shebitky", *Ser* 6 (1980), 221–240.

Young, E., *The Book of Isaiah: Volume 2, Chapters 19–39* (Grand Rapids, 1969).

Young, R.A., *Hezekiah in History and Tradition* (VTSup 155; Leiden, 2012).

Younger, K.L., "Yahweh at Ashkelon and Calah? Yahwistic Names in Neo-Assyrian", *VT* 52 (2002) 207–218

Zamazalova, S., "Before the Assyrian Conquest in 761 B.C.E.: Relations between Egypt, Kush and Assyria," in J. Mynárová (ed.), *Egypt and the Near East – the Crossroads: proceedings of an International Conference on the Relations of Egypt and the Near East in the Bronze Age, September 1–3, 2010* (Prague, 2011), 297–328.

Zawadzki, S., "Hostages in Assyrian Royal Inscriptions", in K. van Lerberghe and A. Schoors (eds.), *Immigration and Emigration within the Ancient Near East. Festschrift E. Lipiński* (OLA 65; Leuven, 1995), 449–458.

Zimansky, P.E, *Ecology and Empire. The Structure of the Urartian State* (SAOC 41; Chicago, 1985).

Zobel, H-J., "יהודה", *ThDOT*, 5, pp. 492–3.

Appendix

Appendix

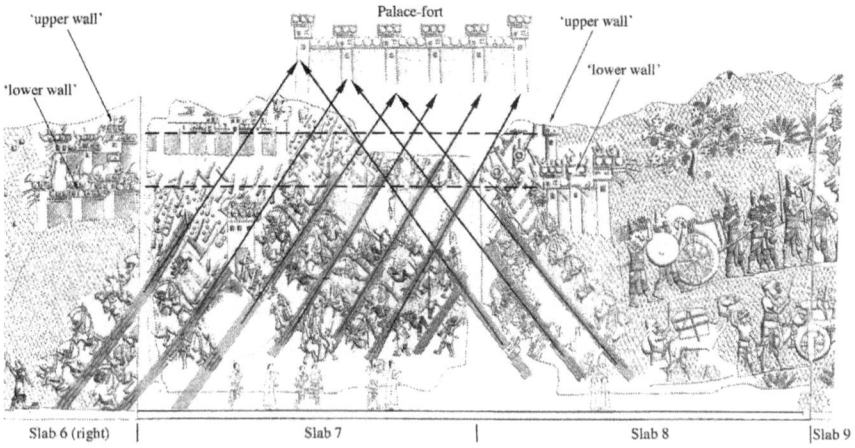

Figure 1: Tentative reassembling of Slabs 2–4, with selective restoration including the now-missing citadel (Uehlinger 2003, p 269)

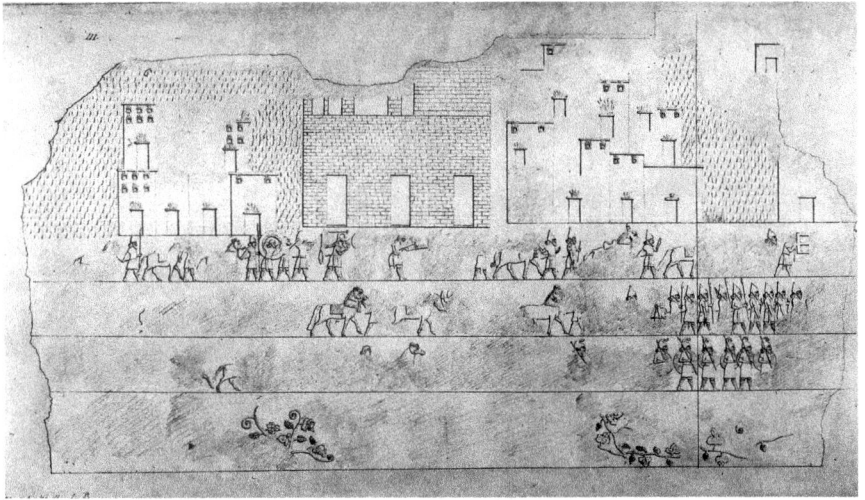

Figure 2: [above:] The city of Ukku; [below:] The city of Dilbat (Barnett 1998, pl. 30; and pl. 49)

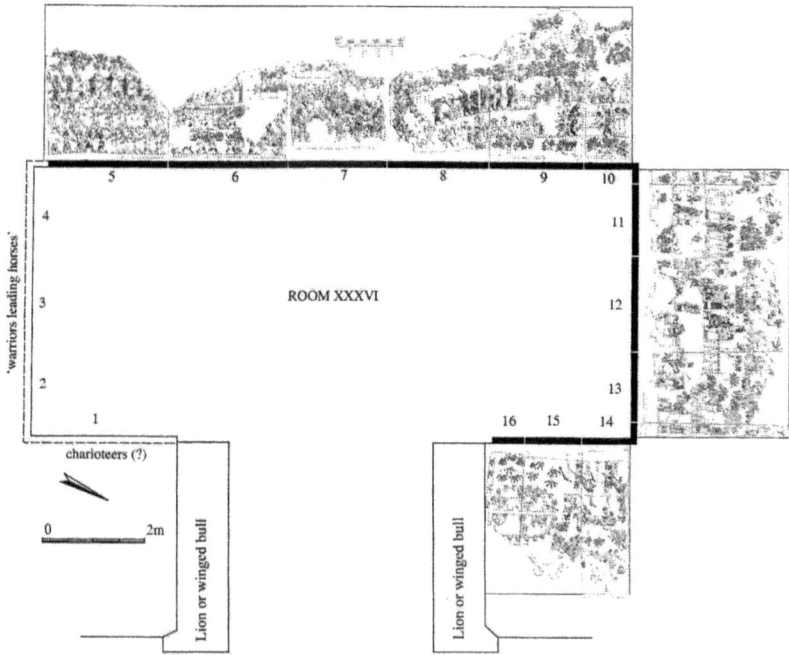

Figure 3: Plan of the Lachish Room (No.XXXVI) in South-west Palace (Uehlinger 2003, p. 276)

Figure 4: City of Alammu (R.D. Barnett 1998, pl. 158)

Figure 5: City depicted in Sennacherib's throne hall (Barnett 1998, pl. 46)

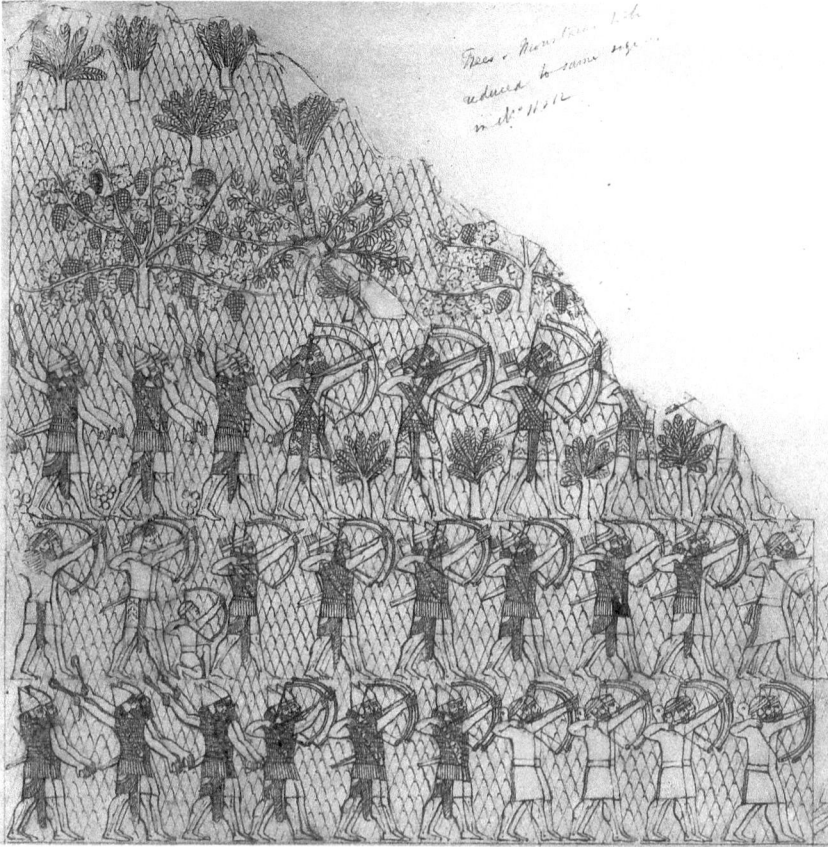

Figure 6: Series of the Lachish reliefs, Slab 1 (Barnett 1998, pl. 324)

Figure 7: Series of the Lachish reliefs, Slab 2 (Barnett 1998, pl. 328)

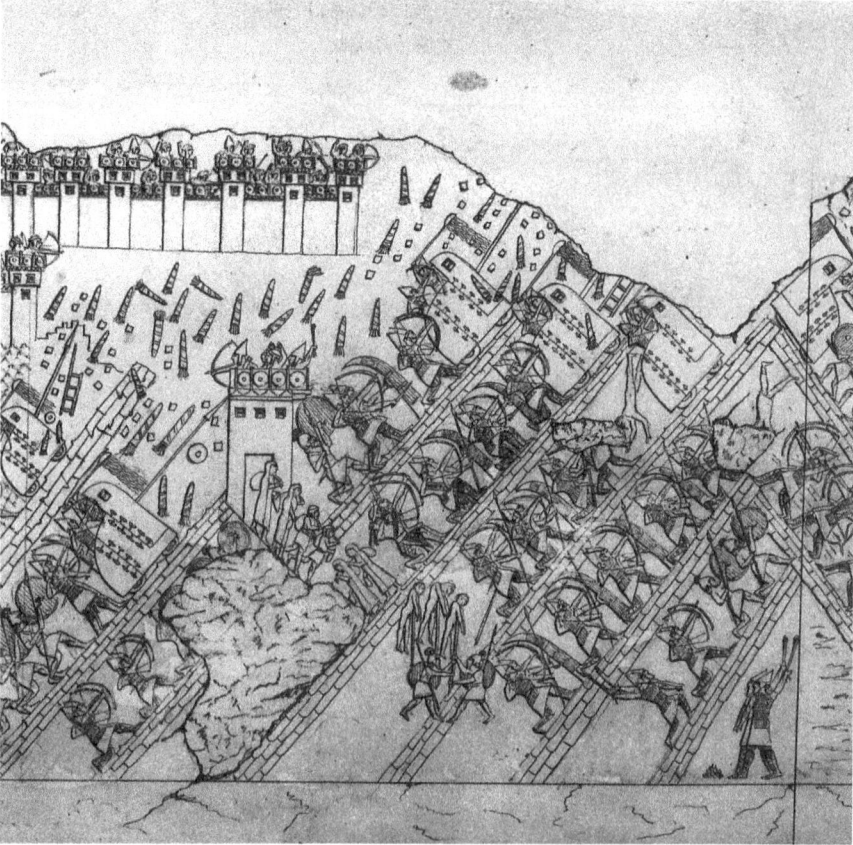

Figure 8: Series of the Lachish reliefs, Slab 3 (Barnett 1998, pl. 330)

Figure 9: Series of the Lachish reliefs, Slab 4 (Barnett 1998, pl. 330)

Figure 10: Series of the Lachish reliefs, Slab 5 (Barnett 1998, pl. 336)

Figure 11: Series of the Lachish reliefs, Slab 6 (Barnett 1998, pl. 338)

Figure 12: Series of the Lachish reliefs, Slab 7 (Barnett 1998, pl. 338)

Figure 13: Series of the Lachish reliefs, Slab 8 (Barnett 1998, pl. 342)

Figure 14: Series of the Lachish reliefs, Slab 9 (Barnett 1998, pl. 342)

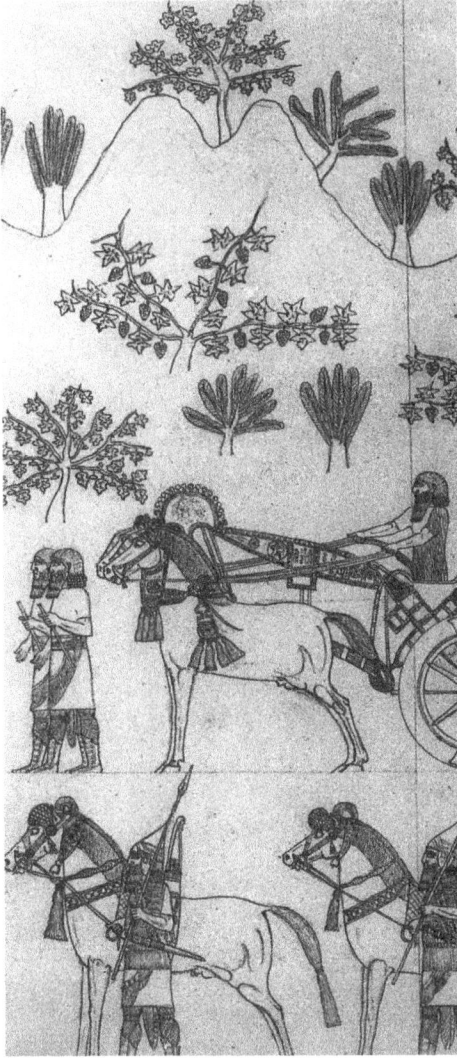

Figure 15: Series of the Lachish reliefs, Slab 10 (Barnett 1998, pl. 346)

Figure 16: Series of the Lachish reliefs, Slab 11 (Barnett 1998, pl. 346)

Figure 17: Series of the Lachish reliefs, Slab 12 (Barnett 1998, pl. 346)

Index of Names

Index of Ancient places

Index of Ancient people